On Being Black

An In-Group Analysis

(Second Edition)

...Essays in Honor of W.E.B. DuBois...

David Pilgrim

" ... timely, informative, and readable. No library or serious scholar of the Afro-American experience should be without it."

Andrew Billingsley
University of Maryland

Wyndham Hall Press

ON BEING BLACK: An In-Group Analysis
(Being Essays in Honor of W.E.B. DuBois)

Edited by

David Pilgrim, Ph.D.
Assistant Professor
Department of Sociology
Saint Mary's College/Notre Dame

SECOND EDITION

(First Edition published in 1986)

Library of Congress
Catalog Card Number
85-052309

ISBN   0-932269-75-3

SECOND EDITION

P · R · E · F · A · C · E

One of the positive trends of the 1980s is the increasing willingness of mainstream publishers to publish books on the black American experience. This is noteworthy because as recently as the late 1970s many publishers regarded "Black titles" as passe', unnecessary, and unmarketable, thus insuring a dearth of books about the contemporary black American experience. This situation changed due largely to the vision of certain smaller academic publishing companies, for example, Wyndham Hall Press, who have consistently published first-rate material by and about black Americans. Fortunately, the example set by many of these presses is being followed now by larger publishing houses, to the benefit of all.

In the three years following the publication of **ON BEING BLACK**, the status of black America has remained relatively unchanged. There have been indicators of progress (Jesse Jackson's serious bid for the Democratic Presidential nomination; more than 2 million new registered black voters; passage of a major civil rights bill; and an increasing number of blacks who are objectively middle-class), and indicators of retrogression (the percentage of the AIDS population that is black increases daily; more black youths are addicted to drugs; violent gangs are terrorizing more black communities; increasing numbers of black families have fallen below the poverty line; and blatant white racism has resurfaced on college campuses, in public accommodations, and in neighborhoods). The status of black America is probably best summarized by the adage: "Everything has changed, but it is still the same."

The objective of this second edition remains the same: to allow black social scientists the opportunity to share their research on the black American experience. All of the chapters from the first edition were retained. One addition is the "Quotient of Black Information" Test, called the "Q.B.I. Test". This test was designed to measure one's knowledge about black Americans

and the black American experience. This instrument was included to stimulate classroom discussions.

I would like to acknowledge the editorial assistance provided
by Charles Pressler and Patricia Pilger, my colleagues at Saint
Mary's College. I am also grateful to Karol Dlouhy for typing
and re-typing portions of the manuscript.

D.P.   Saint Mary's College
Notre Dame, IN   Autumn, 1988

TABLE OF CONTENTS

INTRODUCTION

*My God, the American Negro has finally
come of age; he is capable of self-analysis
and self-criticism.*

In the Preface to the second edition of his sardonic BLACK BOUR-
GEOISIE, E. Franklin Frazier credited the above quote to a liberal
European critic living in South Africa. Both scholars erred. While
it is hardly surprising that a European scholar would be ignorant of
Afro-American scholarship, it is disappointing that Frazier, the fore-
most Black sociologist of the 1950s, would imply that his research
was a pioneering effort -- apparently, Whites do not have a monopoly
on self-aggrandizement.

A century before BLACK BOURGEOISIE scarified the Black middle-
class, Blacks were engaging in critical analysis, of themselves and
the Whites who oppressed them. In 1845, an intrepid ex-slave wrote
NARRATIVE OF THE LIFE OF FREDERICK DOUGLASS, AN AMERI-
CAN SLAVE, WRITTEN BY HIMSELF. Written less than five years
after his escape from this peculiar institution, this laconic reply
to the racist contention that God sanctioned chattel slavery was
one of the earliest published examples of critical analysis by an Afro-
American. Other books in this genre were: THE FUGITIVE BLACK-
SMITH, or EVENTS IN THE HISTORY OF JAMES W. C. PENNINGTON,
PASTOR OF A PRESBYTERIAN CHURCH, NEW YORK, FORMERLY
A SLAVE IN THE STATE OF MARYLAND, UNITED STATES (1849),
and, AUTOBIOGRAPHY OF A FUGITIVE NEGRO: HIS ANTI-SLAVERY
LABORS IN THE UNITED STATES, CANADA AND ENGLAND, by
Samuel Ringgold Ward (1855).

An excerpt from Douglass' NARRATIVE illustrates the ex-slave's
capacity for critical thinking:

"By some means I learned from these inquiries, that 'God, up
in the sky,' made everybody; and that he made **white** people to
be masters and mistresses, and **black** people to be slaves. This
did not satisfy me, nor lessen my interest in the subject. I was
told, too, that God was good, and that He knew what was best
for me, and best for everybody. This was less satisfactory than

1

the first statement: because it came, point blank, against all my notions of goodness. . . I was not long in finding out the true solution of the matter. It was not color, but **crime**, not God, but man, that afforded the true explanation of the existence of slavery; nor was I long in finding out another important truth, viz: what man can make, man can unmake. The appalling darkness faded away, and I was master of the subject" (Quote derived from BONTEMPS, 1966:865-66).

The pervasiveness of structural racism and individual racism forced later Black writers to also limit their research to the "Negro problem." For example, in an effort to debunk the racist myth that Blacks were parasites throughout American history, Black scholars published Afro-American histories. In 1833, George Washington Williams wrote HISTORY OF THE NEGRO RACE IN AMERICA. William Wells Brown, whose books were the linear antecedents of the works of historian John Hope Franklin and novelist Richard Wright, wrote several histories and narrative essays that remain deserving of a readership. Among these were: THE NEGRO IN THE AMERICAN REBELLION, 1868, THE RISING SON, 1874, and MY SOUTHERN HOME, 1880.

In 1896, William Edward Burghardt DuBois, in this writer's opinion the most brilliant mind produced on American soil, completed his THE SUPPRESSION OF THE AFRICAN SLAVE TRADE. This document, his dissertation, was widely acclaimed as the first social scientific work written by an Afro-American and was selected as the first volume of the Harvard Historical Studies series. His natural genius was cultivated by the greatest minds of his age, a virtual hall of fame of instructors, namely, Josiah Royce, William James, Albert Bushnell Hart and George Santayana. In 1899, their prized student published THE PHILADELPHIA NEGRO: A SOCIAL STUDY. Although this was the first social scientific study conducted by any American, it did not guarantee its author's fame. Indeed, White scholars, especially sociologists, have steadfastly refused to acknowledge its historical importance. Unfortunately, most White members of the scholarly community are unaware of its existence.

DuBois' literary career spanned six decades. Indefatigably, he produced some forty monographs and several hundred scholarly articles and critical essays. His ideas about the innate equality of all persons were not palatable to Mr. and Mrs. America, therefore he was blacklisted by mainstream publishing companies. Undaunted, he used "radical" and low-budget presses. This partially explains the lack of esteem enjoyed by DuBois the scholar -- unfairly, he is primarily remembered as a social activist. The single work which brought DuBois his greatest acclaim as a scholar was THE SOULS OF BLACK FOLK (1903). Some books interpret history, this book made history. This collection of essays, written as a rebuttal to Booker T. Washington's nauseous UP FROM SLAVERY, AN AUTOBIOGRAPHY (1900), remains the chief d'oeuvre of Black scholarship. The following is a sample of DuBois' ideas:

"One ever feels his twoness, -- an American, a Negro; two souls, two thoughts, two unreconciled strivings; two warring ideals in one dark body, whose dogged strength alone keeps it from being torn asunder. The history of the American Negro is the history of this strife, -- this longing to attain self-conscious manhood, to merge his double self into a better and truer self. In this merging he wishes neither of the older selves to be lost. . . He simply wishes to make it possible for a man to be both a Negro and an American, without being cursed and spit upon by his fellows, without having the doors of Opportunity closed roughly in his face" (DuBois, 1903/1961:17).

The opening criticism of Frazier should not be read as a personal attack or an indictment against his research -- from most accounts, he was a fine gentleman and a thorough scholar. The intent was to dispel the misguided notion that Black scholarship began with Frazier. There were literally thousands of critically thinking Afro-Americans before 1957, the year BLACK BOURGEOISIE was published. The small number of Black writers cited earlier, with the exception of DuBois, were not atypical. Americans of African descent have always been critical thinkers but White Americans, particularly White publishers, historically have not been objective listeners.

SIGNIFICANCE OF THIS BOOK

All books have some significance, this one has more than most. We are living in a generation of big lies, **White** lies. The biggest lie is that racial membership is no longer the most important determinant of success in America. Sometimes, this lie is spread by social scientists (Wilson, 1980), but in most instances it is propagated by average White Americans who are more concerned about their jobs and neighborhoods than the human rights of Afro-Americans. These "100% Americans" eat breakfast with Bryant Gumbel and dinner with Bill Cosby, and erroneously deduce that most Blacks can assimilate if they are inclined.

The **Big Lie** has given birth to smaller, but equally ominous, progeny. The large number of poverty-stricken Afro-Americans, for example, are seen as indolent parasites. This lie, and the liars who voice it,

3

ignore the overwhelmingly high number of American Blacks who are underemployed -- the vile cycle of poverty is not broken with cashier paychecks from McDonald's, Burger King, or Mac Seafood Restaurant. Most Afro-Americans are systematically excluded from graduate school programs, national political offices, top managerial positions in large corporations, and professional occupations; of course, there is some token representation, but the masses are excluded. It is no accident that Black unemployment has been twice that of whites for 25 years (Parillo, et al., 1985:251).

Afro-Americans are confronted by the legacy of past discrimination and the persistence of modern, more sophisticated, racism. For every Black **welcomed** into the American mainstream five are excluded. The Civil Rights Movement was not fought so that a few Blacks could partake of this nation's social goodies, rather, its objective was to improve the life chances of all Blacks. Today, Blacks are disproportion- ately represented in unemployment lines, shanties, state-run asylums, hospital emergency rooms, prisons, and cemeteries -- annually, Blacks are dying in 50 percent greater numbers than Whites (Hairston and Davis, 1985:25). The Black masses are worse off today than they were in 1963, and these truths must be told.

The Editor

Bontemps, Arna
   1966   "The Negro Contribution to American Letters." In, THE AMERICAN NEGRO REFERENCE BOOK. Edited by John P. Davis, Englewood Cliffs, New Jersey: Prentice-Hall, Inc.

DuBois, W.E.B.
   1961   THE SOULS OF BLACK FOLK. Introduction by Saunders Redding. New York: Fawcett Publications, Inc.

Hariston, George E., and W. Michael Byrd
   1985   "Medical Care In America." THE CRISIS. VOl. 92, No. 8, (Oct.) 25-28.

Parillo, Vincent et al.,
   1985   CONTEMPORARY SOCIAL PROBLEMS. New York: John Wiley & Sons.

Wilson, William J.
   1980   THE DECLINING SIGNIFICANCE OF RACE. 2nd ed. Chicago: University of Chicago Press.

A TRIBUTE TO W.E.B. DUBOIS

A prophet is without honor in his own country. W.E.B. DuBois deserved respect and adulation but he received contempt and ostracism. Because of his uncompromising stance against White supremacy, DuBois was branded as a race-baiting pawn of Communists. Conservatives loathed him, moderates disliked him, and liberals feared him. During a time when passivity was demanded of Blacks, DuBois dared to be an arrogant and outspoken gadfly.

William Edward Burghardt DuBois was born on February 23, 1868, in Great Barrington, Massachusetts, a sleepy, middle-class town. After excelling in the local public schools, he entered Fisk University in 1885 and was graduated in 1888. Pursuing a lifelong dream, he entered Harvard University, albeit as a junior -- Harvard refused to recognize his baccalaureate degree because it was granted by a Black institution. In 1890, he was graduated by Harvard with another baccalaureate degree, and he immediately entered the university's graduate school.

Since Harvard did not recognize sociology as a legitimate science, DuBois selected history as his field of doctoral study -- the emphasis on history would undergird all of his later works. As was the custom, he spent two years studying in a foreign institution, the University of Berlin. When he returned, he completed his doctoral dissertation entitled "The Suppression of the African Slave-Trade to the United States of America, 1638-1870," which was published as the first volume of the Harvard Historical Studies. When he received his Doctor of Philosophy degree in 1896, he became the first Black to receive this award from Harvard and only the fifth Black to receive a doctorate from any American University.

White colleges and universities did not welcome him, therefore DuBois accepted a position as Professor of Greek and Latin at Wilberforce College, a poor Black college in Ohio. In 1897, he left Wilberforce to take a position as an Assistant Instructor at the University of Pennsylvania. His title was a nominal one -- he taught no classes, had no contact with students or professors, and was not given an office. Undaunted, DuBois exploited this "opportunity" by conducting the research which produced THE PHILADELPHIA NEGRO.

DuBois spent 13 years, 1897-1910, as Professor of History and Economics at Atlanta University, a fine Black college which would, under DuBois' tutelage, lay the foundation for social scientific investigation of Afro-Americans. These were productive years for DuBois: he conducted research for the ATLANTA STUDIES, 16 monographs on race relations in southern and border states; wrote THE SOULS OF BLACK FOLKS, which inflamed most Americans; published JOHN BROWN; and, he helped organize the Niagara Movement, the spiritual and political antecedent of the NAACP.

DuBois was one of the original founders of the NAACP and in 1910 he became editor of the organization's newsmagazine, THE CRISIS. Freed from the taxing duties of a college professor, DuBois was able to devote himself to propagating the plight of Afro-Americans. Through his biting essays, DuBois became the undisputed philosopher of the Black protest movement. At its height, THE CRISIS was read by more than 100,000 Blacks and had a tremendous influence on many notable Afro-Americans including Roy Wilkins, Ruby Dee, Langston Hughes, Lorraine Hansberry, and Paul Robeson. THE CRISIS impacted on all Americans; Blacks knew that they had an uncompromising advocate in DuBois, Whites knew that they had a persistent and worthy foe. In addition to several scholarly books, THE NEGRO, DARK-WATER, and THE GIFT OF BLACK FOLK, DuBois founded and edited THE BROWNIES' BOOK, a monthly magazine for Black children which portrayed Black children as intelligent, beautiful and useful.

Intraorganizational disputes over his handling of THE CRISIS led to his retirement from his position as editor. In 1934, he returned to Atlanta University as Professor of Sociology and began the most productive period of his life. During the ten years of his second stint at Atlanta University, DuBois published the following books: BLACK RECONSTRUCTION; BLACK FOLK, THEN AND NOW; DUSK OF DAWN; and COLOR AND DEMOCRACY. Sensing the need for a scholarly journal which would objectively tackle the complexities of Afro-American life, DuBois founded and edited Phylon: The Atlanta University Review of Race and Culture.

In 1944, at the age of 76, DuBois was forced to retire from Atlanta University. He accepted a position as a Consultant for African Affairs with the NAACP. His four year term was unpleasant because of repeated conflicts with the Association's Executive Secretary, Walter White. He performed his duties admirably but was dismissed in 1948.

During the last fifteen years of his life, DuBois became progressively frustrated with America's handling of its racial minorities. Since democracy and capitalism were intimately linked, DuBois saw the Western World as the major obstacle to the uplift of the colored people of the world. He saw the Western nations as imperialistic, materialistic war-mongrels. In 1950, he became Chairman of the Peace Information Center so that he could inform American citizens of world-wide peace initiatives. His bubble burst that year when he was indicted on Federal charge of being an "unregistered foreign agent." Although the charges were later dropped, DuBois' faith in American democracy was effectively squashed. In 1961, after years of personal debate, he joined the Communist Party of the United States. That same year, he accepted an invitation from President Nkrumah to come to Ghana as Director of the Encyclopedia Africana project. In 1963, he became a citizen of Ghana and he died there on August 27 of that year. Paradoxically, DuBois died the day before the great Civil Rights March on Washington.

For most of his life, DuBois loved America. His love transcended the daily reminders of his subordinate status. It was not easy for one so brash and haughty as DuBois, to love a country which despised him; but he loved. The only body which rivaled America for DuBois affection was Black America. Long before the 1960s, DuBois argued that Black was beautiful. He spent his life combating racism and its effects on Blacks. When he joined the Communist Party it was America's shame not his.

To him who much is given, much is required. This book is a tribute to W. E. B. DuBois, the deepest mind produced on American soil. Although we tried to follow his example -- clarity of ideas, systematic observation, thorough documentation, objective analysis of the data, and the passionate presentation of the findings--we can only approximate the high level of his scholarship. As a final gesture of our respect for the "Dean" we have assembled an annotated bibliography of his major books -- he wrote about 40 books and monographs, and more than 200 scholarly articles and essays -- for the benefit of those students who wish to understand what it means to live **under the veil**.

THE SUPPRESSION OF THE AFRICAN SLAVE TRADE TO THE UNITED STATES, 1638-1870 (Harvard Historical Series, I). New York: Longmans, Green and Company, 1896; 335pp.

Probably the first socio-historical analysis of American slavery, this is a stern but objective treatment of the contemptible practices of slave merchants and the suffering of slaves. DuBois claims that thousands of slaves were smuggled into America each year until the Civil War -- there is some evidence that the slave trade continued even beyond this period. The scholarship in this document, his doctoral dissertation, was so thorough that this work was selected as the first manuscript for the Harvard Historical Studies series.

THE PHILADELPHIA NEGRO: A SOCIAL STUDY. Philadelphia: University of Pennsylvania, 1899; 520 pp.

This was the first empirical sociological study conducted by **any** American; DuBois interviewed most of the 5,000 respondents. This study, which laid the foundation for Myrdal's AN AMERICAN DILEMMA (1943), blamed White Americans for the wretched conditions faced by Blacks. His ideas on economic determinism and class struggle, although not refined, were presented here for the first time. White scholars have either ignored this book or belittled its significance.

THE SOULS OF BLACK FOLK: ESSAYS AND SKETCHES. Chicago, Illinois: A. C. McClurg & Company, 1903; 265 pp.

This book is the definitive response to Washington's UP FROM SLAVERY (1900). Written in splendid Biblical rhetoric, this collection of scholarly essays and poetic sketches justifies Reconstruction, refutes the old myth of White supremacy, demands equal opportunities for Blacks, and propagates the cultural contributions of Afro-Americans. One of the most significant books written in the 20th century, this book enjoyed huge popularity in the 1960's.

THE HEALTH AND PHYSIQUE OF THE NEGRO AMERICAN. Atlanta, Georgia: Atlanta University Press, 1906; 112 pp.

This is the first significant multidisciplinary approach to the health problems and biological study of Afro-Americans. Drawing from studies in anthropology, psychology, and medical research, DuBois debunks the myth of genetic deficiencies in Blacks. This was DuBois' only effort in this field, and the work was totally ignored by White researchers. It is safe to say that this work was years ahead of its time.

JOHN BROWN. Philadelphia, Pennsylvania: George W. Jacobs & Company, 1909; 406 pp.

This book is a historical biography which presents Brown as a sane, intelligent, and deeply religious abolitionist. With his typical literary

8

brilliance, DuBois attacks the decadent and demonic institution of chattel slavery. Unlike most biographers of Brown, DuBois portrays Brown's actions as a Christian response to slavery. DuBois wonders why other White Christians did not follow Brown's example.

THE NEGRO. New York: Henry Holt & Company, 1915; 254 pp.

In this small volume, DuBois debunks the myth that Africans were savages by introducing theretofore unknown facts about African culture. He vigorously attacks the racist idea that Africans were the chief beneficiaries of slavery. The idea that Black and White workers should unite against the American elite undergrids the analysis.

DARKWATER: THE TWENTIETH CENTURY COMPLETION OF UNCLE TOM'S CABIN. Washington, D.C.: A. Jenkins Company, 1920; 276 pp.

This collection of ten essays represents DuBois' most vehement denouncement of White racism. Although Whites considered the entire book inflammatory, they were especially offended by two of the essays: "The Souls of White Folk," and "The Damnation of Women." In the former, DuBois lays bare the hypocrisy of White Christians; in the latter, he shows how White men have used Black women as objects of sexual perversion. This book also includes his famous "Credo" where he reconciles his love of God with his vision of civil rights for Blacks.

THE GIFT OF BLACK FOLK; THE NEGROES IN THE MAKING OF AMERICA. Boston, Mass.: The Stratford Company, 1924; 349 pp.

This book chronicles the contributions of Afro-Americans. Although the level of analysis is not thorough by DuBoisian standards, this work introduces theretofore "hidden" achievements by numerous Blacks. DuBois correctly notes that Whites stole or minimized accomplishments by Blacks and then accused Blacks of contributing nothing.

BLACK RECONSTRUCTION IN AMERICA, 1860-1880. New York: Harcourt, Brace, 1935; 746 pp.

A thorough but verbose justification of the roles played by Blacks and Radical Republicans during Reconstruction. DuBois argues that Reconstruction was **neither** the salvation nor damnation of the freedmen, rather, it was a necessary transition from slavery to freedom. He astutely argues that Blacks were not responsible for the problems experienced by the South during this difficult period. This book is preferable to the one-sided accounts of Reconstruction which are produced by other historians -- traditionalists, revisionists, and/or post-revisionists.

BLACK FOLK, THEN AND NOW: AN ESSAY IN THE HISTORY AND SOCIOLOGY OF THE NEGRO RACE. New York: Henry Holt & Company, 1939; 401 pp.

In this sociological, anthropological, and historical study, DuBois refines and expands the ideas presented in THE NEGRO. DuBois expends much energy documenting the achievements of Africans and Afro-Americans. While demonstrating the economic basis of racism, he severely criticizes European imperialism, racial stereotyping, and the myth of Aryan superiority.

DUSK OF DAWN: AN ESSAY TOWARD AN AUTOBIOGRAPHY OF A RACE CONCEPT. New York: Harcourt, Brace & Company, 1940: 334 pp.

With the pen of a poet, DuBois uses his life as a backdrop for critiquing the sociological and psychological aspects of American race relations -- he used this approach earlier in the booklet, A PAGEANT IN SEVEN DECADES (1938). The most interesting section is Chapter Seven, "The Colored World Within," where he introduces his ideas on voluntary segregation as a means for combating the more ominous condition of involuntary segregation.

THE BLACK FLAME -- A TRILOGY: THE ORDEAL OF MANSART, MANSART BUILDS A SCHOOL, and WORLDS OF COLOR. New York: Mainstream Publisher, 1957, 1959, 1961,; 316, 367, 349 pp.

Written when DuBois was in his late eighties and early nineties, he uses historical fiction to show the plight of Afro-Americans since Reconstruction. As usual, DuBois is adamant in his condemnation of the Whites responsible for the subordinate status of Blacks. In these historical novels we see DuBois the consummate scholar: he is historian, psychologist, economist, sociologist, political scientist, and novelist.

AN ABC OF COLOR: SELECTIONS FROM OVER A HALF CENTURY OF THE WRITINGS OF W. E. B. DUBOIS. Berlin, German Democratic Republic: Seven Seas Publishers, 1963; 214 pp.

This book is a collection of excerpts from DuBois' books, scholarly articles, essays, and public speeches. The material is useful for students unfamiliar with DuBois' writings, but this book is inadequate for serious students of DuBoisian thought.

We must study, we must investigate, we must attempt to solve; and the utmost that the world can demand is, not lack of human interest and moral conviction, but rather the heart-quality of fairness and an earnest desire for the truth despite its possible unpleasantness.

W. E. B. DuBois
THE AUTOBIOGRAPHY, 1964

CHAPTER ONE

PRE-COLUMBIAN BLACK PRESENCE
IN THE WESTERN HEMISPHERE*

Almose A. Thompson, Jr.

When one desires to research and study the racial history of the Western Hemisphere, some interesting, complex and perplexing problems are encountered. Admittedly, a Black presence was noted by Columbus and later by other early White European explorers of the New World. This presence was also noted in the folklore, culture and legends of the American Indian. For instance, Leon says: ". . .the memories of them in most ancient tradition induce us to believe that Negroes were the first inhabitants of Mexico."[1]

A rash or unsupported position -- certainly not! But it has made for a hot controversy between both advocate and detractor with respect to who should receive the credit for the discovery of America -- Columbus or Black Africans! The resulting debate has stimulated many to evaluate and re-evaluate existing data, particularly in light of recent and important findings. By and large, this change, the willingness to objectively evaluate and re-evaluate data from other than contemporary or generally accepted frames of reference, can be attributed to several factors.

Racial bias has less effect upon scholarly interpretations than was true in the past. More and more, color blindness is becoming the

---

*This paper originally appeared in NEGRO HISTORY BULLETIN, volume 38, Number 7, October/November, 1975, 452-456.

rule rather than the exception. For instance, Abu-Lughod recently pointed out that "as a result of pressure from African historians, scholars now realize that they must pay more attention to the Arabic literature. . ."[2] We do not know how much they will reveal, but Arabic manuscripts of both Near-Eastern and West Africa archives are being edited for publication. In addition to such in-roads, new and vastly improved retrieval techniques and methodology are being employed to locate and interpret data. It is from this frame of reference that the author will develop a thesis for the origin of the human species in the Western Hemisphere that considers the Black presence at the time of Columbus.

Support for this position has been continuous and encouraging, the most important in-put is a series of recent discoveries which have had the effect of undermining generally accepted theories of human arrival and settlement within the Western Hemisphere. These early inhabitants were a diverse group from the standpoint of cultural and physical characteristics. These characteristics were quite different from those of White Europeans. Consistently, African elements have been found among the early inhabitants.[3] Perhaps, the first White explorers in the New World did not speculate over the origin of indigenous natives because of the mistaken assumption that they had landed in India. Today, however, this topic has become an area of much concern (amid incessant and acrimonious debate).

Speculation as to the arrival of human species in the Western Hemisphere usually revolves around one or more versions of the Siberia/Alaska land bridge theory. In general these theories reckon only with the question of Indian descent. The basic opinions of these advocates is that the Western Hemisphere was first populated by "mongolian" types, about 20,000 years ago. These people are believed to have "walked" from Siberia to North America by way of a land bridge then spanning Asia and North America, somewhere in the area of the Bering Strait.[4] This extrapolation, generally accepted by most scholars, was suggested and accepted when most believed that the human species had been on this planet about one million years. This estimate has subsequently been revised to nearly two and one-half times this figure in light of new findings.[5] Digressing a bit, two of these migration theories generally receive most of the attention of scholars. Though they agree on the essentials discussed above, they differ somewhat on the actual flow and form of this migration, and whether this immigrant population was heterogeneous or homogenous in terms of racial and cultural characteristics. One theory suggests that a homogenous group of immigrants worked their way in one continuous wave to the southern-most tip of South America. The other theory adheres to the "multi-waves of settlers" thesis. Remember, at the time of Columbus, Europeans felt the indigenous population reflected heterogeneous racial and cultural characteristics. However, this claim has been questioned by many contemporary scholars. But, for our purposes, it is not necessary that we take sides in this debate.

Those scholars who hold to the belief in the homogenity of the native American population during the migration period maintain that there was only one exodus wave regardless of its length. On the surface, this position appears reasonable and consistent. Any other stance would necessarily have to be grounded in defense of the Asiatic reservoir sequence of this immigration wave. Otherwise the homogenity theory would have to be discarded.

Nevertheless, if this homogenity thesis is closely scrutinized, it comes apart at the seams -- it cuts little ice. It's most glaring imperfection is its inability to square with the historical and chronological data that relate to this situation. For example, evidence abounds which indicates that the physical types in the Siberian area during this supposed migration period were quite different from what we find today; the ethnic composition of this population underwent radical change from time to time. The inference is clear: if this Western Hemisphere migration was spread over a considerable period a homogenous population could not possibly have been the result.[6]

Furthermore, the estimated date for this migratory trek is not consistent with the geological phenomena for this period. According to Hopkins of the U.S. Geological survey, it has been shown that the great plain, that would have served as the land bridge for this monumental hike, sunk beneath the sea somewhat more than one million years ago and has not risen appreciably since that time.[7]

So there was no land bridge 20,000 years ago! Wait, this drama becomes more clouded. As previously noted, there can be little doubt that the estimates of the human presence in the Western Hemisphere are generally accepted based on man's existence on earth. However, Leakey, an anthropologist unlocking stone age secrets, uncovered man-like fossils at Olduvai Gorge that pre-dated the zinjanthropus, and are estimated to be well over 2,500,000 years old.[8] This finding suggests the need to re-evaluate and to posit new theories which speak to the human presence in this hemisphere. Fortunately, this is being done. During the latter part of 1973, a group of geologists reported evidence of human activity in Mexico believed to have occurred more than 200,000 years earlier. This is unquestionably the oldest indication of human activity in the Western Hemisphere. According to Malde of the U.S. Geological Survey in Denver, the tools found at the site (80 miles southeast of Mexico City) were without a doubt man made. Also, these tools were associated with the nearby remains of such animals as camels, elephants and the long extinct glyptodon, and indicates that these animals were slain by humans. Moreover, several different dating techniques confirmed the age of the geological deposits from which these tools were excavated to be over 250,000 years old. True, there are scholars who do not accept these age estimates regardless of the geological dating processes and/or techniques employed, but the evidence is against them. Undaunted, these scholars feel that these data estimates are inconsistent with traditional views.[9]

If these estimates are not correct, then how do we explain how so many independent geological dating techniques have derived similar "wrong" conclusions? If this "dating" stands up, and it has yet to be disproven, the need for new theories on the migration of man into the Western Hemisphere will be mandated as the old theories will be discredited. This is clear, for not only was there no land bridge between Siberia and Alaska during this period, but there probably were no people in Siberia either.[10]

Black Presence in Pre-Columbian America

Based on available data, Woodson, Winsor, Quatrefages, Dixon, Thacher, Wiener, McCabe, Rogers, Lawrence, DuBois and a host of other scholars believe that sometime during the first few centuries following the death of Jesus Christ, Black African explorers began voyages to the New World: perhaps as part of a worldwide trade network.[11]

According to the data provided by Dixon, Proto-Negroid types have been found among the Pre-Columbian Indians of the Western Hemisphere.[12] Furthermore, vis-a-vis crania examinations, Dixon determined that the dominant element in the whole central and eastern Rhode Island area during the Pre-Columbian period to be astoundingly Proto-Negroid. Continuing, he states "no possibility of historic Negro mixture is admissable."[13] Dixon also found an early Proto-Negroid type present in the Mexican region.[14]

Before leaving the discussion of these Negroid Proto-types, it should be noted that there are other areas in the Western Hemisphere, both in North and Latin America where the Pre-Columbian Black presence has been substantiated via examination of crania; only a couple of examples were provided here to serve as illustrations.

Also it must be noted that these Proto-Negroid types were not generally found in the west coast regions, particularly north of the California-Oregon border.[15] This would seem to suggest that Blacks did not participate in the great migration from Siberia that many still believe took place 20,000 years ago. And if Blacks did not come via this coastal route, and were present in the Western Hemisphere at the time of Columbus' arrival, then Blacks must have arrived as the first explorers of America.

Martyr, a historian who accompanied Balboa mentioned a Black nation located at Darien in Northern Brazil. Prior to this observation, Balboa noted the presence of Blacks in the Panama area. Columbus tells of seeing Blacks on his third voyage. However, during his first visit he was told by natives of a Black group which reportedly had come from the south-east which is the general direction one would sail from this area to reach the west coast of Africa via the north equatorial current. Moreover, these Blacks were reported to have possessed spears with tips of a metal alloy frequently made by West Africans during this period.[16]

Other Black settlements were located among the Yamassi of Florida, around the Orinoco River in Venezuela at St. Vincent in the Gulf of Mexico. Again, special note should be made of the fact that these settlements were reported by White Europeans upon their arrival in the New World.

Legends and Gods

Indian legends also serve as a fount of support for the Pre-Columbian Black presence in the Western Hemisphere. The Black African type was very prominent in the legends of the Mayans, Aztecs, and Incas. The Mayans in particular held ancient Blacks in high esteem. Among their deities were Black Gods, for example, Quetzalcoatl the Serpent and Messiah, and Ex-ahau the War Captain. All of the remaining replicas of these Gods show them Black and wooly haired.

Indian legends abound with stories of Black Gods. For example, there is a giant statue of a Black African type in Ecuador estimated to be 20,000 years old.[19] An ancient Black God worshiped by the Mexicans is Lxtilton, meaning black face.[20] Further, numerous statues depicting Black Indian Gods can be seen in Central America. An authority

15

on Central American Indians, Verril, says that a Black Christ existed in ancient Central America as well as Europe. He points out that:

> In the little church of Esquipultas, Guatemala, is the image of the black Christ to which thousands of Indians journey annually from all parts of Central America and even from Mexico and South America. . . The real urge that leads them to the spot is the ineradicable faith in their ancient gods and religion. The very fact that the image is black has a symbolic significance.[21]

Anthropological Evidence

Black Africans also appear in and on many early designs and artifacts delineating an African Morphology that have been found throughout the Western Hemisphere. For example, five large, solid granite heads, one weighing approximately five tons, have been found at Vera Cruz, Mexico and in the Canton of Taxla.[22] Furthermore, burial mounds have been found in various sectors of the United States in which fossil men comparable to West African types of the Pre-Columbian era have been excavated.[23,24]

Cultural anthropologists have also suggested that Africans pre-date Columbus in America. Their research indicates that there was an exchange of crops between persons living in the Americas and Africa some time before the Portugese and Spanish explorers arrived in America. In other words, when the first White Europeans reached African shores during the mid-fifteenth century they found crops that were indigenous to the Americas. These crops included maize and manihot. Conversely, indigenous African crops observed to be growing in America by the first White Europeans upon their arrival included yams, taros, manioc, tobacco, cotton and peanuts.[25] One logical explanation is that these crops do not spoil easily, therefore they were ideal foods for both ends of a long sea journey. Moreover, these crops were found spread in the Western Hemisphere along the same general route as were the Black settlers previously discussed. Add to this the fact that there were two natural water highways leading to America and returning to Africa, the north and south equatorial currents which lie along this same course, and the full picture almost comes into focus.

Other Data Pertaining to Pre-Columbian Blacks

On his voyage to America, Columbus encountered non-barking dogs of a variety found in Africa.[26] Ogilby, wrote of this variety of African dogs and he specifically noted that they cannot or do not bark.[27]

Wiener has proved that Africans carried baseball to Mexico from the so-called "Dark Continent." Ancient drawings uncovered in Mexico depicted this game being played over five centuries ago.[28]

Wiener also claims that tobacco was in wide use among the Indians when the first White settlers arrived on these shores. He cited Brazil and Central America as the initial places where this crop was planted and cultivated.[29] In support, archaeologists have retrieved ancient Indian pipes decorated with pictures of African elephants, from ceremonial mounds in Ohio and New York.[30]

African Maritime Superiority

Did ancient Africans possess the skills necessary to dominate the seas? The answer is yes. Africans were able to make their own sailing charts with latitude and longitude grids; they frequently sailed out of sight of land while using the compass, charts and the art or science of astronomy. Moreover, their maritime superiority was responsible, in part, for the Moors overrunning Spain in 711.[31]

At the time of Columbus, African navigators were far superior to their White European counterparts. They had established trade relations with China, India, Mediterranean Europe and the Atlantic Islands.

These exploits were made possible through the geographical and astronomical theories of such African writers as Abu Zaid, Masudi, Aldrise, Itakhti, Abulfelda and others. Both Aldrise and Abulfelda stressed the rotundity of the Earth and the latter spoke of possible voyages around the world; during this time Europeans believed that the world was flat.[32] Usually, credit for these maritime advancements and concepts are awarded to Prince Henry the Navigator and Columbus. All history, is somewhat distorted, but this is a conscious deception that has no place in scholarly work.

The Africans laid the cornerstone for the major advances in navigation which took place from the tenth to the fifteenth century. These scientific advancements were put to good use as the Africans engaged in long distance navigations for the purpose of trading precious metals with Mycenean Greeks. Furthermore, Africans possessed highly developed mathematics for the precise standards necessary to support this type of activity. This can be readily discerned by reviewing the nagivational records of the twelfth and thirteenth centuries. During

17

these centuries large expeditions frequently departed from the ports of Cadiz, Barcelona, and Cartagena. Based upon improvements resulting from these and similar voyages, Christian nations remodeled and improved their maritime regulations.[33]

These occurrences should help shatter the myth of European navigational superiority during this period. If not, there are other facts to support the thesis of African navigational superiorty. During the fifteenth century, Prince Henry the Navigator set up a school where Portugese instructors were taught by Moors. Students in this school included Columbus, Vespucci, and Magellan.[34] As a result of this training, Europeans were able to define what they thought to be India on the World map; of course, the Europeans miscalculated often.

When one looks at this obvious maritime superiority against, what were by Columbus' own admission, less developed European skills, it becomes apparent that Africans were also capable of such voyages. Heyerdahl recently proved it could be done. In 1969 he resolved to sail from Africa to the Americas in a reed boat of the type made by ancient Africans. According to the National Geographic, January 1971:

> The hull consists of two main bundles plus a small center one, all lashed together with a continuous spiraling rope. Thin bundles on each side form the gunwales, no metal -- not a nail or screw -- was used.

To make a long story short, he made a successful crossing in 57 days, from Africa to the West Indies. Surely, this was a repeat of adventures carried out by Africans centuries earlier on a continuous basis.

A Word On Detractors

Even in the face of this multitude of evidence, those who contend for Pre-Columbian African exploration are not without their detractors. Much of the reason for this opposition is traceable to the impact made by White scholars who wrote during the fifteenth to nineteenth centuries. Bent upon justifying the slave trade, they became slaves, in turn, to the theory of innate African inferiority. Obviously, these writers worked from a narrow perspective and tended to detract from, rather than appreciate, what was already known in terms of African worldwide contributions. Frequently, Whites have sought convenient means by which to discredit the contributions of the Americans of African descent. White scholars have constructed a "history" which depicts Anglo Saxons as superior beings.

The pragmatic result of such efforts is the daily oppression of non-Whites, particularly Blacks. There was a vague prejudice against Blacks even before the first Whites came to America -- but prejudice against Blacks reached its zenith on American shores. There has always been, inherent within this society, a definite tendency to associate blackness with savagery, heathenism, and a general failure to observe and adhere to the White European standard of conformity and propriety.[37] Therefore it is not surprising that White scholars continue to ignore **any** data which presents Blacks in a favorable light. The data presented in this paper is seen, by Whites, as products of the African imagination, boastful exaggeration or plain lies.[38] Proponents of the thesis that Blacks were here before Columbus have been forced to over-prove their contentions or to mention their ideas vaguely, in passing, for fear of being criticized or ridiculed.[39]

White scholars, consciously or unconsciously, have tended to discredit the accomplishments of Africans and their descendants. In the past when a Black African type achieved greatness it was quickly pointed out or suggested that he was part-White, and that the white blood was responsible for the achievements; or that those involved were Hamites, dark-skinned Whites, Arabs, Hindus, Muslims, Egyptians and other labels intended to avoid the fact that many of these people were Black Africans. In closing, if we can accept as fact the presence of the Vikings in America before Columbus, based upon a few scattered artifacts and some grapevines then we must accept the overwhelming evidence that Africans reached the shores of the Western Hemisphere before Columbus.

Von Daniken provides an appropriate closing thought:

> What I am saying is that at some time or other the technical feasibility of every new idea vitally affecting the life of mankind was not proven. Proof of its practicability was always preceded by speculation of the so-called visionaries who were violently attacked or what is often harder to stomach laughed at condescendingly by their contemporaries.[40]

REFERENCES

1. N. Leon, Historia - General de Mexico: Mexico, 1919, p. 14; Riva - Palacio. Mexico A V Traves De Los Sigos. Mexico, 1887, Vol I, p. 63-67.

2. Oregionian, Portland, Oregon, October 12, 1970.

3. W.E.B. DuBois, THE GIFT OF BLACK FOLKS, Boston, 1924, p. 35-51; Carter G. Woodsen, THE STORY OF THE NEGRO RE-TOLD, Washington, D.C., p. 13-14. Leo Wiener, AFRICA AND THE DISCOVERY OF AMERICA. 1-III. Philly, 1922.

4. Roland B. Dixon, THE RACIAL HISTORY OF MAN. New York: p. 393-406.

5. UPI Release, 11/72: Interview with Richard Leakey, "Skull Dates Man 2,500,000 years Ago." Leakey, son of the famed anthropologist is Director of the Nationai Museum of Kenya.

6. Dixon, **op. cit.**, p. 393-406.

7. William G. Haag, SCIENTIFIC AMERICAN, "The Bering Strait Land Bridge." January 1962, p. 112-113.

8. UPI Release, 11/72: **op. cit.**

9. Virginia Steen-McIntyre, Roald Fryxell, and Harold E. Malde. Paper given by Harold E. Malde "Unexpectedly Old Age of Deposits at Hueyatlaco Archaeological site, Valcequillo, Mexico, implied by New Stratigraphic and Petrographic Findings, Nov. 12, 1973.

10. William G. Haag, **op.cit.** p. 112-113.

11. Carter G. Woodsen, **op. cit.**, p. 13-14; Justin Winsor, CRITICAL HISTORY OF AMERICA, Boston, 1884-1889; W.E.B. DuBois, THE GIFT OF BLACK FOLKS, Boston, 1924 p. 35-51; Roland B. Dixon, THE RACIAL HISTORY OF MAN, New York: 1923, p. 393-406, 436, 451 and 459; B. Thacher, CHRISTOPHER COLUM-BUS, 1903, Vol. 2 p. 379-380; J. McCabe, THE SPLENDOR OF MOORISH SPAIN, London, 1935, p. 179-202; A. Quatrefages, INTRODUCTION A LETUDE DES RACES HUMAINES, Paris,

1889, p. 406; Leo Wiener, Africa and the Discovery of America, Vol. I, 1922, p. 169-170, 172, 174, 175 and Vol. III P. 225-261, 264-266, 314-322; and Harold G. Lawrence, THE CRISIS "African Explorers of the New World," 1962, p. 321-332. N. Leon, "Historia - General de Mexico, Mexico, 1919, p. 14.

12. Roland B. Dixon, THE RACIAL HISTORY OF MAN, New York: 1923, p. 400.

13. **Ibid.**, p. 409.

14. **Ibid.**, p. 441.

15. **Ibid.**, p. 403.

16. C. Jane, VOYAGES OF COLUMBUS, N.H. Hakluyt II Series Vol. LXX, London: 1930, p. 164-165, OREGIONIAN. **Op cit.** Harold G. Lawrence, AFRICAN EXPLORERS OF THE NEW WORLD, p. 321-332.

17. A. Quatrefages, INTRODUCTION A. LETUDE DES RACES HUMAINES, Paris, 1889, p. 406.

18. Leo Wiener, **op. cit.** Vol. I, p. 169-170, 172, 174-175, and III p. 225-261, 264-266, 314-322; J.A. Rogers, SEX AND RACE Vol. I, p. 270.

19. J.A. Rogers, AFRICAS GIFT TO AMERICA, New York, 1961, p. 15.

20. Riva-Palacio, **Op. cit.**, p. 163.

21. A. Hyatt Verril, OLD CIVILIZATIONS OF THE NEW WORLD, Indianapolis, 1929, p. 145.

22. Leo Wiener, p. 322, Rogers **op. cit.** p. 17.

23. The Fourth Annual Report, U.S. Bureau of Ethnology, p. 407-409.

24. Roland B. Dixon, **op. cit.**, p. 436,451,459; A.E. Hooten APES, MEN AND MORONS, London: 1939, p. 183.

25. Ignatius Donnelly, Atlantis, "The Testimony of the Flora and Fauna." New York: 1949, p. 44-52; W.E.B. DuBois, THE GIFT OF BLACK FOLKS, Boston: 1924, p. 4 and 5; M. Jeffereys, SCIENTIA, "Pre-Columbian Negroes in America," XIIC, 1953.

26. C. Jane, VOYAGES OF COLUMBUS, N.H. Hakluyt II Series Vol. LXX, London; 1930, p. 164-165.

27. J. Ogilby, AFRICA, London: 1670.

28. F. Peterson, Sepia, "Africans Beat Columbus to the New World." Vol. 18, #2, 1969, p. 10-13; Leo Wiener, AFRICA AND THE DISCOVERY OF AMERICA, Vol. I-II.

29. Wiener **Ibid.**

30. Peterson, **op. cit.**, p. 10-13.

31. M. Jeffreys, **op. cit.**

32. Lady Lugard, A TROPICAL DEPENDENCY, London: 1906; M. Jeffreys, **op. cit.**; Carter G. Woodsen, THE AFRICAN BACKGROUND OUTLINED, Washington, D.C., 1936, p..56.

33. Lancelot Hogben, MATHEMATICS FOR MILLIONS, 1953, p. 26; Livio Castallo Stecchini, SECRETS OF THE GREAT PYRAMIDS, Edited by Peter Tompkins, Navigational Contribution, 1971, p. 351; Theodor Noldeke, et al. HISTORIAN'S HISTORY OF THE WORLD. Edited by Henry Williams, 1904, p. 273.

34. Lancelot Hogben, **op. cit.**, p. 54-55 and 363; NATIONAL GEOGRAPHIC August, 1964, Vol. 126, #2; May 1965, Vol. 127, #5, August 1966, Vol 130, #2; and September, 1968, Vol. 134, #3.

35. M. Jeffreys, **op. cit.**

36. RELAVENT MAGAZINE, Afro-Studies, No. 47788, 1972, New York: p. 48-51.

37. G. M. Fredrickson, KEY ISSUES IN THE AFRO-AMERICAN EXPERIENCE, "Toward a Social Interpretation of the Development of American Racism, Vol., N.Y., 1971, p. 240-254.

38. Alan H. Broderick, MIRAGE OF AFRICA, London: 1953, p. 53; Janheinz Jahn, AN OUTLINE OF THE NEW AFRICAN CULTURE, New York: 1958, p. 11-38; Basil Davidson, THE AFRICAN SLAVE TRADE, U.S.A., p. XII-XXIV.

39. Eric Von Doniken, GODS FROM OUTER SPACE, p. 2.

40. **Ibid.**

I am by birth and law a free black American citizen. As such I have both rights and duties.

W. E. B. DuBois
THE CRISIS, 1913

CHAPTER TWO

A HISTORICAL ANALYSIS OF THE BLACK POPULATION IN THE UNITED STATES: RACE, CENSUS AND PUBLIC POLICY

Huey L. Perry

The black population is currently the largest racial minority group in the United States.[1] The black population in the United States has undergone some significant changes over the course of its history. This chapter describes and analyzes characteristics of the black population in the United States in selected categories from 1790, the year the first census was taken, to 1980. These categories are: growth, distribution and composition. The chapter focuses on describing and analyzing changes in the black population over the history of census taking in the United States in these three categories. Prior to the summary and conclusion section of the chapter, there is a discussion of the policy consequences of census taking for blacks.

Growth, Distribution, and Composition[2]

Growth

This section provides a brief historical sketch of the growth of the black population in the United States. Available data on the size of the black population pre-date the 1790 census, going back to colonial times. The earliest year for which data are available is 1650 and for that year, which was just a few years after the importation of black slaves began, it is estimated that the colonies contained about 1,600 blacks. Additional estimates put the size of the black population in the United States at 462,000 in 1770 and 562,000 in 1780.[3] If these figures are accurate, this means that the black population in the United States increased by more than a three hundred fifty-fold increase between 1650 and 1780. At the time the first census of the United States was taken in 1790, there were about 757,000 blacks in the country (Table 1). By 1890 the black population numbered 7.5 million, which represented a nearly tenfold increase over the century since the first census.[4] As the bicentennial observance of the first census approaches, the current size of the black population in the United States is 26.4 million, which represents a thirty-four fold increase over the 1790 figure and nearly a $3\frac{1}{2}$ time increase over the 1890 figure.

The growth rate of the black population in the United States since the 1790 census has fluctuated considerably. Between the 1790 census and the 1860 census, the census preceding the civil war, the black population grew at the rapid rate of over 2.0 per year.[5] Table 1 shows that the 1860 black population growth rate of 2.53 is the highest black growth rate in the history of census taking. The two factors accounting for this rapid and sustained growth rate are the artificial (non-natural) expansion of the black population via the continued legal importation of slaves prior to January 1, 1808 and the illegal slave trafficking after January 1, 1808, and the natural increase (excess of births over deaths) of the black population.

After the Civil War, the growth rate of the black population declined owing to the complete cessation of the slave trade and decline of black fertility. Table 1 shows that this trend continued, with only an occasional deviation (in 1900 and 1930), until 1940. Over the decades of the 1950s and 1960s the black population, like the total population in the United States, owing to the post-war "baby boom" experienced a more rapid growth rate, although the black growth rate reached a post-war high in the decade from 1950 to 1960 of 2.29 which approached its all time high of 1860. By 1970, the black growth rate dropped significantly owing to a lower fertility rate.

As Table 1 also shows, blacks constituted a larger proportion (19.3 percent) of the total population in the first census than in any other subsequent census up to 1910 and a much larger proportion of any other census after the 1910 census. Between 1790 and 1930, the proportion that blacks comprised of the total population in the United States declined with each census. The principle factor accounting for this 140 year decline was the significant increase in the white population in the United States resulting from waves of European immigration over this period. The proportion of blacks, however, began to rise after 1940 and by 1980 had reached the twentieth century high of just under 12 percent. This rise was attributable to a significant lowering of the rate of immigration by means of public policy.

Table 1. Total Resident Population for Selected Years: 1790 to 1980

Year	Millions of persons		Percent Black of total	Average annual rate of increase[1]	
	Total	Black		Total	Black
1790.......	3.9	0.8	19.3	(X)	(X)
1860.......	31.4	4.4	14.1	2.97	2.53
1870[2]	39.8	5.4	13.5	2.36	1.94
1890.......	62.9	7.5	11.9	2.29	1.64
1900.......	76.2	8.8	11.6	1.91	1.79
1910.......	92.2	9.8	10.7	1.91	1.07
1920.......	106.0	10.5	9.9	1.39	0.94
1930.......	123.2	11.9	9.7	1.50	1.28
1940.......	132.2	12.9	9.7	0.70	0.79
1950.......	151.3	15.0	9.9	1.35	1.56
1960.......	179.3	18.9	10.5	1.70	2.29
1970.......	203.2	22.6	11.1	1.25	1.77
1980.......	225.2	26.4	11.8	?	?

X Not applicable.

[1] Computed by the formula for continuous compounding, $P_1 = P_o e^{rt}$

[2] Revised to include adjustment of 1,260,078 persons (512,163 Black and 747,915 White) for underenumeration in the Southern States. Unrevised census count is 38,558,371 for the total population and 4,880,009 for the Black population. Unadjusted data are used in subsequent tables because revised figures for States, age, etc., are not available.

NOTE: The 1930 census and subsequent decennial censuses were conducted as of April 1 of the respective year: prior to 1930, the month of enumeration varied.

SOURCE: The data appearing in this table, except the 1980 data, and the above notes are taken from the U.S. Department of Commerce, Bureau of the Census, The Social and Economic Status of the Black Population in the United States: An Historical View, 1790-1971, Current Population Reports, Special Studies, Series P-23, No. 80 (Washington, D.C.: U.S. Government Printing Office). The 1980 data are taken from the U.S. Department of Commerce, Bureau of the Census, 1980 Census of the United States.

Distribution

Prior to World War II, the great majority of blacks in the United States lived in the southern states. Each census from 1790 to 1910 showed that 9 out of every 10 blacks in the United States lived in the South. Although the proportion of blacks living in the South declined after 1910, 3 out of every 4 blacks continued to live in the South by 1940. These numbers reflect the fact of black migration out of the South beginning during World War I and continuing in the post-war years. During the 1920s, the net outmigration of blacks from the South was 749,000 as compared to 450,000 in the previous decade.[6] The first episode of the northward migration of southern blacks was caused in part by the labor supply shortage in the North which in turn was caused by the United States' participation in the War. The fact that many white males in the labor force had to interrupt their participation in the workforce in order to serve in the armed services created a shortage in the nation's manpower supply which was filled by those blacks who did not go to the armed services and women. Other reasons accounting for the northward migration of southern blacks during the 1920s include the decline of agriculture in the South and the intense racial oppression to which blacks were subjected by southern whites. In the 1930s outmigration of blacks from the South continued but at a considerably reduced pace.

During the 1940s, the migration of southern blacks to the North was repeated but this time with a considerably greater magnitude. Not only was this second migration larger than the first but it also lasted longer, continuing well into the 1970s. Over this three decade period, the South lost close to 1.5 million blacks in each of the three decades. Another set of statistics even more vividly reveals the changing regional demographics of the black population in the United States between 1940 and 1970. In 1940, 75 percent of the black population resided in the South; by 1970, only 53 percent of the black population resided in the South.[7] Thus in thirty years the proportion of blacks residing in the South had declined a significant 22 percentage points. The reasons accounting for this second migration were basically the same as those causing the first: a shortage in the northern labor supply created by American participation in World War II and the continued decline of agriculture in the South combined with the continued oppression of blacks.

Most blacks who migrated out of the South during World War I, the interwar years, and World War II moved to the North. The data in Table 2 clearly show this pattern. In 1910 only 10 percent of the

Table 2. Distribution of the Population, by Region for Selected Years: 1790 to 1980

Area and race	1790	1870	1910	1940	1960	1970	1980
BLACK							
United States...millions.	1	5	10	13	19	23	26
percent, total.........	100	100	100	100	100	100	100
South.......................	91	91	89	77	60	53	50
North.......................	9	9	10	22	34	39	58
Northeast.................	9	4	5	11	16	19	18
North Central.............	-	6	6	11	18	20	19
West.......................	-	-	1	1	6	8	9
WHITE							
United States...millions.	3	34	82	118	159	178	185
percent, total.........	100	100	100	100	100	100	100
South.......................	40	23	25	27	27	28	32
North.......................	60	74	67	62	56	54	53
Northeast.................	60	36	31	29	26	25	23
North Central.............	-	38	36	33	30	29	27
West.......................	-	3	8	11	16	18	19
BLACK AS A PERCENT OF THE TOTAL POPULATION							
United States...........	19	13	11	10	11	11	11
South.......................	35	36	30	24	21	19	19
North.......................	3	2	2	4	7	8	9
Northeast.................	3	1	2	4	7	9	10
North Central.............	-	2	2	4	7	8	8
West.......................	-	1	1	1	4	5	7

- Represents or rounds to zero.

SOURCE: The data appearing in this table, except the 1980 data, and the above notes are taken from the U.S. Department of Commerce, Bureau of the Census, The Social and Economic Status of the Black Population in the United States: An Historical View, 1790-1971, Current Population Reports, Special Studies, Series P-23, No. 80 (Washington, D.C.: U.S. Government Printing Office). The 1980 data are taken from the U.S. Department of Commerce, Bureau of the Census, 1980 Census of the United States.

Table 3. Estimated Net Intercensal Migration of Blacks, by Region:
1870 to 1980

(Numbers in thousands. Plus sign (+) denotes net in-migration;
minus sign (-) denotes net out-migration)

| Intercensal Period | South | North | | | West |
		Total	North-east	North Central	
1870-1880.............	-60	+60	+24	+36	(NA)
1880-1890.............	-70	+70	+46	+24	(NA)
1890-1900.............	-168	+168	+105	+63	(NA)
1900-1910.............	-170	+151	+95	+56	+20
1910-1920.............	-454	+426	+182	+244	+28
1920-1930.............	-749	+713	+349	+364	+36
1930-1940.............	-347	+299	+171	+128	+49
1940-1950.............	-1,599	+1,081	+463	+618	+339
1950-1960.............	-1,473	+1,037	+496	+541	[1]+193
1960-1970.............	-1,380	+994	+612	+382	+301
1970-1980.............	-1,378	+983	+786	+372	(NA)

NA Not available.

[1] Figure revised since prior publication.

NOTE: The net migration estimates for the period 1870-1940 were developed
by the national census survival rate method; the estimates for 1940-1970
were prepared by the vital statistics method. See "References for Tables"
for further information.

SOURCE: U.S. Department of Commerce, Bureau of the Census; and, Everett S.
Lee, et al. Population Redistribution and Economic Growth: United States,
1870-1950, Vol. I, The American Philosophical Society, Philadelphia 1957.
(See appendix A for copyright source.), cited in Current Population Reports,
Special Studies, Series P-23, No. 80 (Washington, D.C.: U.S. Government
Printing Office). The 1980 data are taken from the U.S. Department of
Commerce, Bureau of the Census, 1980 Census of the United States.

black population lived in the North (5 percent in the Northeast and
6 percent in the North Central), as compared to the 89 percent of
the black population that lived in the South. By 1910, however, the
proportion of the black population living in the North had more than
doubled to 22 percent (11 percent each in the Northeast and North
Central), while the proportion of blacks living in the South had declined
to 77 percent. Over this period, the West had only 1 percent of the
black population in the United States. These facts are understandable
given that the overwhelming majority of large plants and factories
needing the South's unskilled and low skilled black workers were in
the North. Although the proportion of the total black population
living in the North experienced another substantial increase of 12

Table 4. Distribution of the Population by Urban-Rural Residence and Nativity for Selected Years: 1980 to 1980

Year and race	Total popula- tion (thou- sands)	Percent residing in--			Foreign born		Native	
		Urban areas	Rural areas		Num- ber (thou- sands)	Percent of total popula- tion	Num- ber (thou- sands)	Percent born in South[1]
			Total	Farm				
BLACK								
1890........	7,489	20	80	(NA)	20	-	7,469	[2]93
1910........	9,828	27	73	(NA)	40	-	9,787	93
1940........	12,866	49	51	35	84	1	12,782	[2]89
1950........	15,045	62	38	21	114	1	14,931	[2]83
1960........	18,849	73	27	8	125	1	18,723	75
1970........	22,539	81	19	2	253	1	22,286	49
1980........	26,495	87	14	2	268	1	26,218	49
WHITE								
1890........	55,101	38	62	(NA)	9,122	17	45,979	28
1910........	81,732	49	51	(NA)	13,346	16	68,386	29
1940........	118,702	57	43	22	11,419	10	107,282	30
1950........	134,478	64	36	15	10,095	8	124,383	30
1960........	158,838	70	30	7	9,294	6	149,544	30
1970........	178,119	72	28	4	8,734	5	169,385	29
1980........	226,546	75	27	3	8,348	4	21,523	29

- Represents or rounds to zero.

NA Not available.

[1]Census Bureau evaluation studies for recent census (1960 and 1970) show that the figures for Blacks born in the South have been seriously understated.

[2]Partially estimated.

NOTE: The current definition of the urban population includes urbanized areas and places of 2,500 or more outside urbanized areas. This concept has been in effect since 1950 when substantial revisions were made.

SOURCE: The data appearing in this table, except the 1980 data, and the above notes are taken from the U.S. Department of Commerce, Bureau of the Census, The Social and Economic Status of the Black Population in the United States: An Historical View, 1790-1971, Current Population Reports, Special Studies, Series P-23, No. 80 (Washington, D.C.: U.S. Government Printing Office). The 1980 data are taken from the U.S. Department of Commerce, Bureau of the Census, 1980 Census of the United States.

percentage points to 34 percent in 1960, the 1970 figures reflected a more modest increase (5 percent) and the 1980 figures virtually no increase. Over these three decades, the proportion of blacks living in the South dropped to 60 percent in 1960, 53 percent in 1970, and 50 percent in 1980. By 1960, a significant number of those blacks leaving the South had begun to migrate to the West as the West had 6 percent of the total black population in that year; by 1970, 8 percent; and 1980, 9 percent. Table 3 provides additional support for these points. A substantial number of those southern blacks who migrated to the West settled in one state -- California.

As pronounced as the above migratory patterns were between the 1940s and 1970s, the movement of blacks during this period consisted of more than just a simple interregional migration. There was also during this period an overlapping rural to urban movement. Thus, blacks not only moved from the South to the North and West; they also moved from the farms to the cities, especially to the cities in the North and West. Prior to 1940, the great majority of the black population in the United States resided in rural areas. According to the 1890 census, which was the first census containing urban-rural data for blacks, 80 percent of the black population resided in rural areas as Table 4 shows. Table 4 further shows that by 1970, eighty years later, the situation had completely reversed itself as 81 percent of the black population lived in urban areas. Table 4 shows that the greatest spurts in the urbanization of the black population occurred between 1940 and 1960.

The combined effect of the interregional and the rural-to-urban population movements exerted a tremendous impact on redistributing the black population in the United States over the course of the twentieth century. "...By 1970, only 53 percent of Blacks lived in the South and 81 percent lived in urban areas".[8] By 1980, the proportion of blacks living in the South had declined to an all time low of 50 percent, with a record high of 87 percent of blacks residing in urban areas.

There is a sub-pattern to the general pattern of blacks being urban dwellers and that sub-pattern is that urban blacks concentrate in increasing numbers in central cities of the largest metropolitan areas. The proportion of blacks of the total central city population rose from 16 percent in 1960 to 21 percent in 1970 and to 24 percent in 1980 (See Table 5). The proportional increases of blacks in the metropolitan areas of 1 million or more people were even greater during this period: 19 percent in 1960, 25 percent in 1970, and 30 percent in 1980, as Table 5 also shows that Blacks are not suburban dwellers

Table 5. Black as a Percent of Total Population Inside and Outside
by Size of Metropolitan Area: 1960, 1970, and 1980

(Data shown according to the definition and size of metropolitan
area in 1970)

Type of Residence	1960	1970	1980
United States.......................	10.6	11.1	11.4
Metropolitan areas[1].....................	10.7	11.9	13.3
Central cities........................	16.4	20.5	23.8
Central cities in metropolitan			
areas of-- 1,000,000 or more.....	18.8	25.2	29.9
Less than 1,000,000...............	13.2	14.9	18.8
Suburbs.................................	4.8	4.6	5.2
Suburbs in metropolitan areas of--			
1,000,000 or more................	4.0	4.5	5.6
Less than 1,000,000..............	5.9	4.8	4.8
Nonmetropolitan areas..................	10.3	9.1	8.8
In counties designated metropolitan			
since 1970.......................	(X)	7.7	NA

X Not applicable.

NA Not available.

[1] Excludes Middlesex and Somerset Counties in New Jersey.

NOTE· Standard metropolitan areas as a statistical concept were first
used in the 1950 census. However, data for 1950 have not been reconstructed
according to the 1970 definition of metropolitan areas.

SOURCE: The data appearing in this table, except the 1980 data, and the
above notes are taken from the U.S. Department of Commerce, Bureau of the
Census, The Social and Economic Status of the Black Population in the United
States: An Historical View, 1790-1971, Current Population Reports, Special
Studies, Series P-23, No. 80 (Washington, D C.: U.S. Department of Commerce,
Bureau of the Census, 1980 Census of the United States.

to any significant extent. Between 1960 and 1980 the percentage
of blacks living in all suburbs, remained low, ranging between 4
and 6 percent over this period.

In the 1970s, a new pattern of black migration emerged. In this decade,
the South experienced a decline in the volume of black outmigration
and an increase in black immigration. In other words, the data suggest
that the long established pattern of a net outmigration of blacks
from the South had begun to reverse itself, with more blacks coming

31

Table 6. Interregional Migration of the Population 5 Years Old and Over:
March 1970 to March 1975

(Numbers in thousands. Minus sign (-) denotes decrease)

Migration status and race	South	Northeast	North Central	West
BLACK				
Immigrants....................	302	118	150	153
Outmigrants..................	288	182	202	51
Net migration...............	14	-64	-52	102
WHITE				
Immigrants....................	3,730	920	1,569	2,155
Outmigrants..................	1,939	2,160	2,714	1,561
Net migration...............	1,791	-1,240	-1,145	594

SOURCE: The data appearing in this table, are taken from the U.S. Department
of Commerce, Bureau of the Census, The Social and Economic Status of the
Black Population in the United States: An Historical View, 1790-1971,
Current Population Reports, Special Studies, Series P-23, No. 80 (Washington,
D.C.: U.S. Government Printing Office).

into the South than leaving the South. As Table 6 shows, during the
five year period from 1970 to 1975, 302,000 blacks migrated into
the South while only 228,000 migrated out of the South, making for
a net migration gain of 14,000. The reason for this new pattern of
black migration is often explained in the context of the frostbelt
(or snowbelt) versus the sunbelt phenomenon, that is, the relocation
of people and businesses from the harsh weather, high taxes, and
declining cities of the North where organized labor is generally strong
to warmer climate, lower taxes, and the growing cities of the South
and Southwest where organized labor's presence is virtually negligible.[9]
As Table 7 shows, this pattern continued apace with a slight increase
between 1975 and 1980.

Table 7. Interregional Migration of the Population 5 Years Old and Over:
March 1975 to March 1980

(Numbers in thousands. Minus sign (-) denotes decrease)

Migration status and race	South	Northeast	North Central	West
BLACK				
Immigrants....................	384	168	205	192
Outmigrants..................	327	258	263	82
Net migration................	17	NA	NA	136
WHITE				
Immigrants....................	5,853	1,121	2,659	3,681
Outmigrants..................	2,458	3,163	3,533	1,987
Net migration................	2,137	-1,734	-1,574	786

NA Not Available.

SOURCE: The data appearing in this table, except the 1980 data, and the
above notes are taken from the U.S. Department of Commerce, Bureau of the
Census, The Social and Economic Status of the Black Population in the United
States: An Historical View, 1790-1971, Current Population Reports, Special
Studies, Series P-23, No. 80 (Washington, D.C.: U.S. Department of Commerce,
Bureau of the Census, 1980 Census of the United States.

Composition

This section focuses on the age and sex composition of the black
population in the United States. The age distribution of the black
population in the United States has shown substantial change over
the past 100 years. The thrust of the change is that the median age
of the black population over the last century has increased. In 1870,
the median age of the black population, as Table 8 shows, was a youthful 18.5 years. Over the next seven decades from 1870 to 1940, the
median age of the black population increased by 6.6 years to 25.1
years. This marked increase in the median age of the black population
was primarily attributed to the decline in black fertility. The median
age of the black population dropped slightly during the decade of
the 1960s and increased slightly during the decade of the 1970s, undoubtedly reflecting the impact of the post-war baby boom and the
decline in fertility in its aftermath.

Table 8. Black Population by Age and Sex for Selected Years:

(Numbers in thousands)

Age and Sex	1870	1910	1940	1960	1970	1980
Total Black Population	4,880	9,798	12,866	18,849	22,580	26,495
AGE						
All ages...........	100	100	100	100	100	100
Under 5 years..........	16	13	10	14	11	9
5 to 9 years...........	13	13	10	13	12	10
10 to 14 years.........	13	12	10	10	12	13
15 to 19 years.........	11	11	10	8	11	11
20 to 24 years.........		10	9	6	8	10
25 to 34 years.........		16	17	13	12	13
35 to 44 years.........	46	11	14	12	11	9
45 to 54 years.........		7	10	10	9	9
55 to 64 years.........		4	5	7	7	7
65 years and over......		3	5	6	7	7
Age not reported.......	-	-	(X)	(X)	(X)	(X)
Median age.............	18.5	20.8	25.1	23.5	22.4	24.5
SEX						
Male...................	2,393	4,856	6,269	9,098	10,748	12,569
Female.................	2,487	4,942	6,596	9,751	11,832	13,926
Males per 100 females..	96.2	98.3	95.0	93.3	90.8	91.0

- Represents or rounds to zero.

X Not applicable.

SOURCE: The data appearing in this table, except the 1980 data, and the
above notes are taken from the U.S. Department of Commerce, Bureau of the
Census, The Social and Economic Status of the Black Population in the United
States: An Historical View, 1790-1971, Current Population Reports, Special
Studies, Series P-23, No. 80 (Washington, D.C.: U.S. Government Printing
Office). The 1980 data are taken from the U.S. Department of Commerce,
Bureau of the Census, 1980 Census of the United States. The age and sex
data appearing on this table are in reverse order from its appearance in
the reference source.

Another way of documenting the change in the age composition of
the black population over time is by examining the lower and upper
ranges of the black population in terms of their proportion of the
total black population. The proportion of the black population below
the age of 15 has varied from census to census since 1910, commensu-
rate with changing fertility levels. As Table 8 shows, the proportion
of the black population below the age of 15 declined from 38 to 30
percent between 1910 and 1940, climbed to 37 percent in 1960, dropped

34

to 35 percent in 1970 and to 32 percent in 1980.[10] Unlike the below 15 years of age category, the proportion of the black population 65 years of age and older, as Table 8 shows, has constituted a small but continually increasing portion of the total black population since 1910. Between 1910 and 1980, the percent of the black population 65 years of age and older increased from three percent to seven percent which amounts to more than a doubling of the population over this 70 year period. This continual increase in the upper range of the black population is due to a decline in fertility rates as well as medical advancement.

With regard to the gender composition of the black population in the United States, census data show a consistent pattern for over 100 years. As Table 8 shows, black females have outnumbered black males since 1870. In the 1970 census, there were over 1 million more females than males in the black population; in the 1980 census, more than 1.3 million more females than males. The sex ratio (the number of males per 100 females) of the black population during the last seven censuses has varied from 96 in 1870 to a high of 98 in 1910 to a low of 91 in 1970 and in 1980. In some quarters, this is an alarming pattern with many troublesome implications, not the least of which is the difficulty of black women to find suitable mates. However, a study by the United States Census Bureau cautions that female overrepresentation in the black population as suggested by the sex ratio may be overstated owing to the relatively greater uncoverage (or underreporting) of males than females in the decennial census. The study indicates that, for example, the estimated 1970 sex ratio of 91 based on census returns corrected for undercoverage is 95.[11]

The above point about the undercoverage or underreporting in census returns leads to a much discussed subject in recent years, that is, the extent to which the black population in general is accurately counted in the United States Census and the political and policy implications for the national black community of blacks being undercounted. This article now turns attention to an examination of this important subject.

Political and Policy Implications of the United States Census Count of the Black Population

It has become a well established fact in the political and social sciences that government rules and practices are not neutral, that is, their impact on various groups in society is not the same.[12] The same applies to the function of the United States Census in counting the nation's population. The point is that the census count is not an insignificant activity. Rather, the census count is a very important activity full of policy implications for various population groups. The allocation of federal aid to cities and states is heavily influenced by census data and statistics calculated on the basis of census data.

William P. O'Hare writes:

...How often unemployment rates are published, the subgroups or geographic areas for which unemployment rates are calculated, and the quality of the statistics produced are all policy decisions. This area of public policy receives little attention, and it may seem like a rather arcane topic. But the numbers produced by the federal statistical system are used to distribute billions of dollars in federal aid. In fiscal year 1979, for example, statistical data were instrumental in the distribution of $122 billion through over 150 domestic assistance programs.[13]

As O'Hare accurately notes, these statistical data are the primary method for determining whether particular federal programs are succeeding or failing. It is also true, as O'Hare observes, that reappointment and redistricting of the United States Congress as well as most state and local jurisdictions are based on data from the Census Bureau, which is a major arm of the federal statistical system.[14] O'Hare further notes that the population figures produced by the Census Bureau are used by other federal agencies to calculate various indices and rates.[15]

Integrally related to the question of the importance of census data and statistical data based on census data is the accuracy of the census data as regards various population groups. Many black interest group leaders, public officials and academic researchers have long felt that blacks are undercounted in the census. Black interest group leaders and black public officials must take their concern further; that is, they must seek to have input into the planning by the Census Bureau for the decennial census. The questions that are asked and those that are not asked on the census form can materially affect not only how black interest group leaders and black public officials perform their jobs but more importantly the well-being of their constituents.

Summary and Conclusions

As the 200th anniversary of the first census nears, there are some definite demographic patterns characteristic of the black population in the United States. The nation's black population is a highly urbanized black population with 81 percent of the population residing in urbanized areas with the great majority of these residing in central cities. The black population is evenly divided between the South and the non-South with 50 percent in the South and 50 percent in the non-South. A very significant recent trend is that the time-honored pattern of black net outmigration from the South came to an end during the decade of the 1970s. Now there are more blacks coming into the South than there are blacks leaving the South. One of the significant implications of this emerging trend is the potential for increased black political power in the South.

Age-wise, the median age of the black population is increasing with the percentage of persons under 15 years of age getting smaller and the percentage of persons 65 years old and over getting larger. With regard to the sex composition of the black population, the 100 year plus pattern of females outnumbering males remains unchanged. In fact, the ratio of men to women has actually increased over the decades. This statistic gives rise to a number of troublesome implications. Especially significant in this regard is the difficulty black females experience in finding suitable social and marriage partners.

Finally, this study confirms the relevance of census data for public policy formulation and in turn for minority interests. It is clearly in the interest of the black interest group leaders and public officials and that of their constituents for black interest group leaders and public officials to participate in the planning process of the Census Bureau. Federal aid allocation and reapportionment and redistricting for the United States House of Representatives as well as most state and local jurisdictions are based on census data. Census taking is clearly an important, policy relevant activity in which every effort should be made that the black population be accurately enumerated.

FOOTNOTES

1. The position of blacks as being the largest racial minority in the United States may not continue beyond the next decade-and-a-half as some demographers predict that by the turn of the twenty-first century Hispanics will have become the largest racial minority group in the country.

2. These categories are used in the U.S. Department of Commerce, Bureau of the Census, THE SOCIAL AND ECONOMIC STATUS OF THE BLACK POPULATION IN UNITED STATES: AN HISTORICAL VIEW, 1790-1971, Current Population Reports, Special Studies, Series P-23, No 80 (Washington, D.C. U.S. Government Printing Office). This chapter relies heavily on data presented in this volume.

3. U.S. Bureau of the Census Department of Commerce and Labor, A CENTURY OF POPULATION GROWTH IN THE UNITED STATES: 1790-1900 (Washington, D.C. Government Printing Office, 1909), p. 8.

4. U.S. Bureau of the Census, THE SOCIAL AND ECONOMIC STATUS OF THE BLACK POPULATION IN THE UNITED STATES, p. 6.

5. **Ibid.**

6. **Ibid.**, p. 7.

7. **Ibid.**

8. **Ibid.**

9. For a thorough discussion of this lively debate see Kirkpatrick Sale, POWERSHIFT: THE RISE OF THE SOUTHERN RIM AND ITS CHALLENGE TO THE EASTERN ESTABLISHMENT (New York: Random House, 1975) and David C. Perry and Afred J. Watkins, eds., THE RISE OF THE SUNBELT CITIES (Beverly Hills: Sage Publications, Inc., 1977).

10. These figures are obtained by summing the figures in the respective columns for 10 to 14 years, 5 to 9 years, and under 5 years categories in Table 7.

11. U.S. Bureau of the Census, EVALUATION AND RESEARCH PROGRAM OF ESTIMATES OF COVERAGE OF POPULATION BY SEX, RACE, AND AGE: DEMOGRAPHIC ANALYSIS, PHC (E)-4, 1973, p. 28.

12. For a thorough discussion of this concept, see Edwin Dorn, RULES AND RACIAL EQUALITY (New Haven: Yale University Press, 1979).

13. WIlliam P. O'Hare, "Statistics and Public Policy", FOCUS, April, 1983, p. 7.

14. **Ibid.**

15. **Ibid.**

The future of American Negroes is in the South.

W. E. B. DuBois
BEHOLD THE LAND, 1946

CHAPTER THREE

EXODUS FROM THE PROMISED LAND: REVERSAL OF A HISTORICAL PATTERN OF BLACK MIGRATION IN THE UNITED STATES

Isaac A. Robinson

The literature on internal migration in the United States yields a paucity of current research on the geographical mobility of the black population (Strangler, 1975). The current foci of demographers, journalists and urban planners are the rise of the "New South" and the immigration of white business executives and their families from the northern region (Rice, 1981; Abbott, 1981). Some research has also focused upon the immigration of elderly whites into sunny retirement centers in the South (Bigger, 1979), however the immigration patterns of blacks have been largely ignored. It is interesting to note that this inattention has occurred during one of the most significant periods in the history of black migration in the United States. Recent trends indicate a growing immigration of blacks to the South -- a reversal of the historical pattern of outmigration from the region. It appears that the migration pattern of the black population in the United States has come full circle over several historical periods.

Given the lack of substantive research on present-day migration patterns of the black population of the United States, this essay will examine the current period of black migration within a historical perspective. The essential focus will be upon identifying and analyzing the major social, economic, and political factors associated with migration patterns over three historical periods. The first period, immediately after the Civil War until 1910, witnessed very little movement of the black population. The second period extended from World War I through the 1960s and was known as "the Great Northern Migration". The third period, beginning with the mid-1970s, saw a net immigration of blacks to the Southern region for the first time since the forced immigration of slaves into the region (Grant, 1962).

Conceptual Frame of Reference

One useful tool for explaining the interregional movement of blacks within the United States is the push-pull/intervening obstacles theory. This theory explains migration in terms of positive and negative factors at points of origin and destination weighed against the relative effort or cost of overcoming the obstacles that lie between the two points (Lee, 1966:47-57).

Essentially, the push-pull/intervening obstacles theory suggests that specific factors attract people to an area -- while other factors repulse people from an area. A major factor that tends to hold people in an area is "natural inertia" -- that is, the tendency to remain in one's present location because of the unfamiliarity of new areas and the comfortableness of familiar relationships in the area of origin. The pull (attraction) factors in an area of destination are generally related to social and economic conditions -- the promise of better jobs, better housing, and more opportunities for upward mobility. The intervening obstacles are the barriers that make it difficult to reach the desired area. These barriers may be laws restricting movement, the distance to be traveled, or the social and economic cost of making the move (Lee, 1966:47-57).

When this attraction-repulsion concept is applied to the three major periods of black migration within the United States, the influence of interregional push-pull factors become apparent. The period from slavery through the Emancipation Proclamation and until 1910 saw little interregional movement among the black population. However, after 1910 blacks began a tremendous migration from the South, a movement that continued through the 1960s. After 1970 this historical pattern at first declined and then reversed.

Delineating the Southern Region

There are several popular perceptions of what geographical area constitutes the southern region. The most popular commercial delineation of the region is the area making up the bottom half of the United States -- generally following the 37th parallel from the northern border of North Carolina through the lower one-third of California. For this paper, the South is conceptualized as those states in the region spanned from Delaware in the South Atlantic Division to Texas and Oklahoma in the West South Central Division (See Table 1). This conceptualization was borrowed from the U.S. Bureau of the Census.

41

Table 1

Regions and Geographic Divisions as
Defined by the U.S. Bureau of the Census

REGION	DIVISION	STATES
North East	New England	Maine, New Hampshire, Vermont, Massachusetts, Rhode Island, Connecticut
	Middle Atlantic	New York, New Jersey, Pennsylvania
North Central	East North Central	Ohio, Indiana, Illinois, Michigan, Wisconsin
	West North Central	Minnesota, Iowa, Missouri, North Dakota, South Dakota, Nebraska, Kansas
South	South Atlantic	Delaware, Maryland, District of Columbia, Virginia, West Virginia, North Carolina, South Carolina, Georgia, Florida
	East South Central	Kentucky, Tennessee, Alabama, Mississippi
	West South Central	Arkansas, Louisiana, Oklahoma, Texas
West	Mountain	Montana, Idaho, Wyoming, Colorado, New Mexico, Arizona, Utah, Nevada
	Pacific	Washington, Oregon, California, Alaska, Hawaii

Migration Before 1910

From the first forced immigration of blacks to the United States
in 1619 until around 1910, the black population rarely moved (Myrdal,
1944:183). Before the Civil War blacks were the property of white
slave owners, and free movement by them was illegal. The few trans-
fers of the black population during this period were related to the
buying and selling of slaves among white owners from plantation

42

to plantation and from state to state, primarily within the South (Grant, 1962:13). Some blacks escaped to the West, to the North, and even to Canada. However, this illegal movement represented a minute proportion of the slave population and has little statistical significance in terms of migration trends (Woodson, 1962:18-38).

Blacks continued to remain concentrated in the rural South for the period immediately following the Civil War and the ratification of the Thirteenth Amendment to the Constitution (Kennedy, 1930:30). This lack of movement lasted for the next four decades even though the legal restrictions on travel had been removed. Such migration as occurred consisted of short distance moves within the South or to states immediately adjacent thereto. For example, in 1820, 92.8 percent of the total black population of the United States resided in the South; by 1910, 89 percent were still there. Although the North had a general reputation of providing greater personal liberty during this period, the northward migration of blacks was only a trickle (Grant, 1962:14).

The end of the Civil War saw many blacks uprooted by the break-up of the large southern plantations. Many blacks were thus reduced to refugee status and around 72,500 were resettled in government camps in the District of Columbia, New York, Pennsylvania, and Massachusetts. Most blacks, however, remained in the South, migrating to many of the larger cities. In 1890 only 15.3 percent of southern blacks lived in cities; by 1910 the numbers had increased to 22 percent (Woofter, 1969:26).

Several hypotheses have been posited to explain why so few blacks left the South following the Civil War. Some hypotheses attribute this slow outmigration to southern blacks' fear of leaving their families, friends, and familiar places to go to new locations (Henri, 1975). A more useful hypothesis, however, attributes the slow outmigration of blacks to a reverse relationship between black migration to the North and the immigration of white Europeans to that area. Thomas stated that:

When immigration of foreign workers was in full spate the North-ward movement of Negroes was at a low ebb and vice versa. The rate of increase in the foreign-born population rose sharply from 20 percent to 32 percent in 1889 - 90 whereas the growth of the Negro population in the North fell from 36 to 14 percent. During the period 1910-30, when immigration was drastically reduced, first by World War I and then by the Immigration Restriction Act of 1924, an extraordinary increase took place in the number of Negroes enumerated in the North, 44 percent in 1910-20 and 67 percent in 1920-30 (Thomas, 1972:42).

Even though the black population was relatively free to move after 1870, the oppressive conditions in the South after the Civil War were not a strong enough repulsion factor for heavy outmigration of blacks. This situation can perhaps be explained in terms of the lack of strong attraction factors in other areas during the 1870-1910 period, especially in the northern states, where white European immigrants provided a labor supply for the rapidly developing industries in that region.

The Great Exodus from the South after 1910

From 1910 through the 1960s the black migration from the South swelled into one of the largest and strongest movements of people in the nation's history. The decrease in the numbers of European immigrants marked by World War I and the 1924 legislation restricting immigration, the increasing oppression of blacks in the South, and the attraction of jobs in northern industry are all considered major influences in releasing this migration stream (Henri, 1951:195).

The increased job opportunities in the North paralleled increasing discrimination, proscription, and mob violence toward blacks in the South. During this period, the South had developed a system for the social control of the black population. This system was first manifested in the form of mob violence, of which lynchings were the most prevalent incidents. Between 1889 and 1940, 3,449 blacks were lynched in the South (Myrdal, 1944:560). In addition, between 1896 and 1915, all southern states passed laws that disenfranchised their black populations. Other laws established racial segregation in schools, public accommodations, and all areas of social life (Meier, 1968:164). This period also witnessed the resurgence of the Ku Klux Klan, which became the primary informal enforcement agency of "Jim Crow" laws and the southern caste system. Thus, the combination of increasing job opportunities in the North and increasing oppression in the South set the stage for the great exodus of blacks from the South after 1910.

The greatest outmigration occurred between 1910 and 1930. Between 1890 and 1910 the number of blacks in the North increased by 46.6 percent, but between 1910 and 1930 the increase soared to 134.4 percent. In addition, blacks tended to migrate to certain states --

New York, New Jersey, Pennsylvania, Ohio, Illinois, Michigan, and the District of Columbia. The proportion of the total population increases in these states attributed to black immigration was 76 percent in 1910-20, 79 percent in 1920-30, 68 percent in 1930-40, and 70 percent in 1940-50 (Thomas, 1972:143).

Several authors have identified specific factors that served as strong pull factors for migration from the South during the 1910-30 period. One of these authors emphasized the influence of both labor agents sent South by northern industries to recruit black workers and black newspapers published in the North; some of the labor agents were salaried employees of large industrial companies while others were independent employment agents (Henri, 1975:187). The independent agents charged fees of $3 to $6 per new immigrant for their services, which included finding a job and housing for him.

The relatively high cost of transportation was a major obstacle for many blacks who wanted to migrate. For instance, the rail fare in 1910 was $22.52 per person from New Orleans to Chicago -- or over $135 for a family of six. A relatively short trip -- Norfolk, Virginia, to Pittsburgh, Pennsylvania -- cost a family of six $73 (Henri, 1975:66). Northern industries often paid the fare of those migrants who were coming to them to take specific jobs and then took the cost of the trip out of their wages.

Trains were backed into several Southern cities and hundreds of Negroes were gathered up in a day, loaded into the cars, and whirled away to the North. In February, 1917, a special train was sent to carry 191 Negro migrants from Bessemer, Alabama, to Pittsburgh at a cost to a coal company of $4,491.95 (Henri, 1975:60).

Another writer reported that the desire to leave the South was so great that many blacks deserted their jobs and went to the trains without notifying their employers or their families. Between 75,000 and 100,000 blacks went by rail to Pennsylvania to work for the Pennsylvania and Erie Railroad, while many more found work in Pennsylvania's steel mills, munitions plants, and other heavy industries (Baker, 1964).

Among the black newspapers published in the North, the CHICAGO DEFENDER is generally recognized as having played an important role in attracting southern blacks to the North. In the early 1900s this newspaper served as a major communications link between the

45

North and the South, its principle news and editorials being directed toward southern blacks. By 1920 the DEFENDER'S circulation had soared to 283,571, with about two-thirds of its readers outside of Chicago (Spears, 1967:143). Through accounts of job opportunities, improved social conditions, and success stories of recent migrants from the South, the paper made southern blacks aware of their plight and encouraged them to migrate North. Many of the DEFENDER'S headlines equated the flight from the South by blacks with the Israelites' flight out of Egypt (Spears, 1967:134-37).

There is considerable dispute regarding the number of blacks who left the South during the Great Northern Migration. Estimates range from 500,000 to 1,000,000 (Henri, 1975:201). The vast differences in the estimates were probably due to the undercounting of the black male population and the including of mulattoes in the white population. Although the exact number of black outmigrants during this period is uncertain, census data reflect a tremendous increase in the northern black population between 1910 and 1930. For instance, between 1900 and 1910 the black population of the North reportedly increased by 16.7 percent over the preceding decade; between 1910 and 1920 the increase was 43.3 percent; and between 1920 and 1930, 63.6 percent (Henri, 1975:201-05).

Implications of the Great Northern Migration

The historical record of black migration from the South continued steadily through the 1960s. Immediately after World War I the balance of attractions in the North and repulsions in the South maintained the outmigration pattern. The percentage of the black population who lived in the Northeast and North Central increased from 21.6 percent in 1940 to 39.2 percent in 1970. During this same period, the percentage of blacks who lived in the South decreased from 77 percent to 53.2 percent (Thomas, 1972:154).

The primary direction of migration from the South followed two well-defined streams to large industrial cities in the Northeast and North Central regions. By 1970 the black population of New York City was 1.5 million; Chicago had 1.15 million; and Philadelphia had 700,000 (Thomas, 1972:155). In 1970, 68 percent of the population in Washington, D.C. was black; in Detroit the figure was 47 percent, Baltimore had 45 percent black population, and St. Louis was 46 percent black. This relatively sudden shift in the rural/urban distribution of the black population precipitated a new set of problems associated with urban life. Blacks were concentrated in the ghettoes of these large

46

cities. The problems of unemployment, inadequate housing, family disorganization, and crime became endemic in these areas (Thomas, 1972:155-60).

In 1910 only 27 percent of the Negro population was classified as urban in comparison with 48 percent of the white population. By 1940 the Negro population was 49 percent urban, the white population 58 percent; by 1950 the corresponding percentages had risen to 62 and 63 percent. By 1960, 73.2 percent of the Negroes and only 69.6 percent of the whites fell into the urban category (Smith, 1970:503).

This heavy influx of blacks to the large northern cities became a major factor in the migration of whites and middle-class blacks. The past two decades have seen both a migration of whites from the industrial North and a concomitant movement of whites to the South. This "white flight" from the northern urban areas was followed by a similar exodus of business and industry to the South.

Reverse Migration to the South after 1970

The South has shown an overall net immigration since the decade following World War II (Fligstein, 1981:8-19). Between 1950 and 1975 the population of the South increased by an average of 3.78 million compared with 2.96 million for the North Central and 1.96 million for the North East (Bigger, 1979:2). Given this overall pattern, the South continued to show a net outmigration of the black population through the early 1970s. The period from 1970-75 showed a net immigration of blacks to the South of 14,000 compared with a net outmigration from the South of 385,000 for the five previous years (see Table 2). This new trend of black immigration to the South increased in momentum through the 1975-80 period as 415,000 blacks migrated to the South from the North East, North Central, and West while 220,000 migrated from the South. The period 1980-83 shows a slowing in the overall pattern in black migration with a continuing net immigration to the South (see Table 2). This brief but historically significant period of net immigration represents the beginning of a reversal in a pattern that extends back to the pre-Civil War era.

Factors Associated with Reversal and Implications

General improvement in the social and economic climate of the South over the past two decades coupled with the positive spin-offs of the Civil Rights era appear to be major factors influencing the reversal

47

Table 2

Black Migration Patterns 1958-83
by Southern Origin and Destination
(numbers in thousands)

Time Period	Black Migrants From South to Regions				Black Migrants to South From Regions				Net Migration
	North East	North Central	West	Total	North East	North Central	West	Total	
1958-1960	77	88	78	243	26	51	23	100	-143
1960-1965	332	249	210	791	125	109	89	323	-468
1965-1970	325	338	204	867	203	149	130	482	-385
1970-1975	79	123	86	288	158	122	22	302	14
1975-1980	50	94	76	220	192	121	102	415	195
1980-1983	96	107	131	334	150	130	96	376	42
Total	959	999	785	2743	854	682	462	1998	

Source: U.S. Bureau of the Census, Current Population Reports, Series P-20, No. 113, p. 28, table 13; No. 118, p. 30, table 13; No. 127, p. 39, table 9; No. 134, p. 48, table 14; No. 141, No. 150, p. 50, table 14; No. 156, p. 49, table 14; No. 171, p. 47; table 14; No. 188, p. 46, table 13; No. 193, p. 48, table 13; No. 210, p. 47, table 13; No. 235, p. 48, table 13; No. 262, p. 61, table 29; No. 273, p. 72, table 29; No. 285, p. 102, table 36; No. 305, p. 111, table 39, No. 353, p. 116, table 42; No. 377, p. 131, table 42; No. 393, p. 131, table 42 "Mobility of the Population of the United States", U.S. Government Printing Office, Washington, D.C.

of the historical trend of outmigration of blacks from the South (Drey-fuss, 1977:39-41). These positive factors associated with the South and the negative effects of general deteriorating social and economic conditions in the North East and North Central regions seems to have reversed the balance of push and pull factors associated with the northern and southern regions. Between 1960 and 1975 the North East showed a 57.8 percent increase in real personal income, a 10.9 percent increase in population, and a 13.7 percent decrease in manu-facturing employment (BUSINESS WEEK, 1978:92). In stark contrast to the relatively slow rate of growth in the northern region, the South gained 23.3 percent in population, 114.3 percent in real personal in-come, and 43.3 percent in manufacturing employment. The May 17, 1978 issue of BUSINESS WEEK pointed out that:

> Continued economic decline and fiscal crisis is likely for cities and states of the industrial North. . . The per capita income of Charlotte, N.C., among other southern cities, has exceeded that of New York City as well as that of most other large cities in the Northeast and Midwest, from Hartford to Milwaukee.

Factors associated with the phenomenal growth of the South mentioned most frequently in the literature, include civilian and defense spending by the federal government, hospitable weather conditions in the region, and a "favorable business climate" (Bernard and Rice, 1983; Bigger, 1979). The outbreak of World War II resulted in a gradual shifting of military installations and the shifting of contracts for weaponry and other hardware from the North East and North Central to the southern region. This trend has lead some to argue that the economic backbone of the southern region is now defense spending (Sutton, 1978:30). Several recent studies have documented the disproportional share of defense spending received by states in the southern region. Richard S. Morris reported that the Northeastern states which contain 45 percent of the American population receives 28 percent of the national defense spending while the southern region with 38 percent of the population receives over 50 percent of the national defense budget. The South has also received large outlays of federal funds for interstate highway construction, urban redevelopment -- including expensive downtown civic centers and stadiums, and the southern location of federal regional offices. These federal expenditures have impacted substantially upon income redistribution into the southern region (Morris, 1980:147).

The South has also become known for what has been termed "a good business climate." A 1975 survey ranked the 48 mainland states on

31 criteria of business climate -- some of which included the availability of energy, water, transportation, and qualified workers. Eight southern cities ranked in the top ten and none in the bottom ten ranks. Many states in the South have offered tax concessions to businesses and have made public funds available for the erection of facilities for leasing by new industries at low market prices. A good example of this is the Research Triangle Park in North Carolina which has attracted a stream of high tech industries from the northern region. The fact that southern industries are for the most part nonunionized has also not gone unnoticed by northern firms (Bernard and Rice, 1983).

The attraction of young high paid workers to the South has created shifts in income and accelerated the region's growth. New markets have been created that have attracted a wider variety of businesses and industries -- manufacturing, finance, advertising, wholesaling, and a vast array of personal services industries. Increases in taxable income have created new sources of revenue for supporting the public services that have accompanied urban growth in the South.

The recent reversal in the historical migration pattern of blacks may indicate that basic changes in the social, political, and economical structure of the South are having positive effects on the black population. The region is now being referred to as the "New South" or "the Sunbelt", indicating a changing view of the region. For decades called variously the "Bible Belt", the "Cotton Belt", the "Black Belt", the South is now fast becoming the nation's new center of economic activities as the traditional emphasis on race, religion, and farming is slowly diminishing in many locations (Dreyfuss, 1977:39-41; Wilson, 1978).

There is some evidence that the successes of the Civil Rights Movement of the 1960s and the ensuing legislation in the areas of voter's rights, school desegregation, and discrimination in employment has resulted in substantial economic gains for some blacks in the South. For example, sixty percent of the minority firms are located in the southern region, and of the 2,500 black elected officials in the United States in 1970, more than 2,000 lived in the South (Dreyfuss, 1977; EBONY, 1971:68-70). The presence of black mayors in Birmingham, New Orleans, Atlanta, and Charlotte, all historical bastions of institutionalized racism, highlights the improved status of blacks in the South.

Characteristics of New Southern Immigrants

During the period 1975-79, over 70 percent of Black immigrants to

Table 3

Characteristics of 1975-79 Black Migrants
to the South Compared with the 1979
Black Population of the South
(numbers in thousands)

Demographic and Socio-economic Variables	Black Migrants to the South (1975-1979)		Black Population of the South (1979)	
Occupations				
16 Years & Older	N	%	N	%
Professional, Technical				
Managerial	36	26.28	694	13.87
Sales Workers	2	1.46	231	4.61
Clerical & Kinder Workers	26	18.96	675	13.01
Craft & Kinder Workers	14	10.22	472	9.03
Operatives	12	8.76	804	16.07
Transportation Operatives	3	2.19	252	5.04
Laborers	15	10.95	516	11.31
Farm Workers	4	2.92	159	3.06
Service Workers	25	18.24	1201	24.00
Total	137	100.00	5004	100.00
Employment Status				
16 Years & Older	N	%	N	%
Employed	128	83.66	4975	89.34
Unemployed	25	16.34	560	10.66
Total	153	100.00	5535	100.00
Poverty Status 4 Years & Older				
Persons in Families	N	%	N	%
Above Poverty	201	73.89	2285	71.38
Below Poverty	71	26.11	916	28.62
Total	272	100.00	3201	100.00

51

Table 3 (Continued)

Demographic and Socio-economic Variables	Black Migrants to the South (1975-1979)		Black Population of the South (1979)	
Age	N	%	N	%
Less than 5 years	8	2.72	1310	10.22
5 to 14 years	79	26.87	2769	21.60
15 to 24 years	64	21.77	3076	24.00
25 to 34 years	87	29.59	1099	8.57
35 to 44 years	28	9.52	1326	10.34
45 to 64 years	13	4.42	2130	16.63
65 years/older	15	5.10	1108	8.64
Total	294	100.00	12818	100.00
Sex				
4 Years & Older	N	%	N	%
Male	159	50.31	6639	41.27
Female	157	49.69	7407	58.73
Total	316	100.00	14046	100.00
School Years Completed				
25 Years & Older	N	%	N	%
Elementary: 0 to 8 years	25	15.35	2311	41.20
High School: 1 to 3 years	21	12.90	1411	25.19
4 years	61	37.52	1190	21.12
College: 1 to 3 years	33	20.12	144	2.57
4 or more years	23	14.11	554	9.82
Total	163	100.00	5610	100.00

Source: U.S. Bureau of the Census, General Economic on Social Characteristics, United States Summary, Census of Population, Chapter C, Volumn 1, December 1980, p. 113, table 40; p. 246, table 215; p. 248, table 216.

52

the South were between 5 and 34 years of age indicating that the group contained large numbers of young adults just starting families and careers (see Table 3). There was almost an even split between males and females which departs from the traditional pattern of male selectivity. Almost 35 percent of the immigrants had four or more years of college while over one quarter were employed in professional and managerial jobs (see Table 3). Table 3 indicates that the new immigrants were atypical of the black population of the South. They tended to be younger, better educated, and employed in more prestigious occupations. Slightly more immigrants were unemployed than blacks in the regions indicating that many were migrating South in search of job opportunities. For this group the South could become the "new promised land" of opportunity and upward mobility.

Implications and Conclusions

Assuming that the current reversal of the historical South-to-North migration is not a temporary phenomenon, a major change in the distribution of the black population of the United States could be in the making. As of 1975, over half of all blacks lived in the South. A sustained period of heavy immigration could raise the proportion of blacks residing in the South to that of the post Civil War era -- to around 85 percent of all blacks (Schaefer, 1979:142).

In the final analysis the question must be addressed as to whether the improving social and economic conditions of the southern region will have a "drip-down effect" for the black community. The South has a tradition of general political and social conservativism and pronounced institutional racism towards its black population. The new white immigrants to the South have generally been northern business and professional suburbanites who are more likely to be Republican and conservative. These groups can be expected to oppose government spending on human services programs that benefit the black community directly while endorsing greater funding for the military installations clustered in the southern region (Bernard and Rice, 1983:20).

The general economic condition of blacks in the South continues to lag far behind that of southern whites. In 1980 the medium income for the southern white family was $20,631 compared with $11,629 for black families in the region. During the same year, almost one third of all black families had incomes below the poverty level compared with less than one tenth of white families. Given the generally depressed economic condition of most blacks in the South, the new

53

black immigrants to the region could be members of the new "privileged class of blacks" identified by Wilson in his provocative study of race and socioeconomic status in the black community (Wilson, 1978:151).

BIBLIOGRAPHY

Abbott, Carl
1981   THE NEW URBAN AMERICA: GROWTH AND POLITICS
        IN SUNBELT CITIES. Chapel Hill: The University of North
        Carolina Press.

Baker, Ray Stannard
1964   THE NEGRO GOES NORTH. New York: Harper and Row
        Publishers.

Bernard, Richard M. and Bradley R. Rice
1983   SUNBELT CITIES: POLITICS AND GROWTH SINCE
        WORLD WAR II. Austin, Texas: University of Texas Press.

Bigger, Jeanne C.
1979   "The Sunning of America: Migration to the Sunbelt."
        POPULATION BULLETIN 34 (March):1-42.

Dreyfuss, Joel
1977   "The Sun Also Rises: Blacks in the Sunbelt," BLACK EN-
        TERPRISE (January): 39-41.

Fligstein, Neil
1981   "Going North: Migration of Blacks and Whites from the
        South 1900-1950." New York: Academic Press.

Grant, Robert B.
1962   THE BLACK MAN COMES TO THE CITY. Chicago: Nelson-
        Hall Company.

Henri, Florette
1975   BLACK MIGRATION: MOVEMENT NORTH 1900-1920.
        New York: Columbia University Press.

Johnson, James H. and Walter C. Farrell, Jr.
1982   "Implications of Black Move to the South". BLACK ENTER-
        PRISE 12 (January).

Kennedy, Louise V.
1930   THE NEGRO PEASANT TURNS CITYWARD: EFFECTS
        OF RECENT MIGRATION TO NORTHERN CITIES. New
        York: Columbia University Press.

Lee, Everett S.
1966   "A Theory of Migration". DEMOGRAPHY 3 (3):47-57.

Meier, August and Elliot M. Rudwick
1968   FROM PLANTATION TO GHETTO. New York: Hill and Wang.

Morris, Richard S.
1980   BUM RAP ON AMERICAN CITIES. Englewood Cliffs, N.J.: Prentice-Hall, Inc.

Myrdal, Gunnar
1944   AN AMERICAN DILEMMA, Vol. 1. New York: Harper and Row, Publishers.

Rice, Bradley R.
1981   "Searching for the Sunbelt". AMERICAN DEMOGRAPHY 3 (March):22-23.

Schaefer, Richard T.
1979   RACIAL AND ETHNIC GROUPS. Boston, Mass.: Little, Brown and Company.

Smith. Lynn T. and Paul E. Zopf, Jr.
1970   DEMOGRAPHY: PRINCIPLES AND METHODS. Philadelphia, Pa.: F. A. Davis Company.

Strangler, Gary S., et al.
1975   "Black Return Migration to Two Non-Metropolitan Areas of the South". Paper presented at the Rural Sociological Section of the Annual Meeting of the Southern Association of Agricultural Scientists, New Orleans, Louisiana, February, 1975.

Sutton, Horace
1978   "Sunbelt vs. Frostbelt: A Second Civil War?" SATURDAY REVIEW 5 (15):28-37.

Spears, Allen H.
1967   BLACK CHICAGO: THE MAKING OF A GHETTO, 1890-1920. Chicago: University of Chicago Press.

"The Second War Between the States." 197 (6) BUSINESS WEEK (May 17)

"The South Today." 1971 EBONY (August 26).

Thomas, Brinley
1972   MIGRATION AND URBAN DEVELOPMENT. London: Methuen and Company Ltd.

U.S. Bureau of the Census
1980   General Social and Economic Characteristics, United States Summary: 1980. Washington, D.C.: GPO.

U.S. Bureau of the Census.
1980   Statistical Abstract of the United States: 1980. Washington: GPO.

Walker, Alfred J.
1978   "Intermetropolitan Migration and the Rise of the Sunbelt". SOCIAL SCIENCE QUARTERLY 59 (December):553-661.

Walker, Alfred J.
1980   "Good Business Climate, the Second War Between the States". DISSENT 27 (Fall):476-485.

Wilson, William J.
1978   "The Declining Significance of Race." Chicago: The University of Chicago Press.

Woodson, Carter G.
1970   A CENTURY OF NEGRO MIGRATION. New York: AMS Press.

Woofter, T.S., Sr.
1969   NEGRO PROBLEMS IN CITIES. New York: Negro University Press.

For we know that as the world grows better there will be realized in our children's lives that for which we fight unfalteringly but vainly now.

W. E. B. DuBois
THE CRISIS, 1912

CHAPTER FOUR

AFRO-AMERICAN FAMILY: CONTEMPORARY ISSUES AND IMPLICATIONS FOR SOCIAL POLICY

Carlene Young

As we approach the twenty-first century with all of its technological sophistication and confront basic changes in the social, economic, and political fabric in the United States, we need pause and assess the status and direction of fundamental institutions in our communities. Institutions evolve as patterns of behavior or organized means of achieving commonly defined goals and basic needs for a particular group or society. They reflect core values, experiential bases, and unique perspectives of their members.

One such institution in the Afro-American community experience, which has been central to its survival, perpetuity, and character, is the family. The signal importance of the Afro-American family has never been missed nor underestimated by policy makers, researchers, and other observers of the human condition. In most instances, the Afro-American family has been historically singled out for analysis as a dysfunctional pathological entity.

It is interesting to note that the African family warranted the attention of slave owners so much so that laws were passed in slaveholding states which forbade marriage and the establishment of families. The precedent was therein established for subsequent analysis of the family as deviant and incapable of sustaining its members. Yet there is abundant evidence that these laws were resisted and super human efforts were made by children and parents to establish cohesive units which mirrored their remembered experiences (Blassingame, 1978; Douglas, 1855/1969; Guttman, 1976). African heritage and continuity of patterns, structure, behavior, values and belief systems have been well documented by a number of scholars (DuBois, 1908 (1969), Herskovits, 1941 (1958); Sudarkasa, 1980, 1981; Nobles, 1981; Radcliff-Brown, 1950).

It is too often forgotten that many Africans brought to this land, although enslaved, were in varying ranges of adulthood; members of kinship communities with values, norms, expectations of behavior, and had formal institutions with prescribed roles and functions. These behaviors and memories were not all forgotten. Obligation to kin and fellow slaves were part of the lessons taught children. These kin obligations formed the basis for later development of mutual self-help organizations as found in churches, lodges, and neighborhoods.

Early studies of the Afro-American family chose to ignore and/or deny the validity of this remembered past and its influence on the newly formed communities (Frazier, 1939; Moynihan, 1965). The determination that Afro-American families were (are) unfailingly disorganized, unstable, fragmented, hopelessly mired in a culture of poverty, buffeted aimlessly by uncaring welfare, pimps, and social misfits is a direct outgrowth of the premise established and promulgated during slavery. This premise purported that (a) Africans came fron inferior stock and land; (b) slavery was ennobling; (c) there were no institutions, beliefs, culture or practices which were worthy of acknowledgement/acceptance by Euro-Americans and finally, (d) the Africans were destined to serve the needs and interests of their white masters.

Once these assumptions have been prooffered and incorporated into the laws, institutions, and social mores of a people, it is difficult to analyze the subject group from a different or objective perspective. So it should come as no surprise that prevailing sentiment reinforces the originally biased premise. Present day analysis has for the most part continued along that same continuum.

This paper, then, attempts to delineate some of the key issues which significantly impact on Afro-American family life and the implication of these issues on social policy decisions.

The current status of Afro-American families is once more the focus of national scrutiny and debate. Although there is a legacy of majority two-parent families, the current trend is one of increasing numbers of female headed households and teen-age pregnancies. While this is part of a broader societal trend, there is no question that the impact of these conditions on the Afro-American community is severe. As a result of public sentiment which views the poor as creators of their own condition, the analysis of black families has come full circle. Once again authoritative voices conclude that the condition of Afro-American families is merely the result of their love affair with the welfare system and the largesse of a liberal democratic government (Sowell, 1975; Gilder, 1981).

These commentators on the condition of Afro-American families selectively ignore the structural changes in the economy, job opportunities, patterns of urban development, health care issues, resources, and opportunities available to Afro-Americans. Proponents of this school of thought came to be known as the culture-of-poverty theorists. The government popularized this concept with the U.S. Department of Labor report authored by Daniel P. Moynihan (1965). The central tenet of the report -- that family deterioration was the major factor in illegitimacy, juvenile delinquency, low achievement, adult crime, and the essential ingredient in the perpetuation of the cycle of poverty and deprivation. The argument that distinctive lower class values were transmitted to each subsequent generation, engendering a psychological incapacity to take full advantage of increased opportunities became the sine qua non for government strategies to deal with the "problem" and the rationalization for continued inequality. The responsibility for the degradation associated with poverty is thereby placed upon the people and the cultural subsystem which they develop to surmount their isolation and deprivation. The danger to society, inherent in this approach, is put forth by William Ryan (1971) in his treatise on BLAMING THE VICTIM. He sees it as an ideology that "so distorts and disorients the thinking of the average concerned citizen that it becomes a primary barrier to effective social change." The veneer of humanitarianism mask its true nature, that is, a denial of any obligation to change the opportunity structure and quality of life for those defined as different -- strangers and savages.

> The stigma, the defect, the fatal difference -- though derived in the past from environmental forces -- is still located **within** the victim, inside his skin. . .the humanitarian can have it both ways. He can, all at the same time, concentrate his charitable interest on the defects of the victim, condemn the vague social and environmental stresses that produce the defect (sometime ago), and ignore the continuing effect of victimizing social forces (right now). It is a brilliant ideology for justifying a perverse form of social action designed to change, not society, as one might expect, but rather society's victim. (Ryan, 1971:7)

Public opinion has generally supported this point of view. National polls indicate that 53 percent of adults questioned report that the poor are at fault for their condition while only 22 percent believe the social structure is at fault (Parrillo, 1985:36). Other explanations which point out the structural conditions and social relationships which perpetuate poverty receive little attention.

Subscribing to the culture-of-poverty thesis as opposed to entrenched structural factors results in exceedingly different approaches to social/ economic issues, proposed solutions, and opportunity structures. According to Ryan "the formula for action becomes extraordinarily simple: change the victim" (Ryan, 1971:8).

Although this "culture of poverty" has never been scientifically demon- strated, the rhetoric continues to hold the imagination of white Amer- ica and spokespersons for Reagan administration policies such as black economists Thomas Sowell and Walter Williams. These proponents ignore the social structural oppression and endorse what Kinder and Sears (1981) describe as a style of racism which combines antiblack anxiety and hostility with traditional American moral values such as individualism and self-reliance or what has been termed "symbolic racism." According to Kinder and Sears (1981), this latest version of white racism ". . .simply reflects the latent racial hostility that over three hundred fifty years of racism has imbued in American culture." These beliefs and attitudes serve to cement the unequal circumstances.

> By the sustaining conditions of poverty, we are referring to the institutional structures and social relationships in American society that prevent the poor from gaining access to adequate financial resources and social rewards. There are at least five such factors in our society that act to sustain poverty: (1) ecologi- cal and demographic trends; (2) the limited opportunity structure for the poor; (3) patterns of racial discrimination; (4) deficiencies in community resources for the poor; and (5) agency-client rela- tionships (Ferman, 1968:316).

Opportunity Structure

Those who persist in making the comparison between European immi- grants, other racial minorities in the United States, and Afro-Ameri- cans, with respect to upward mobility, progress, and degrees of assimi- lation, must pay attention to historical precendent established by the system of Jim Crow laws and social practices, the changing indus- trial base, and racial violence and intimidation particularly in the era of lynchings and Klan activities.

The masses of European immigrants entered the U.S.A. during the period of the Industrial Revolution when the demand for unskilled labor was at its apex and ideologies of white supremacy and racism were entrenched in the society. Although the ranking system of nativists preferred Anglo-Saxons, the social structure expanded to accommodate lower class and "darker swarms" from southern and eastern Europe. Americanization or assimilation was the proposed solution for these immigrants with schools serving as one of the key agents of socialization and effecting Anglo-conformity. The introduction of Asian immigrants was also accompanied by racial discrimination and hostility. However, there was neither resistance to the development and maintenance of family units, nor the obstacles to the implementation of value structures which appear consonant with white, Anglo-Saxon protestant virtues. Because the Cubans and Vietnamese refugees arrived possessing the education and occupational experience of the middle class, they succeeded in overcoming early native concerns and did not encounter the same degree of negativism as had earlier groups (Parrillo, 1985:40).

One of the structural factors which differentiates the European/Asian immigrant, their economic development and subsequent ability to work themselves out of poverty has to do with the availability of masses of unskilled jobs. Blacks, on the other hand, migrated to cities at a time when there was decreasing need for unskilled workers and institutionalized racism excluded them from securing jobs except during wartime production and strike breaking efforts. Labor unions adhered to the discriminatory practices prevalent in the job market and were successful in excluding Afro-Americans from trade and industrial unions. These unions, on the other hand, enabled Ethnic Americans to gain almost exclusive control of the craft and trade unions and climb the ladder of success. Denial of admission to apprenticeship programs has been one of the most effective means of keeping blacks in low-paying, unskilled jobs.

Discriminatory practices in the governmental sector contributed to the maintenance of white superiority and black subordination as effectively as the segregation which characterized the private sector.

Urbanization

Afro-Americans are primarily an urban people concentrated in inner cities. According to the 1980 census, approximately 81 percent of black Americans live in metropolitan areas with the South retaining 53 percent of the total black population. While blacks moved to central cities, whites, including industry and commerce, were relocating in the suburbs. This "suburban drift" has resulted in a poverty stricken core of black residents surrounded by rings of affluent whites who maintain control of the resources, institutions, and decision making apparatus.

As businesses and industry move to the suburban rings so does the tax base thereby limiting allocations for public education, including qualified experienced teachers, adequate supplies, and facilities. There is also a reduction in the labor market which further limits the opportunity for employment. Available jobs are most often low-paying, part-time and economically exploitative.

The relocation of manufacturing industries and changes in basic technology is having a profound effect on the employment picture for white and black Americans. Economists predict a shift in employment (hi-tech services) opportunities from manufacturing jobs (19%) to service-oriented jobs (58%) in the coming decades (Dingle, 1985). Future job opportunities for blacks aspiring to achieve middle-class are proportionately threatened.

. . .Black blue collar workers will be besieged by technological advancements and troubled by the relocation of basic manufacturing plants, away from urban corridors. The bulk of the black population and certainly the black labor force is not going to find employment in these older industries (Dingle, 1985).

The impact of joblessness on black families is heightened even more, however, when we consider that black men were even more likely to be out of work than black women. Analysts theorize that availability of domestic service jobs helped to mitigate somewhat the unemployment situation of black women. But such women were likely to have low incomes, increasing the likelihood that they would become heads of households with dependent children (Harris, 1982).

High poverty levels are to some extent due to the following factors: (1) scarcity of jobs in central cities; (2) black women are younger and have younger children; (3) the gap between black and white unemployment rates appear to be widening; (4) racial discrimination; (5) enormous increase in white females in the labor force. Socio-cultural patterns, cultural transmissions, psychological impairment, including low self-esteem, fatherless families, inability to plan and defer gratification are components of the 'cultural determinism' which is self-perpetuating according to culture of poverty proponents. However, no measure of motivation, achievement orientation or middle-class cultural transmissions can alter the reality of fundamental changes occurring in the technology.

Income

Since 1970, the median income of black families has decreased from $13,325 to 12,674 in 1980 while median income for whites rose slightly, $21,722 and 21,904 respectively (U.S. Bureau of Census).

THE STATE OF BLACK AMERICA, 1983 reports that the "absolute decline in black living standards was limited to the 40% of the black families with the lowest incomes while the standard of living of upper income black families increased moderately" (Swinton, 1983:53). Black families continue to consist of a majority of married couples (54%). This represents a decline from 66 percent in 1970. However, the increase in single female-headed households increased dramatically from 30% to 42% during the decade from 1970 to 1980. Although some members of the black middle class did prosper, their economic stability is still in question. Middle-class black families are far more dependent on two incomes than are their white counterparts. Future job opportunities in basic manufacturing industries -- the leading employers of middle-income blacks -- seem threatened by new structural and technological changes (Dingle, 1985).

The labor market position of blacks is generally reflective of the overall condition in U.S. Society.

. . .blacks have consistently experienced a relatively disadvantageous labor market position in good times and bad. Black workers typically have higher rates of unemployment, obtain fewer high paying jobs, more low paying jobs, and have lower wage rates than whites. The combination of obtaining less work and lower paid work results, as we have seen, in blacks obtaining significantly smaller amount of income from labor than whites (Swinton, 1983:62).

For almost thirty years (since 1959) the unemployment rate for blacks has been twice that of white counterparts -- with the exception of 1975 and 1963 for males and females respectively.

The unemployment rates of black workers has been above 12 percent every year since 1975. For black teenagers, unemployment has been above 34 percent in each of these years. . . The high rates of unemployment now being experienced by black workers under age 35 have never been observed in post-war history (Swinton, 1983:66).

Since wage earnings are the primary form of income for Afro-Americans, employment or the lack thereof, is an essential barometer of the conditions to which a people are subjected.

The systemic nature of unemployment which has plagued the black community since Emancipation cannot be explained away as merely a lack of productivity. Full employment for Afro-Americans ended with slavery. The employment and wage differential which exist between black and white Americans is more accurately a reflection of the persistent, institutionalized, inequality which has never been substantially challenged or changed. As dire as the unemployment figures are they present only a partial view of the predicament which confronts Americans of African ancestry. Unemployment figures are reported from only those persons actively seeking employment and do not include discouraged workers.

Another indicator of the life's chances available to blacks is the labor force participation rate which measures the proportion of the population in the work force whether employed or unemployed. The participation rate for all males has declined. However, the trend for black males over the past twenty years has decelerated from 83 percent in 1960 to 71 percent in 1980 when less than three-fourths of the black male population were even in the labor force (McGhee, 1983:9). While black women have increased their participation rate from 48 percent in 1960 to 53 percent in 1980, white women have soared from 37 percent in 1960 to 51 percent in 1980. McGhee (1983:10) explains the significance of this phenomena by pointing out the impact this increase of white females in the labor force has had on black employment.

. . .the increase in the number of white females in the labor force between 1960 and 1980 represents more people than the entire black force (male and female) of 12.5 million persons. This enormous increase. . .is part of the explanation for the continuing high levels of unemployment among blacks.

Family Structure

The multigenerational, interdependent kinship system which serves to provide emotional and economic support for its members has dominated Afro-American family life for generations. This extended family structure which had its antecedents in the African experience, was molded and shaped by the crucible of slavery and refined in the segregated enclaves of the Jim Crow era. Social scientists have traditionally determined that the extended family is merely an adaptation to the break up of families during slavery and/or adjustments to urban, poverty-stricken ghettos. These interpretations are limited by the paucity of contact and understanding of a culture different from the Anglo-Saxon model of middle-class aspirants -- the nuclear family.

Emphasis on consanguineal relationships as opposed to conjugal ties is fundamental to this difference. The function of kin, grandparents, aunts, uncles, cousins, and "play" relatives is central to the development of the child in the Afro-American family. Moral training, role relationships, gender identification, coping skills, belief systems and value orientations are part of the transmission processes which form the systematic nature of the extended family. Ignorance of the dynamics of these involvement and the predilection to over-categorize or stereotype persons of African ancestry as inferior human types has resulted in distortions. These distortions are then rationalized and legitimatized by scholarship and political exigency.

The emphasis on household organization and on adaptation results in overlooking important aspects of family organization and structure, such as the maintenance of family ties through space and time by means of conscious and ritualized practices in funerals, reunions, and regular visiting patterns. (Aschenbrenner, 1975:6).

Family ties are not limited by locale or physical proximity. Although there is a base household with a dominant family figure who directs joint family activities coordinates mutual self-help efforts, and allocates scarce family resources (Martin & Martin, 1978).

The continuity and cohesiveness which characterize extended family networks are presently jeopardized by a number of factors which include lack of adequate housing, popularizing individualism and material success while minimizing the importance of kin, rearing of children in isolated urban settings and increasing membership in the subterraneans (extra-legal class) (Drake & Cayton, 1965; Billingsley, 1968; Blackwell, 1985) and underclass.

The precedent setting work of Billingsley which authoritatively delineates variations in Afro-American families according to systems analysis and household composition is a useful tool for analysis of the transitional process. His typology of the black family into incipient, simple, and attenuated, whether nuclear or extended, is illuminating in view of the complexity and diversity of role relationships which involve all members.

One of the major limitations in discussions about the Afro-American family is the lack of acknowledgement of the diversity among low-income peoples. There is no single mode of behavior which can be attributed to all people within that classification. The variations of experiences and perceived realities within the working poor, non-working poor, and those attempting to achieve a middle-class lifestyle certainly includes a desire for improved conditions for themselves and their children.

Hylan Lewis (1976) notes that field reports document the fact that low-income urban black parents do not prefer or approve of the circumstances in which they now live and in which their children are being reared. They share many of the ideals of the broader society. Yet they must maintain some resilient hopefulness in the possibility of change in their life's chances and, at the same time, adapt to the present circumstances. Hyman Rodman (1963) refers to this as a **stretched** value system, that is, a sharing of general values by all social classes in society, but lower classes while not rejecting these values "come to tolerate and eventually to evaluate favorably certain deviations from middle-class values." In this way they need not be continually frustrated by their failure to live up to unattainable values.

Single Parent Families

Increased attention has been focused on the one-parent family. During the past decade, from 1970-1980 the national trend demonstrates a rise in this social category. In 1970, more than 8 million children -- 11.9 percent of the total U.S. population under age 18 -- lived in one parent families. By 1979, while the total number of children was down by about 10 percent, the number living with one parent had grown to over 11 million -- 18.5 percent, or almost one in five. There were 19.7 percent living with one parent in 1980.

This trend is even more pronounced in the Afro-American community where two-parent families are declining rapidly with divorce playing a significant role in the phenomena. In 1980, over half (55.5 percent)

67

of black families consisted of a married couple, with or without any children. However, the accelerated rate of decline in this structure is such that "it is not unreasonable to predict that unless the downturn is immediately checked, two parent units will be in the minority within the black community by the 1990 census, if not before (Blackwell, 1985:93).

In 1970, 58.1 percent of black children compared to 89.2 percent of white children lived with both parents. By 1980 44 percent of black children lived with their mothers, only 2 percent lived exclusively with their fathers, and 12.1 percent lived with neither parent, most often grandparents (Blackwell, 1985:95). McGhee points out the reason that black women are heads of households.

> Only about one-fourth of them have never been married. Nearly three-fourths . . .are either married with an absent spouse (28.7%), widowed (22.2%), or divorced (21.9%). Clearly, then these are not single women deliberately having babies in order to get the state to support them through the welfare payments as has been often charged. The evidence points, instead, to women making a commitment to a man and starting a family based on that commitment (McGhee, 1983:16).

The financial constraints under which single female head of households operate is increasingly a matter for concern. U.S. Civil Rights Commission projects that, if the trend continues, by the year 2000, the only poor will be women and children. These households have the lowest median incomes of any family types. Between 1960 and 1981 the number of below-poverty-line households headed by women jumped 54 percent. Poor families headed by black women increased at twice that rate.

> Those families are poor not just because they are headed by women, they are poor because the women who head them are either unemployed, underemployed, or not in the labor force at all. Nearly half (48%) of all female household heads worked full time in 1980, which disputes the common perception of all female households heads as poor and dependent upon welfare for their income (McGhee 1983:16).

In 1980, the labor force participation rate for black females was 53 percent. While 59.6 percent of wives in black families were in paid labor force.

Generations of social scientists have sought to attribute juvenile delinquency, crime, confused sexual identity and other pathologies to the female headed household and "missing" father. This correlation has never been demonstrated. The assumption that since the structure is different therefore the function and role interactions must be deficient is not supported by evidence. The belief that children reared in black female headed households have little or no contact with male role models ignores the dynamics of interaction among extended family members, age-graded groups, 'play relatives', and the mother's boyfriend or companion. The lack of a father to serve in the capacity of permanent (consistent) provider and nurturer constitutes a level of disadvantage which cannot be construed, by definition, as pathology or basis for role identity problems. Other variables which come into play must be investigated before such a determination can be made with any validity.

Teenage Pregnancy

The epidemic of teenage pregnancy is now a world wide problem (see Development Forum, Feb.-March, 1985) and "one of America's major public health problems" according to Dr. Allan Rosenfield, Director of the Center of Population and Family Health at Columbia University.

The severity of the impact of this problem on the black community has not yet been adequately assessed, however, its manifestation is cause for prudent examination and concerted action. Complications which result from lack of information about requisite health care and nutrition, adequate housing, availability of employment, income and educational attainment for teenage mothers, have a disproportionate effect on the black community particularly since blacks under 19 years old constitute 40 percent of the total black population.

According to the 1980 census, black youth, 15-19 years olds were 11.3 percent of the population and the median age of the black population was 25 years, compared to 41 years for the white population. A number of factors contribute to the youthfulness of the black population. These include consistently higher birth rates which resulted in more children and a shorter life expectancy than for white counterparts. Although these differences have been narrowing, there remains a persistent disparity in life expectancy rates.

The rate of out-of-wedlock pregnancies while declining for blacks and increasing for white teenagers is approaching parity.

The number of out-of-wedlock live births to non-whites under the age of 19 peaked at 139,000 in 1977 and is now on the decline. . .while the number of out-of-wedlock births for white females under the age of 19 has risen steadily over the past decade to a peak of 111,700 in 1978, an increase of 73% in eight years (McGhee, 1982:180).

This pattern of involvement in no way mitigates the urgency of the situation which is tantamount to being condemned to a life of severe hardship, sustained periods of poverty, and limited educational and occupational achievement. The issue is not only that unwed pregnancies are rising at such rapid rates but that the age of these mothers is lowering.

These are precisely the groups that are more vulnerable by any standard of measurement employed to determine economic, social, and health problems and who are forced by their pregnancies either to discontinue or interrupt formal education (Blackwell, 1985:102).

Although the extended family plays a key role in the absorption and support of these families, 56 percent of black female headed families are officially poor compared with 35 percent of all families headed by women who live in poverty.

Hill (1972:38) found that most out-of-wedlock black babies (90%) were kept by parents and relatives while only 7 percent of white babies born out-of-wedlock were kept by the parent and kin in existing families. One of the major strengths of black families identified by Hill is the strong kinship bonds manifested in the capacity to absorb other individuals into the family structure and informal adoptions. Self-help is the characteristic pattern of most black families. His data show relatives providing about one-third of the total income of female-headed households while public assistance accounted for 13 percent.

Summary

This paper suggests a frame of reference for developing approaches to understanding issues relevant to the Afro-American family as it adapts to structural forces in the society.

The objective conditions under which the majority of Afro-Americans are forced to live represent hardship, isolation, rejection and a perpetual state of poverty amidst booming reports of growth, affluence, and prosperity. The gap is widening between those two Americas -- one black, one white -- one poor, one affluent. More than 40 million Americans live in families with incomes of less than $10,000 a year -- that is, $192 a week, before taxes. The official standard of poverty for a family of four is income less than $10,178 for the year. The attitudes of most Americans have hardened against those perceived to be a drain on the system. "A recent CBS-New York Times poll found that, when asked who they worry about most, families getting too little or too much, 2-1 majority said it worries most about those getting 'too much'." Among black respondents, revealingly, the numbers are the reverse: by 2-1, blacks worry most about those getting too little help (Kaiser, 1984).

The mood and focus of the nation is not empathetic to acknowledging or addressing the issues which are impacting on Afro-American families as delineated in this paper. Nonetheless, the implications for urgently needed social policies are readily apparent. While Afro-Americans are characterized to a great extent by lack of power, it is no less true that they, the largest racial group in the U.S., are interwoven into the social fabric of this nation and cannot be merely relegated to the waste heap of humanity and ignored.

The general approach of the government to policy issues concerned with Afro-American affairs has been at best one of benign neglect. Disregard for the economic, social, political, and psychological well-being of black citizens is apparent in the deterioration of services, resources, and quality of life available to inner city residents.

Policy issues which are relevant to the output (educational, cultural); performance (economic, population); security (well being, health); and structural (family, church); cohesiveness of Afro-Americans are summarized briefly:

Health related services based on prevention and health mainten-ance.

Targeted reduction of infant mortality rates in inner cities through pre-natal care and support services.

Identification, selection, training of capable youth as early as junior high school to become physicians and other health care personnel to serve the impoverished.

71

Agencies serving family planning needs provide services for unwed adolescent fathers as well as unwed adolescent mothers.

Housing loan programs to enable and support home ownership among the poor, especially single parent families.

Job creation initiatives targeted to enable teenagers to enter the technology/information age.

Availability of public hospitals limited by national trend of closures and restricted access.

Training of mental health personnel to recognize and effectively deal with mental health/stress issues relevant to Afro-Americans.

Monies allocated to maintain men in prison for one year, reallocated to train and educate.

Community clinic programs to inform and educate youth about diet, nutrition, parenting, sexual responsibility.

Affordable child care centers to enable single parent households to complete education, receive job training or work.

Income support programs that provide direct assistance rather than in-kind.

Revise eligibility requirements for aid and training to adjust for structural inequities and institutional racism.

Support self-help efforts of the extended family with direct aid, community, and organizational programs.

Communities organize to provide safe neighborhoods for residents and children.

Supplementary educational services provided by churches.

Accountability of schools to educate Afro-Americans.

Meaningful employment opportunities available to female heads of households.

Survey poor to determine priority of needs and proposed solutions.

BIBLIOGRAPHY

Aschenbrenner, Joyce.
LIFELINES: BLACK FAMILIES IN CHICAGO. New York: Holt, Rinehart and Winston, Inc., 1975.

Billingsley, Andrew.
BLACK FAMILIES IN WHITE AMERICA. Englewood Cliffs, New Jersey: Prentice-Hall, 1968.

Blackwell, James E.
THE BLACK COMMUNITY, 2nd Edition. New York: Harper and Row, 1985.

Blassingame, J.
THE SLAVE COMMUNITY. New York: Oxford University Press, 1972.

Dingle, Derek T.
"Seeking A Foundation For Stability." BLACK ENTERPRISE. January, 1985.

Douglass, Frederick.
BONDAGE AND MY FREEDOM. New York: Dover Publication, 1969.

Drake, St. Clair and Cayton, Horace.
BLACK METROPOLIS. New York: Harper and Row, 1965.

DuBois, W.E.B.
THE NEGRO AMERICAN FAMILY. Atlanta University Press, 1908; Cambridge, Mass: MIT Press, 1969.

Ferman, Louis A.; Kornbluh, Joyce and Haber, Alan, Editors.
POVERTY IN AMERICA. Ann Arbor: University of Michigan, 1968.

Frazier, E. Franklin.
THE NEGRO FAMILY IN THE UNITED STATES. Chicago: University of Chicago Press, 1966.

Gilder, George.
WEALTH AND POVERTY. New York: Basic Books, Inc., 1981.

Gutman, Herbert G.
THE BLACK FAMILY IN SLAVERY AND FREEDOM, 1750-1925.
New York: Pantheon Books, 1976.

Harris, William H.
THE HARDER WE RUN. New York: Oxford University Press,
1982.

Herskovits, Melville.
THE MYTH OF THE NEGRO PAST. Boston: Beacon Press, 1958.

Hill, Robert.
THE STRENGTHS OF BLACK FAMILIES. New York: Emerson
Hall Publishing Co., 1972.

Kaiser, Robert G.
"An Alarming Picture of Poverty in the U.S. Today," SAN FRANCIS-
CO CHRONICLE, November 28, 1984.

Kinder, Donald R. and Sears, David O.
"Prejudice and Politics: Symbolic Racism versus Racial Threats
to 'The Good Life'," JOURNAL OF PERSONALITY AND SOCIAL
PSYCHOLOGY. 40 (1981): 414-31.

Lewis, Hylan.
"Culture, Class and Family Life Among Low-Income Urban
Negroes," EMPLOYMENT, RACE, AND POVERTY. Edited by
Arthur Ross and Herbert Hill. New York: Harcourt, Brace and
World, Inc., 1967.

Martin, Elmer P. and Martin, Joanne M.
THE BLACK EXTENDED FAMILY. Chicago: University of Chicago
Press, 1978.

McGhee, James D.
"The Black Teenager: An Endangered Species," THE STATE OF
BLACK AMERICA. New York: National Urban League, 1982.

_____
"The Changing Demographics in Black America," THE STATE
OF BLACK AMERICA. New York: National Urban League, 1983.

McNatt, Robert.
"Black American Is In A State Of Crisis," BLACK ENTERPRISE.
January, 1984.

Moynihan, Daniel P.
THE NEGRO FAMILY: THE CASE FOR NATIONAL ACTION.
Washington, D.C.: U.S. Department of Labor, 1965.

Nobles, Wade.
"African American Family Life: An Instrument of Culture," THE BLACK FAMILY. Harriette McAdoo, ed. Beverly Hills, Calif.: Sage Publications, 1981.

Parrillo, Vincent.
STRANGERS TO THESE SHORES. New York: John Wiley and Sons, 1985.

Radcliff-Brown.
AFRICAN SYSTEMS OF KINSHIP AND MARRIAGE. London: Oxford University Press, 1950.

Rodman, Hyman.
"The Lower Class Value Stretch," SOCIAL FORCES. 42 (1963), 205-215.

Ryan, William.
BLAMING THE VICTIM. New York: Pantheon Books, 1971.

Sowell, Thomas.
RACE AND ECONOMICS. New York: Logman, Inc., 1975.

Sudarkasa, Kasa, Niara.
African and Afro-American Family Structure; A Comparison," THE BLACK SCHOLAR. Vol. 11, Nov.-Dec. 1980, pp. 37-60.

_____
"Interpreting the African Heritage in Afro-American Family Organizations," THE BLACK FAMILY, ed., McAdoo, Harriette, Beverly Hills, Calif.: Sage Publications, 1981.

Swinton, David H.
"The Economic Status of the Black Population," THE STATE OF BLACK AMERICA. New York: National Urban League, 1983.

Turner, Jonathan H.; Singleton, Royce; and Musick, David.
OPPRESSION: A SOCIO-HISTORY OF BLACK-WHITE RELATIONS. Chicago: Nelson-Hall, 1984.

Few groups of people are forced by their situation into such cruel dilemmas as American Negroes.

W. E. B. DuBois
THE CRISIS, 1913

CHAPTER FIVE

A NEW EMERGING PATTERN OF BLACK FAMILY FORMATION

Joseph W. Scott

Traditionally in America one expects that courtship between unmarried adults would precede love, and love would precede marriage, marriage would precede sexual intercourse, sexual intercourse would precede pregnancy and childbirth, and childbirth would precede childrearing done by the same couple who started out courting. In short, it is widely expected that sexual intercourse, pregnancy, childbirth and child-rearing would occur within the same marriage and family. This process eventuates in what demographers call a "stable family" defined as:

> one in which a man and woman marry and head their own households and have children which would be born into and raised in a household which contains both their parents (Bianchi and Farley, 1979:538).

This process of American family formation is on the decline in general and it is particularly on the decline among low income blacks in the United States. In recent decades, there has been a consistent shift away from the traditional sequence of love, marriage, childbirth and childrearing carried out in a single husband-wife family. Increasingly all of these sequential events are becoming separated in social time and social location. For instance, an emerging revised sequence is for courtship to lead to love, love to sexual intercourse, sexual intercourse to pregnancy and childbirth, and these to postpartum courtship which eventuates, perhaps, but not always so, into marriage (as often as not) between the couple who conceived the child out of wedlock in the first place. During the postpartum courtship and quasi-marital period, childrearing is usually carried on by grandparents and other relatives or fictive kin. Most of such children live much, if not most of their lives, apart from their natural parents but within extended family networks especially that of the mother.

In sum, a revised sequence of black family formation is beginning to thrust itself onto the American societyscape, and it is becoming, possibly, the most common sequence of family formation in the black community today. The supporting evidence is as follows.

Childbirth

Today, more than half of all births of blacks are occurring without benefit of marriage -- out of wedlock. In fact, fifty-eight percent of all black first births are to unwed mothers who overwhelmingly elect to keep their babies and remain unmarried upon discovering their pregnancy (Glick and Norton, 1977:6). Fifty-five percent of black births are to unmarried mothers. The figure for whites is 9.4 percent. It should be noted that the rate of increase for white unmarried mothers is 66 percent higher than for black women. Over ninety-five percent of the babies born to black teenagers occur out of wedlock largely because blacks (in contrast to whites) still refuse to marry in order to "legitimize" premaritally conceived births. Whites more than blacks mask premarital pregnancies through so-called "shotgun" marriages (Zelnik and Kantner, 1980:231ff).

Blacks who have children out of wedlock, however, eventually do marry but not because of and not immediately after the onset of pregnancy: only about four percent of the black teenage women do this.

But, in the early 1900's blacks, compared to whites, had higher rates of teenage marriages (Sklar and Berkow, 1974:80). However, in the 1960's this tendency began to reverse itself, and by 1970, more white teenagers than black were marrying in their "teens." Since the 1960's, among teenagers in general and among Blacks in particular, there has been a declining propensity to marry at all. In point of fact, the ever-married rate among black teenagers has already dropped to its lowest level ever during this whole century. One consequence is that close to fifty percent of black teenage women in some urban areas begin motherhood without benefit of marriage before the age of twenty.

Black males and females, as stated, eventually marry. Thus, most teenage mothers will marry despite the fact that there is a serious shortage of black men of marriageable age. Jackson (1971) and Scott (1980) have all reported that the sex ratio for blacks of childbearing ages is around 85 (eighty-five males per hundred females). Additionally, Scott and Stewart (1978) have shown that there has been some considerable systemic institutional decimation of black American males: more of them losing their lives in the military, in industrial accidents, in poor health delivery systems, and in police violence against blacks. What also cannot be overlooked is that blacks are also killing blacks at an alarming rate. All of these losses have the effect of creating a shortage of black males of marriage age, giving rise to man-sharing and varieties of consensual polygamy.

Marriage

Marriage seems to be an institution of declining popularity among blacks (Bianchi and Farley, 1979:539). They seem to be postponing marriage or not marrying at all in ever decreasing proportions; that is, the proportions of black men and women who are making the transitions from singlehood to marriedhood are decreasing. The proportions who are marrying and continuing to live with their spouses are decreasing. While the proportions of never-married is increasing, the proportion of those marrying at the younger ages is decreasing.

Fewer than half of all adult women are in the status of "wife." Only about fifty percent of the adult males are in the status of "husband." More and more black men and women are choosing to remain single even though they are still mating and having children.

The fastest growing category of women forming single-parent households is the never-married category. From 1960 to 1973 the percentage of change was 66 percent, going from 12 in 1960 to 20 in 1973. During this period there was a 25 percent change among those separated and divorced, going from 40 percent in 1960 to 49 percent in 1973 (Rodger-Rose, 1980:37). Additionally, blacks also seem to be disrupting their marriages more frequently by separations and divorce.

Parenthood

Out-of-wedlock pregnancies and births, like all others, begin with sexual intercourse. Black teenagers, in larger proportions than white teenagers, start sexual activity earlier but whites engage in it more pervasively (Kantner and Zelnik, 1980:231-232). Almost half of those blacks who have started did so before age 16. The average age is 15.5 for blacks and 16.2 for whites.

Zelnik and Kanter (1980) in a national survey found that about two-thirds of all the black teenagers and two-fifths of all the white teenagers had experienced premarital intercourse. By age 19, however, around 89 percent of the blacks had experienced premarital sexual intercourse, compared to about 65 percent of the whites. For both groups most of the coitus was without contraceptive devices.

According to this same national survey (by Zelnik and Kantner, 1980) 45 percent of the black teenagers and 29 percent of the white teenagers who had experienced sexual intercourse had had at least one out-of-wedlock pregnancy. Black teenagers tended not to resolve their pregnancies by abortion or adoption. About 96 percent of the pregnant black teenagers refused to marry before the outcome of pregnancy as compared to only 80 percent for whites.

Blacks are starting sexual intercourse earlier, even though they are not having sex more often or with more people. White teenagers have more sex partners than do black teenagers.

Since most black adult women eventually become mothers, most households with childbearing women have dependent children in them. Marriage, being of declining utility, is less and less the choice of adult blacks. Only around 50 percent of the adult black men and even fewer adult black women (as we said) are living in husband-wife families.

Blacks are not marrying as much as before, but they are mating as much as ever. Premarital intercourse is on the rise. Pregnancy is a common outcome from these activities among young black women because they are reluctant to contracept. For instance, from 1940 to 1960, the percentage of black women who made the transition to motherhood by age 25 rose from 57 to 76 percent with childlessness decreasing from 30 to 11 percent. From 1960 to 1975 the transition to motherhood by age 20 was 43-45 percent and by age 25, 73-75 percent (Masnick and McFalls, 1978:4). All of this is happening despite the decreasing popularity of marriage or decreasing capability of marriage maintenance among black adults.

With such low rates of marriage and a declining number of husband-wife families more babies could be expected to be born outside of marriage, and this is precisely what is happening among blacks. Contributing to this total are marital disruptions and babies being born between marital unions. The proportions of separations and divorces are increasing among black women; well over 20 percent of black adult women live under these conditions. No less than ten percent of the babies born come from these women who are no longer wed, according to the Population Reference Bureau.

The consequences for black children are predictable: at present, less than half of the black children, under 18, live with two parents of any kind. Kantner and Zelnik (1973) found that only 35 percent of black sexually active teenagers lived in a father-headed household. Glick and Norton (1979) reported that three-quarters of all children in America living with never-married mothers are black.

The great majority of all single-parent households have children in them, which should not be surprising given the fact that most black women have had at least one pregnancy by age 25. With more never-married black women having children out-of-wedlock, and more black women becoming divorced or separated, more single women with children are setting up independent households rather than live as "relatives" with their parents; single-parent families are almost as common as two-parent families. In point of fact, nearly 50 percent of black families are single-parent families.

Childrearing

Since there has been a general decline of black adults of marriageable age living in husband-wife families, childrearing patterns have been altered. In 1960, 86 percent of the white adults and 72 percent of the black adults lived in traditional husband-wife families. By 1976, those figures had dropped to 80 percent for whites and 55 percent for blacks (Bianchi and Farley, 1979:538). Concomitantly more black households have come to be female-headed households. There has been a corresponding decrease in the number of black women who are wives -- by 1977, only 44 percent were in this status. Disruptions of marital relationships have contributed most to this total, but unmarried motherhood has also contributed substantially.

At the lowest socioeconomic levels, blacks often have to rear their children in different ways and in different loci than those (blacks or whites) from the middle classes. Rogers-Rose (1980) reports that black adults who earn over $15,000 generally live in husband-wife families and have their children living with them, while those who are at the level of $4000 and below have fewer than one in five of their children with both parents. Since most blacks live at the moderate to low income levels in the U.S. less than half of the black children can be expected to be living with both natural parents.

The Population Reference Bureau in 1976 reported that less than half of the black children were living with two parents (including stepparents) and fewer than half of all black children, 45 percent, were living with their natural parents. In 1978, almost as many black children under 18 were living with their mothers, 44 percent, only, as were living with two parents. In 1980, 43 percent of black children had two parents present. In all of the United States, half of all children living with relatives other than their biological parents were black. Forty-four percent of black children in 1980 lived only with their mothers and for whites, 13.5 percent. The proportion of black families with women as heads is 47 percent; for white familes, 13.4 percent. Black single mothers include never-married, 29%; separated 37%; widowed 9%; and divorced 25% (for whites the figures are 7%, 29%, 12%, and 53% respectively).

We can safely estimate that at least half of all Black children are reared apart from their natural parents for some considerable part if not all of their growing years.

Who rears the children if not the natural parents? The answer most often given is that the grandparents do, especially the grandmothers. Aunts and uncles come in a close second. Since agency adoptions and induced abortions are still not very popular ways of resolving "unwanted" or "unplanned" pregnancies, "informal adoption" among black relatives and fictive kin as well as "shared childrearing" have emerged as functional alternatives to exclusive childrearing by both natural parents.

Most Blacks, when interviewed verbally, support the traditionally accepted sequence of love, marriage, sex, parenthood and childrearing occurring in that order and confined in a specific space and time. But the social, economic and demographic circumstances of life which are too numerous to enumerate here create a different factual order from the ideal accepted order for a large segment of the black community.

Summary and Conclusions

The revised black family formation process described above is an adaptive response in part to economic and demographic deprivation. Demographically, there is a shortage of black males, especially in the marriage ages. Reasons for this development have already been mentioned. Accordingly a substantial number of young black women with or without children will not be able to form husband-wife families even under the most favorable economic circumstances. Man sharing is emerging as a distinct reality for many lower socioeconomic level women although not for them exclusively. My own research would suggest that single never-married mothers have the greatest possibility of becoming the consensual "second wives" of black men who are already contractually married and who are intent upon maintaining themselves in those relationships.

Economic deprivation however seems to be the greatest causal factor in the emerging alternative black family formation process. Scientific research has established that economic cycles influence marriage rates, marital disruptions, and other aspects of family life, and science has long established that socioeconomic resource levels are correlated with the number of children born in a family, the rates of children born outside of marriage, that is, before the first marriage and between serial marriages.   Husband-wife families and single-parent families also fall into patterns of socioeconomic status. Finally, it is accepted in the scholarly community that economic resources influence the rate of marriage especially among teenage mothers and fathers.

Given the meager resources of most low socioeconomic level blacks and given the fact that most of the first born out-of-wedlock children are to teenagers who have few if any economic resources, marriage, by them has to be delayed or abandoned altogether. Since most teenage pregnancies and births are unplanned and untimed, parenthood, therefore, often begins before the socio-emotional bonds between the young couples have ripened and developed to the point where commitments such as marital commitments can be confidently made. The tendency therefore is to postpone marriage and continue the courtship after the birth of the baby. The baby often becomes the "linking pin" between couples who might otherwise drift away from each other over time as they reach late adolescence and young adulthood. Because teenagers have little or no resources and are still dependent themselves, they are not in a position to take full financial and social responsibility for their actions -- raising a young new born baby. Such a baby is therefore, usually raised by the mother's mother or the mother's aunt, sometimes for the duration of the childrearing period, and sometimes until the young mother, with or without a spouse, is economically endowed enough to survive on her own or with minimum assistance. Given the fact that unemployment among black teenagers and young adults is so precarious, the setting up of an independent household usually has to wait until they reach their middle or late twenties. Nevertheless, family life goes on outside of marriage: love, sexual intercourse, childbearing and childrearing do not wait; they continue unabated until such time as marital or quasi-marital relationship is possible.

Clearly, more economic resources would facilitate earlier marriages and more stable husband-wife families. Better economic circumstances might even encourage aspirations which would delay early sexual activity, pregnancy and childbirth. The higher the socioeconomic level of resources among blacks (and whites) the lower is the premarital sex and pregnancy and childbirth rate; so economic deprivation is partly a cause of the revision of black family formation, which was once thought to be the exception and now has become the rule. At its broadest level, the changing formation of the black family results from the persistence of economic, educational, and social discrimination.

REFERENCES

Bianchi, Suzanne and Reynolds Farley
    1979   "Racial Differences in Family Living Arrangements and Economic Well-Being: An Analysis of Recent Trends," JOURNAL OF MARRIAGE AND THE FAMILY, 41 (Aug.):537-551.

Farley, Reynolds and Albert Hermalin
    1971   "Family Stability: A Comparison of Trends Between Blacks and Whites," AMERICAN SOCIOLOGICAL REVIEW, 36 (Feb.):1-18.

Glick, Paul C. and Arthur J. Norton
    1977   "Marrying, Divorcing and Living Together in the U.S. Today," POPULATION BULLETIN, Vol. 32, No. 5 (Population Reference Bureau, Inc., Washington, D.C.).

Glick, Paul C. and Arthur J. Norton
    1979   "Marrying, Divorcing, and Living Together in the U.S. Today," POPULATION BULLETIN, Vol. 32, No. 5 (Population Reference Bureau, Inc., Washington, D.C.).

Jackson, Jacquelyne
    1971   "But Where Are The Men?" THE BLACK SCHOLAR 3 (Dec.): 30-41.

Kantner, John F. and Melvin Zelnik
    1973   "Contraception and Pregnancy: Experience of Young Unmarried Women in the United States," FAMILY PLANNING PERSPECTIVES, 5 (Winter): 21-55.

Masnick, George S. and Joseph A. McFalls, Jr.
    1978   "Those Perplexing U.S. Fertility Swings" PRB REPORT (Population Reference Bureau, Inc., Washington, D.C.).

Rodgers-Rose, La Frances
    1980   "Some Demographic Characteristics of the Black Woman: 1940 to 1975," in La Frances Rodgers-Rose (Ed.), THE BLACK WOMAN, Beverly Hills, Ca: Sage Publications, 29-42.

Kantner, John F. and Melvin Zelnik
　　1973　"Some Demographic Characteristics of the Black Women"
　　1940 to 1975," in LaFrances Rodgers-Rose (Ed.) THE BLACK
　　WOMAN, Beverly Hills, California: Sage Publications, 29-42.

Sklar, June and Beth Berkov
　　1974 "Teenage Family Formation in Postwar America," FAMILY
　　PLANNING PERSPECTIVES, 6 (Spring):80-90.

Scott, Joseph W.
　　1980 "The Sociology of the Other Woman," BLACK MALE/FEMALE
　　RELATIONSHIPS, 2 (1):30-32.

Stewart, James and Joseph W. Scott
　　1978　"The Institutional Decimation of Black American Males,"
　　THE WESTERN JOURNAL OF BLACK STUDIES, 2 (Summer):82-92.

Zelnik, Melvin and John F. Kantner
　　1978　"First Pregnancies to Women Aged 15-19:　1976-1971,"
　　FAMILY PLANNING PERSPECTIVES, 10 (Jan/Feb.):11-20).

To be a poor man is hard, but to be a poor race in a land of dollars is the very bottom of hardships.

W. E. B. DuBois
THE SOULS OF BLACK FOLK, 1903

CHAPTER SIX

SOCIO-DEMOGRAPHIC PREDICTORS OF RURAL POVERTY: A REGIONAL ANALYSIS

Alton Thompson
Betty J. Traub
Randall P. White

Introduction

Social scientists have continued to focus their research on the topic of rural poverty. Three considerations mark this inquiry. The first is a concern with the quality of life among impoverished groups in the rural population. Secondly, poverty is seen as a persistent force that affects the motivation and behavior of those affected. The final concern involves the link between poverty and many social problems (crime and delinquency, family and generational problems, prejudice and discrimination and unemployment). Collectively, these concerns indicate a need to fill the crucial void in our knowledge concerning the sociodynamic processes of families and individuals in poverty, while concurrently implementing programs which reduce poverty.

The preceding concerns, together with the Economic Opportunity Act of 1964 (in which President Johnson declared a War on Poverty), have resulted in a plethora of studies which focus on the economic and social problems of the poor, particularly the urban poor. Despite

*This research was supported by the United States Department of Agricultural, Research Grant No. NCX-061-5-79-150-1, The Isolation of Factors Related to Levels and Patterns of Living in Selected Areas of the Rural South. An extended version of this paper is published in SOUTHERN RURAL SOCIOLOGY, Volumn 1, 76-96 (1984).

the establishment of the National Advisory Commission on Rural Poverty (1967), a unit that was charged with recommending action "to provide opportunities for the rural population to share in America's abundance. . .," there has been a lack of attention given to rural poverty (Bould, 1977:471); poverty remains a major societal problem (Rogers, 1977; Chadwick and Bahr, 1973; Horton and Leslie, 1973; Osmond, 1978; Daft, 1980; Hoppe, 1980; Cho, 1982). Some researchers, such as Gans, contend that poverty has not been eradicated because it is functional; that is, it serves useful functions for members of society such as creating a job market for penologists, criminologists, social workers and public health workers. The poor also perform the low-paid "dirty-work" and other menial tasks (Gans, 1972:272-79). Other frequently cited reasons for the continued existence of poverty include: lack of mobility, low educational attainment, family structure and size, structural constraints, social disorganization, selective outmigration and population redistribution, alienation, anomie, and cultural differences. Thus, poverty appears to be a multifaceted phenomenon that is woven deeply into the fabric of American society; however, to date, the theories are inadequate and the data are skimpy. Social science research on the poor has failed to provide a body of codified knowledge. Miller contends, for example, that "the data upon which generalizations are wrought are indeed very scanty. . .not only do the data collide with each other, but they are based on studies of restricted, constricted situations. . ."(1970:169). In a similar vein, Allen states that "the theory is woefully inadequate for problems presented by poverty" (1970:149). The need for theory and research in furthering our understanding of poverty still persists, and consequently, it is necessary to go beyond descriptive studies of the poor. With this in mind, the focus of the present study was to determine the extent to which eight socio-demographic variables -- race, sex of head of household, age, farm/nonfarm status, education, occupation, number of children, and willingness to travel for employment -- are predictors of a family's level of poverty.

Methodology

The data for this research were derived from 2,580 structured interviews obtained as part of a regional project entitled, "The Isolation of Factors Related to Levels and Patterns of Living in Selected Areas of the Rural South." A multistage cluster sample was used to select the respondents from thirty racially-mixed, low median income, rural counties in ten contiguous southeastern states -- Alabama, Arkansas, Florida, Georgia, Kentucky, Mississippi, North Carolina, South Carolina, Tennessee and Virginia. Sample sizes were assigned in proportion to the size of the county's population.

Direct discriminant analysis was used to determine those characteristics which distinguish between rural residents in and out of poverty.
The objective of this analysis is to weigh and linearly combine the
discriminating variables -- race, sex of head of household, age, farm/
nonfarm status, education, occupation, number of children and willingness to travel for employment -- in a manner that renders the group
as distinct as possible.

Findings

In 1975, although three-fourths of all rural poor were white, poverty
was more pervasive among rural blacks. Approximately forty-one
percent of all rural blacks, but only twelve percent of all rural whites,
had incomes below the minimum subsistence level. Further, more
than ninety percent of all low income rural blacks lived in the South
(Hoppe, 1980:7). This finding is evident in Table 1 as 61.3 percent
of the black respondents are impoverished compared to 31.3 percent
of the white respondents.

Besides race, families with a female head of household are more
likely to be impoverished than families with a male head of household.
Women who are heads of families typically have many handicaps
when it comes to securing an adequate living. For example, the presence of minor children in the home may make it extremely difficult
for mothers to work outside the home; moreover, the token amount
of child support paid, if paid at all, by the father usually does not
permit a decent standard of living. Also, women tend to be confronted
with discriminatory hiring practices and consistently lower wages
(Horton and Leslie, 1973:337; Wheelock, White and Phillips, 1982:2-3).
The feminization of poverty is manifested in the sample data by the
finding that 61.4 percent of the female heads of household live below
the poverty income threshold level compared to 32.7 percent of the
male heads of household.

Poverty among the rural elderly is exacerbated by the problems associated with aging. Older persons not only live on fixed incomes, but
tend to have greater transportational, nutritional, and health care
needs. In fact, the most often cited reason for poverty among the
elderly is the inadequacy of welfare, social security and other public
assistance programs on which they are heavily dependent (McKee
and Robertson, 1975:263). The elderly poor have few resources and
consequently, little hope of escaping poverty. In this sample, the
poor respondents are, on the average, older than the nonpoor respond-

ents (55.7% and 47.5% respectively); however, large standard deviations tend to obscure this difference.

Poverty appears to be more prevalent among farm residents. The present data show that sixty-one percent of the farm residents are below the poverty level as compared to 38.2 percent of the non-farm families. The mechanization and commercialization of agriculture have greatly decreased the likelihood of farm residents escaping poverty. Recent demonstrations by the American Agricultural Movement (AAM) seem to suggest that farming as a viable occupation or as a route out of poverty is at best, unpromising, hopeless or bleak.

The present study also includes two social status variables, education and occupation, and a fertility variable, number of children. An inverse relationship has been found between these variables and poverty status (Tien, 1961:243; Horton and Leslie, 1978:332-333; Bourvier and Lee, 1972:4). Being poor typically means being poorly educated, at best, a semiskilled occupation, and a large number of children. The data in Table 1 reflect this differential in that rural poor persons have an average educational level of about eight years and an average occupational scale value of 24.5, values that are below the levels of the rural non-poor. The average number of children for the poor and non-poor sample respondents are 3.8 and 2.4, respectively.

A close examination of "pockets" of poverty indicates that high under-employment rates are usually responsible for the low average incomes of the poor (Schiller, 1973:37). Persistent, localized subemployment of this kind is generally the consequences of economic and technological changes; for example, the displacement of small farmers and occupational workers by automation. Given this relationship, willingness to travel is included in the analysis to ascertain if the poor in this sample are more or less likely to travel to employment outside of their immediate area than the non-poor. Table 1 suggest that the poor, on the average, travel shorter distances. The question remains as to the importance of this factor in discriminating between the poor and nonpoor. Of course, several other factors not addressed in this study such as availability of transportation, cost, etc. could be the key.

In summary, the literature, along with the data in Table 1, suggest that poverty tends to be concentrated among blacks, female heads of household, the elderly, poorly educated, low or semiskilled workers, farm workers, families with large number of children and perhaps, families that are less willing to travel to employment outside of their immediate area.

Conclusion

This research has been undertaken with the aim of testing eight socio-demographic variables as predictors of rural poverty. The results are supportive of previous studies as education, occupation, sex, race, number of children, farm status, age and willingness to travel for employment are found to distinguish the poor from the non-poor. The composite portrayal of a rural poor head of household is a poorly educated, semi-skilled, female, black farm resident with a large number of children. Age and willingness to travel for employment, however, do not sufficiently contribute (although statistically significant) to the separation of the two groups.

Despite the multi-billion dollar budget of more than ten major programs developed by the War on Poverty, poverty differentials are still discernible. Based on this analysis, solutions to rural poverty in the South revolve chiefly around increases in the educational and occupational levels of the population and increasing opportunities for female head of households. Solutions will be difficult given the present state of the economy, the requirements of the presentday job market, and the Reagan administration's cutbacks in financial aid to institutions of higher education. The War on Poverty reduced the level of poverty (Horton and Leslie, 1977:326-327), but a concerted action by local, state, and Federal agencies in areas of post secondary education, job opportunities and training and reduction of wage disparity between men and women is critically necessary to help rural families raise their level of living above minimum subsistence.

TABLE 1

PREDICTOR VARIABLES BY POVERTY STATUS

Variables	Poverty Status	
	Poor	Nonpoor
RACE:		
Black	61.3	38.7
White	31.1	68.9
SEX:		
Male	32.7	67.4
Female	61.4	38.6
FARM STATUS:		
Farm	61.0	39.0
Nonfarm	38.2	61.8
OCCUPATION[1]	24.5*	39.8*
	(14.7)	(23.3)
AGE[1]	55.7*	47.5*
	(18.7)	(16.5)
EDUCATION[1]	7.8*	11.2*
	(3.4)	(3.5)
NUMBER OF CHILDREN[1]	3.8*	2.5*
	(3.1)	(2.1)
WILLINGNESS TO TRAVEL[2]	17.4**	23.4**
(Miles)	(8.4)	(12.6)

---

[1]The starred value is the mean and the parenthesized value is the standard deviation.

[2]The double-starred value is the median and the parenthesized value is the quartile deviation.

91

REFERENCES

Allen, Vernon L.
1970 "Theoretical Issues in Poverty Research," JOURNAL OF SOCIAL ISSUES, 26:149-167.

Bould, Sally
1977 "Rural Poverty and Economic Development: Lessons from the War on Poverty," JOURNAL OF APPLIED BEHAVIORAL SCIENCE, Vol. 13, No. 4 (Oct.-Dec.), pp. 471-488.

Bouvier, Leon and Everett S. Lee
1972 THE BEARING OF CHILDREN, The Center for Information on America.

Carlin, Thomas A., Robert A Hoppe, Linda M. Ghelfi and Janet W. Goffin
1979 ASPECTS OF WELFARE AND POVERTY IN RURAL AMERICA: TWO BRIEF ISSUES. Economic Development Division, Economics, Statistics, and Cooperatives Service, U.S. Department of Agriculture, Washington, D.C.

Chadwick, Bruce A. and Howard M. Bahr
1973 "Rural Poverty." Pp. 182-195 in Thomas R. Ford (ed.) RURAL U.S.A.: PERSISTENCE AND CHANGE. Ames, Iowa: Iowa State University Press.

Cho, Woong K.
1982 SOCIO-ECONOMICS AND PSYCHOLOGICAL ATTRIBUTES OF RURAL POVERTY IN MISSISSIPPI. Research Bulletin Number 17, Alcorn State University.

Daft, Lynn M.
1980 "The Rural Poverty Commission: Ten Years Later," RURAL DEVELOPMENT PERSPECTIVES (March), pp. 4-6.

Gans, Herbert J.
1972 "The Positive Functions of Poverty," AMERICAN JOURNAL OF SOCIOLOGY, Vol. 78, pp. 275-289.

Gilbert, Ethel S.
1969 "The Effect of Unequal Variance-Covariance Matrices on Fisher's Linear Discriminant Function," BIOMETRICS 25:505-516.

Grinstead, Mary Jo and Sandra Scholtz
1976 "Poverty, Race and Culture in a Rural Arkansas Community," HUMAN ORGANIZATION, Vol. 35, No.1 (September), pp. 33-44.

Hair, Joseph F., Jr., Ralph E. Anderson, Ronald L. Tatum, and Bernie J. Grablowsky.
1979 MULTIVARIATE DATA ANALYSIS. Tulsa, Oklahoma: Petroleum Publishing Company.

Hauser, Robert M. and David L. Featherman
1977 THE PROCESS OF STRATIFICATION: TRENDS AND ANALYSES. New York: Academic Press, Inc.

Hollings, Ernest F.
1973 "The Rural Poor," CURRENT HISTORY, Vol. 64, pp. 258-273.

Holman, Robert.
1974 "The American Poverty Programme," JOURNAL OF SOCIAL POLICY, Vol. 3, No. 1 (January), pp. 21-38.

Hoppe, Bob.
1980 "Despite Progress, Rural Poverty Demands Attention," RURAL DEVELOPMENT PERSPECTIVES, (March), pp. 7-11.

Horton, Paul B. and Gerald R. Leslie
1978 THE SOCIOLOGY OF SOCIAL PROBLEMS. Englewood Cliffs, New Jersey: Prentice-Hall, Inc.

Klecka, William R.
1975 "Discriminant Analysis," in SPSS: STATISTICAL PACKAGE FOR THE SOCIAL SCIENCES. Nie, Norman H. et al. New York: McGraw Hill, pp. 434-467.

Lachenbruch, Peter A.
1975 DISCRIMINANT ANALYSIS. New York: Hafner Press.

Lewis, Oscar.
1966 "The Culture of Poverty." SCIENTIFIC AMERICAN 215:19-25.

Miller, S.M.
1970 "Poverty Research in the Seventies." JOURNAL OF SOCIAL ISSUES 26:169-173.

McKee, Michael and Ian Robertson
1975 SOCIAL PROBLEMS. New York: Random House, Inc.

Osmond, Marie W. and Charles M. Grigg
1973 "Correlates of Poverty: The Interaction of Individual and Family Characteristics," SOCIAL FORCES, Vol. 56, No. 4 (June), pp. 1099-1120.

Rogers, Tommy W.
1977 "Extent and Distribution of Poverty in Mississippi," THE MISSISSIPPI GEOGRAPHER, Vol. 5, No. 1 (Spring), pp. 11-23.

Schiller, Bradley R.
1973 THE ECONOMICS OF POVERTY AND DISCRIMINATION. Englewood Cliffs, N.J.: Prentice-Hall, Inc.

Tabachnick, Barbara G. and Linda S. Fidell
1983 USING MULTIVARIATE STATISTICS. New York: Harper and Row, Publishers, Inc.

Tien, H. Yuan
1961 "The Social Mobility Fertility Hypothesis Reconsidered: An Empirical Study," AMERICAN SOCIOLOGICAL REVIEW, Vol. 26, pp. 159-166.

Wheelock, Gerald C., Randall P. White and Robert L. Phillips
1982 "Sample Design and Multilevel Objectives: Ten Southern State Household Survey in Low Income, Rural Counties," paper presented at the Rural Sociological Society, San Francisco, California.

The problem of work, the problem of poverty, is today the central, baffling problem of the Northern Negro.

W. E. B. DuBois
THE BLACK NORTH IN 1901

CHAPTER SEVEN

ALIENATION AMONG RETIRED AND SOON TO BE RETIRED BLACK MEN

Anne Squarrel Jenkins

This study has as its purpose the examination of the relevance of contemporary theories of alienation to the life experiences of black men who are either retired or near their retirement dates. The underlying framework for this work, as for others of the genre, is Marx's conceptualization of alienation.

In his definition of estranged, or alienated labor, Marx approached the concept on two levels. First, he described alienation in terms of structural conditions of labor. Second, Marx described estrangement, or the psychological consequence for those who work under conditions of structural alienation. Where the conditions of work are rationalized, as in a modern assembly plant, the workers are used as objects in the machinery of production and that which they produce has no meaningful relevance to themselves. There is nothing of their own uniqueness or creativity in what their work produces. Therefore, rather than work being a source through which the workers may express themselves, work becomes the means by which the worker is reduced in value. Since the worker cannot see himself in his product, the product is made alien to him, and he is made alien to himself.

In contemporary usage, alienation has been operationalized to include the ideas of meaninglessness, isolation, powerlessness, and self-estrangement. Contemporary writers, such as Robert Blauner (ALIENATION AND FREEDOM), have used Marx's thesis to measure alienation in modern workers. Generally, they have found varying degrees of alienation among workers -- especially among the working classes.

This work represents an effort to guage the representativeness of such works as Blauner's as descriptions of the feelings and lives of working class black men. Thus, in an effort to draw comparisons, I undertook to observe twenty black men who worked or had spent their lives working under conditions which are thought to contribute to personal alienation.

All of the respondents are people who have roots in the working class community of Chester, Pennsylvania. They are men who have held blue collar jobs all of their working lives. They have been machinists, maintenance men, construction laborers, and clerks. These men have worked in various plants and mills in and around Chester, each for a single employer for more than twenty years. Ten are retired and ten are still working. All are fifty years old or older. Most of the men are Southern born but more of the working men than retired men were born in Chester. Although their present income levels vary greatly, depending largely upon how long ago they retired, the physical settings of their homes appear very similar. Among the retired men there were only two high school graduates. Most of the retired men had only grammar school education. Most of the working men had a little more education, but on average, only a few grades more. None of the still-working men was a high school graduate. One of the retired men was divorced, one was widowed, but the rest were married men in marriages of long standing. Of the working men, only one was divorced while the others were involved in old, apparently stable marriages or relationships. All but two own the homes in which they live. The retired men tended to live in older neighborhoods where the external appearances of their surroundings are in deterioration. Inside, all of their homes are comfortable, neat, and among the currently working men, contemporarily stylish featuring the furniture and decor desirable to working class people in the city.

No attempt was made at obtaining a random sample. I began by asking men with whom I was familiar to talk to me and they, in turn, suggested others whom they knew from the age categories which I requested. From their referrals, I chose men who reflected as wide a range of occupational experiences as possible. I have lived in this community for over twenty years and have personal knowledge of the life styles and living conditions of men from this category. Therefore, it is with a reasonable amount of confidence that I accept the responses of the respondents as representative.

Interviews of approximately one and a half to two hours each were held with the men. Although I did not use a questionnaire, I had decided upon topics to bring up to guide the discussion with each man. The men were encouraged to reminisce and to stress whatever seemed significant to them, all touched on questions which I had decided beforehand to ask. The result, in many cases, was sociologically fascinating. From autobiographical tapes, which I later analyzed and coded, I extracted material for the development of this work.

All of the men whom I interviewed had worked at their last jobs for many, many years, and most for more than twenty years. Except for two men who had farmed, the last or present jobs are similar to the kinds of jobs they have worked at all their lives. I reasoned, therefore, that those respondents nearing retirement would experience feelings of powerlessness, futility, social disconnectedness and discontentment. Further, I reasoned that men who had retired after having lived such lives would experience retirement with negative feelings. Perhaps they would evidence a sense of bitterness and injustice to themselves. Having sacrificed their youth and ambition in earning profits for others under harsh, unrewarding conditions, they might now feel cast aside like any less than useful commodity. Having lived their lives under the impersonal dominance of the demands of production where much of the order of their daily lives was centered around going to work, being at work, and organizing to facilitate getting to work the next day, it seemed reasonable that now in retirement they should experience their days as uneventful and empty.

Since over their lives their most pressing obligations and responsibilities were the production needs of their work places, it seemed probable that commitments to interpersonal relations with family and friends would have had to take secondary places, especially at times when overtime work or swing shifts interferred, or when slow downs and lay-offs reduced income. In other words, if work under conditions of what Braverman has called monopoly capitalism is personally alienating, those who have worked longest and in the most negative conditions should experience its effects to an even greater extent. Their "objectification" should have been most complete.

Alienation As A Structural Condition Of Work

The literature defines non-alienated working conditions as those which involve creativity and intellectual involvement of the worker with the product. Alienation of the work-place occurs when both the products and the producers of labor are secondary to the profit which each represents. Neither product nor worker are viewed as having intrinsic value.

To find empirical indications of whether the work of the men met the conditions for alienated labor, I asked them to describe their jobs. These men generally described jobs which were the hardest, dirtiest, hottest, most dangerous and least desirable within their companies. This was especially true among those already retired. More of those still working had jobs requiring some responsibility for supervision of others. Two were foremen at a shipyard, one a clerk-assistant-manager in a State Store (Liquor Store). Only two worked as unskilled laborers, **per se**. Over the years, all had worked or were still working as small, rather anonymous and expendable links in a large production machine.

An Historical Perspective of Alienated Work From the Eyes of Black Men

Mr. Be recalled for me the ethnic structure of work with the railroad which was his first permanent job after coming to Chester in the twenties. The Irish, he said, had the supervisory positions in those days. The Italians, many of them recent immigrants, had the positions of gang leaders and laborers. The black men, who were more recently hired than the others, had the laboring jobs. (Anecdotally, Mr. Be related the way black workers had been enticed out of the south by roving railroad recruiters, who promised them jobs, while risking arrest for themselves for luring Southern black laborers to the North.) Mr. Be described a self-sufficient life of a farmer when crops were good, but a life of poverty and indebtedness when they were not. Boll weevils made farming unprofitable on his father's farm. Mr. Be, therefore, came North on his own seeking higher wages. In Chester, he recalled, there was no wage differential by race for the same job, but there was a differential by job, with black men getting the lowest paying jobs. In six months after getting a job with the railroad, Mr. Be was made a foreman "because," he said, "I was a close observer." The Italian man, who was his foreman at first, could not read or write in English, and the Irish supervisor, who was also from South Carolina, noticed Mr. Be performing many of the foreman's functions. Expressing some hostility toward Italians as outsiders and usurpers, the supervisor made Mr. Be foreman over an all black crew of twenty-seven men. Proudly, Mr. Be described his crew as the best and as "troubleshooters" sent out to handle the hardest problems. Mr. Be remained a foreman until the Depression. When, he said, "In 1928, me and the whole crew was layed off." He told me about a railroad worker's status:

People didn't look up to you if you were working on the railroad. They were what you called the gangster. . .the gandy dancers.

98

. . I wouldn't have stayed there, not unless I'd gotten this foreman's job. The foreman, he's up there in the money. My salary was $2,100. a year, and that was a lot. . .

Feeling himself prosperous, Mr. Be went triumphantly back to South Carolina in 1927 to marry. Further, he told me:

Railroad was a leftover job. It was an Italian job, and the Italians were getting wise, and they were leaving. . . When the Italians commenced to leaving, the railroads went South and got the blacks. Italians, when they learned to talk a little in English, were able to move out and get better jobs. The black fellows, if they wanted to get out of the South, they had to take it. There wasn't anything else for them to do. They had the cheapest paying jobs, but it was better than share cropping. Share croppers don't make nothing. The white man say, 'Well, next year, Sammy. Get it on the book.' Now, you're going to work for nothing. You owe it all back.

Mr. Ba., another retired man in my sample, had been able to get the job he held until retirement when he first came to Chester over fifty years ago. Asked to describe his work during the early years, he said:

Anything the man told you to do, you did. Loaded cars, filled barrels. . . I worked myself up from there to be a leader. (He became a third-class millwright and union official by retirement). It was a good job. It's Allied Chemical, about the best paying plant there is except Sun Oil and Phoenix Steel. We are the highest paid in phosphates and acid. It was dangerous. See, it's acid, chemicals, explosions and all that was bad. When I first went there I seen many a man who in three days time his clothes practically fell off him because he had to work in what he had and that acid eats the clothes up. You furnished your own gloves and shoes but now they furnish those things. When I first went there all of us (black men) were assigned to one building as laborers. I was the second black man ever assigned to building #9. (machine shop). All the rest was Pollocks (his usage) and Italians. They worked blacks in there, (#9). If they got stuck, they worked in there, but you had to come out. You weren't assigned there. When I first went there, there wasn't no union, and we didn't get the same pay as the Pollocks and Italians.

From the beginning, then, it appears that the working black men

99

of Chester worked under conditions which would be considered structurally alienating given commonly held definitions. On the basis of what the men told me, therefore, structural alienation will be taken as given.

Powerlessness As A Factor Of Alienation

Power in the workplace is defined in terms of the amount of control the worker has over the pace of work and the resulting degree of pressure which the work exerts, the worker's freedom to move about, and the ability of the worker to control techniques and rates of production.

In these terms, we would have to define the working men in my sample as powerless. They neither held nor sought the ability to control the productive forces on their jobs. From Mr. Ba. the union man to Mr. St. the construction laborer, the right to control the forces of production was hardly an expressed concern. Except for the crane operator, however, the men felt that they were able to move around with opportunities to go to the bathroom, smoke or to talk with their fellow workers. Most of them however, did not seem to view pace and pressure as problems in their work. In fact, they generally felt that they liked the work to move steadily along, that time went slowly when the pace was slow. Mr. W., the refinery worker, told me with some pride.

> You're always moving around. You have to be alert. Now sometimes it's hectic, but most of the time the pace is right, depending on trouble caused by the kind of crude coming in. It's dangerous. It could blow if we weren't alert. At times, it's hard because some valves take two men to close. It's hot with flames in there. But you and the five guys on your shift are cooperating. That's what I think about when I think of work: cooperation and being together and teamwork.

The retired men had generally less responsible jobs during their working years. Like the working men, however, they did not attach too much priority to the factors which are most often used to define powerlessness. Typical of the retired, Mr. Sh. said:

> I like to work -- not fast but to continue the whole day. It keeps your mind occupied, and your body in shape. Sitting around brings on arthritis. Keeping busy, I feel better. If its monotonous, it gets tiresome. You have to learn to develop a certain type of rhythm. Then you don't get tired. Most of my jobs had steady rhythm.

100

The younger working men did generally express a greater sense of not being able to control their working conditions than did the retired men. Rather than being directed at their working conditions, however, their feeling was directed toward racial discrimination, which kept them working at undesirable jobs. Mr. D., the welder at the shipyard told me that he had been ill and his doctor ordered him off the job he had held and enjoyed. The supervisor put him and another, younger, white man to work in a department where there are strong fumes which he feels aggravates his condition: He told me:

That union is not worth a nickel. Someone like me, say I'm not going to do a job, I'm gone. They don't care if you die. Now that white boy went in with me, he complained 'It's bad for my health', and he (supervisor) told me, 'That's your job.'

Mr. N., the crane operator was most bitter about his Delaware based company's racial policies. He said that in one section of his department no black workers have positions above helpers, even though they had to train the new white men just moving into the higher positions. "They know the jobs. They do the jobs under a different title, but they can't pass the (written) qualifying test in order to get the title and the pay."

Mr. P. and Mr. A. were both recently elevated to higher positions and both expressed bitterness that it came under government pressure so late in their careers. Mr. A. told me:

Colored people didn't have the opportunities when I was young. Ten years ago, I couldn't have the job I have. I even turned down opportunities because they said if I took a bid and failed I'd have to go back to the bottom on the job I'd left (loss of job security and seniority benefits). I didn't have education and I was afraid it was too hard until the Human Relations people stood behind me and made me take the job. This job used to be two jobs. One man kept the records and another man got the order filled. Then the company said one man could do the records as he filled the orders. When the Human Relations practically forced me to take this ten years ago, they scared me. The government did it. Not the company. The company would never let a black man get ahead.

Among the retired men, what might have been a sense of powerlessness, in the face of race discrimination, now comes out as kind of philosophical resignation, "Wasn't no need to be bitter. You complain and lost your job. You got your satisfaction. Now, who was going to take care of your family?" Sometimes they even seemed to evidence a sense of pride! That is, they seemed to have a sense of having endured to survive in spite of odds which they perceive that others did not face. The race issue was a recurrent theme among all of the men, but none of them seemed to express a feeling of personal diminishment.

I reasoned that if the men had developed a sense of personal powerlessness with regard to their work, it should have characterlogical implications beyond the arena of work. Therefore, I asked all of them questions relevant to problem solving and their ability to cope. It was interesting that both working and retired men felt able to cope with their day to day problems. They strongly felt the poverty around them but at the same time felt themselves adequate to meet their daily needs. Among the retired men, most usually said that the government would have to be responsible for major crises because ordinary people could not, but they seemed to state this as reality for all people and not as something which made them feel individually powerless.

Few were directly involved in politics, but all were registered, regular voters with obvious distaste for others who were politically apathetic. Most expressed a keen interest in the current Presidential elections. They often spoke of Roosevelt's administration as being responsible for bringing them as far as they had gotten. Although the working men tended to admit some anxiety about their ability to cope with maintaining a decent life-style after retirement, the already retired men were impressive in their serenity. Mr. De. said:

"I don't worry about nothing. Everything's going all right. I used to worry when I first came off. Then, the checks started coming in. I get mine and my wife gets hers. Our bills get paid and we eat just the same. No, I don't worry about nothing.

Mr. Be. told me:

The first thing you want to do is get your income together. Once you have done that you will be happy. But when you first retire you have sleepless nights, thinking about how you are going to make it. It's rough at first. Then you get used to it. You have to change. You can't do it over night either. You have to keep cutting down.

I asked if his life changed a lot.

It seems that it makes it easier because as time goes on you see how you can do it. You get confidence.

The continuous thread of all their discussions seemed to imply a sense of practical, qualified mastery. They could handle their lives if the government lent support on the really big economic problems. There was little indication that these men felt devoid of the personal resources which they needed to contend with their daily living experiences. After enduring the demands and pressures of their jobs, they felt able to adapt to most other things in the sense of any other environmental conditions. The evils of racism they could survive. The economic shortages of retirement were solvable problems. As one working man, Mr. Sp. told me, "It's never been how much a person gets. It's how you manage what you've got. That's what counts whether you're retired or working." Most of these men, especially the retired, felt able to manage.

Meaninglessness

Another aspect of alienation is that highly fragmented, rationalized work, in which workers contribute a minute part to the finished product, gives the worker a sense of purposelessness. Craftsmen work on individuated products, usually completing the whole process of a product's creation. They are responsible for and credited with the quality of the finished product. These factors are missing in the rationalized specialized production structures of modern mills and plants. Workers in modern work environments spend the best part of their days engaged in activities which add nothing to their lives but, rather, take a toll by dulling their minds and eliminating any sense of satisfaction in accomplishment.

To gauge the sense of meaninglessness among the men of my sample, I discussed with them their attitudes toward work as a concept, how important they thought their jobs were to the total operation, their fantasies about being rich and not having to work, about working other places, and about their time perception. Again, I was searching to determine whether for the retired men, there was a sense of void.

All of the retired men and nine of the ten working men felt that their jobs were important to the total operation of their plant's productivity. All of the retired men and most (eight of ten) of the working men felt that their jobs were important. They expressed a sense of satisfaction in their own abilities to master their jobs and to perform well.

Some of the questions and answers cited below reflect this sense that their jobs were meaningful and important to them:

"How important was your job to the whole operation?", I asked each man.

Mr. L. - As far as humanity is concerned, not important. But State Stores provide the state with its greatest source of income.

Mr. F. - (yard man directing train deliveries for General Steel). Hadn't been for us, the plant couldn't run. That was the starting point.

Mr. J. - (pitman for Phoenix Steel). How important was it! Jesus Christ Almighty! Listen! My job was to set these pits and have these molds to take care of the heat when it comes. If we lost it (the heat) they done lost maybe $100,000. Maybe more!

Most of the men viewed the concept of work favorably, but few of them saw work as their greatest source of personal satisfaction. Mr. Be. told me, however, that though he thought the people in the community gave him prestige because of the work he did in his church, he got his greatest personal satisfaction from his job.

Mr. Sh. - Anything a man undertakes to do -- even housework -- a man should be proud. I doubt a man who doesn't work can have a happy life.

Mr. Ba. - I believe I was born and cut out for a leader. God has a use for me, and everything I attempt to do in the Lord, I make good.

Mr. J. - You can't compare jobs. I think a man is just as much important in one place as he is in another.

"If money were no problem," I asked, "if you were rich and had always been rich, would you rather work or not work?"

Mr. F. - I don't know that I ever thought about it. Maybe I'd want to do a little something, but I think I'd rather have the money.

Mr. J. - I ain't never wanted to work. Let me tell you I've been working hard all my life, but I never wanted to work. I **had** to work and I did work. You know by my record (only time missed was at the deaths of his parents) I did work.

Mr. D. - I'd rather not work. (Also Mr. St.)

Mr. W. - A man's work helps him be respectable and meet responsibilities. It's a place where he can do his best. I'd rather work.

Mr. L. - A job is necessary to 99%. 55% of the people are dissatisfied with their jobs but 85% of them are afraid to give it up. You've got to work, but doing something you want to do is the best.

Mr. H. - I like my job because it's not physically hard, but if I could get the necessary financial help I wouldn't work.

Mr. P. - A person should have something to do to keep busy even if they have money.

Mr. Be., Mr. Ba., Mr. R., and Mr. K. all would rather work.

Mr. A. - I prefer work regardless to how much money I have. I might have taken some work on a part time basis. I would coast around the world.

Mr. N. - Oh, I'd rather have worked. It's lots of fun. You have pride in your ability.

Mr. T. - I think. I'd rather have worked and get the experience, but I would have retired at least five years earlier.

Mr. Sh. - Money doesn't excite me. I enjoy working with my hands.

Mr. De. - I'd rather be retired.

Mr. Wil. - I wouldn't want to idle though I believe most people wouldn't want to work. (Mr. Sp. also said he wouldn't be idle).

Mr. Sa. - I would have to have something to do.

The picture we get is not that of men who found no meaning in their working experiences. Generally, they favored work as a concept. However, they hardly appear to embody Weber's description of the ideal capitalist worker who is driven by some internal force or spirit while viewing work as an intrinsic good itself.

This is not to say that the men didn't take pride in their work and their abilities. Several above have spoken to the point. Another question that I asked was: "How important is a man's job to his own feelings about himself as a man". Mr. P's answer was typical, I think: "It's a part of him. He should take pride in his job." But perhaps Mr. Ba's response give a better insight into the thinking of these men about work:

"Work gives prestige, but not only work on the job. I do a lot of work and get a lot of prestige, in the church. The church comes first, and then the job.

Mr. Ba. was my second interview, and after that, I asked all of the men to tell me if there was anything more important than a job in making a man feel worthwhile. Mr. Be., my first interviewee had already told me that he got more personal satisfaction from the job but that he felt, like Mr. Ba., that his community status and prestige came from the work he did in his church and community.

Their responses tallied thusly:

ANYTHING MORE IMPORTANT THAN WORK
IN MAKING A MAN FEEL WORTHWHILE

Working Men			Retired Men		
No	Yes	Vague Answer	No	Yes	Vague Answer
4	5	1	3	6	1

Both sets of men see work as important to their self images, although the working men seem to put slightly (might be sample error) more importance on the job. But then I asked, of those groups that you named that you belonged to (categories were job, family, community organizations, religious affiliations), which gave you the most personal satisfaction. Here, I took the cue from Mr. Be. who clearly saw a difference between the components of self image and sources of reward and recognition. As Mr. Wil. told me, "Work is necessary but other things bring just as much satisfaction. I always try to be a man among men, and that's where my status comes from."

The tally of their responses was:

GREATEST PERSONAL SATISFACTION

Working Men

Work	Family	Church/Community	No. Ans.
0	3	6	1

Retired Men

Work	Family	Church/Community	No. Ans.
2	1	5	2

106

It was clear that few of the men saw work as an end in itself. None of the working men and only two of the retired men (one of these was divorced with no family living in Chester and no community affiliations except nominal church membership) saw the job as their greatest source of personal satisfaction.

The meaning of work seemed to be as a place where the men could earn a livelihood for themselves and families and where they could gain pride in their ability to perform among people who appreciated those abilities. Pride in work and earning power was a recurrent theme but pride in communal recognition was even greater. I asked many of them how they felt about the poor and people who didn't work. Mr. W's answer captures the spirit of most of their responses:

> A man's pride is a big thing, and if you can't keep it going, you lost it. I'd rather work and be respectable than to have people give me. People on relief have respect, but they lose confidence. If they could have gotten off relief quick they wouldn't lose their respect. I think a person who doesn't want to work has to be sick -- physical or mental -- and I think about them the way I do sick people. There are reasons for it, 90% would like to have their respect -- a job. I don't blame them. The government could do more.

Having work meant having respectability which comes of being self-sufficient. Having a job makes a man feel worthwhile, but the reward is not only the work itself but also in the recognition which it brings from the community. The meanings of their lives, to which they attach personal satisfaction, comes largely from the community. The work on the jobs bring money, but they see what they do in the community as meaningful work, also. Most significantly, it is the community based work which they feel brings them status and personal satisfaction. Mr. L. put it so: "You are judged by others. Your greatest status comes from your community activities. Unless you are a public figure, others don't know what your job is. That never comes up."

Social Isolation

This aspect of alienation is related to the external nature of modern production. According to this concept, the worker is denied a sense of membership in the work situation and is unable to identify or is uninterested in identifying with the organization and its goals. It was in this area that the men with whom I talked seemed most nearly to fit the commonly accepted description. It was not so much that they evidenced a sense of loss of identification with the production goals of their companies or that they felt something was lost to them in the anonymity of their relationship to the finished products. It simply seemed to me that the whole idea was to them irrelevant, even frivolous. In fact, those in supervisory positions, although they said they liked their jobs, felt a sense of accomplishment, saw their jobs as important to the success of the company, stressed the demands of responsibility and its repressive nature. Among the retired, when they spoke of the benefits of retirement, they mentioned freedom from the demands of schedule. No more time clocks to punch, ability to plan a whole day doing things which were personally meaningful. One wife told me how her husband had been so much more helpful at home and how their relationship had benefited from having more time and not sitting around sleeping when he was home. Except for the two men who owned the farms, I got no sense that they were consciously aware of any deprivation or feelings of injustice about retirement. Seven of the ten working men maintained active community participation in two or more organizations. Six of the retired men, including one who was (83) years old, participated actively in two or more community organizations. Of the remaining four, Mr. J. was in ill health and seldom left the neighborhood. However, the interview took place on his front porch and, we were often interrupted by people who stopped their cars to yell hello and pass pleasantries (further, Mr. J's grandson is a very well known civil rights and political personality, and his wife told me that Mr. J's counsel and advice are often sought by that grandson as well as their other children and grandchildren). Mr. N. maintains nominal church membership, attending about once a month and Mr. D. attends church weekly and sometimes goes to Golden-Age Club meetings. The fact is that the non-involvement with the finished products of their jobs did not appear to be too important a matter to the men at all in terms of promoting isolation. It apparently had no relational implications for their participation in their communities.

Self-Estrangement

If it were possible to measure "clock-watching," this would be one of the best objective indicators of this mode of alienation. Therefore, I asked the working men about whether time passed slowly and whether their days were interesting while at work. Time, they said, passed quickly unless the pace became unusually slack, then time passed very slowly. All but one called his days interesting. All denied being bored most of the time. Similarly, the retired men felt their lives were generally interesting. Time, they said goes about the same now as when they were working. Most days, they told me, were interesting, even though, from time to time, they felt bored. I asked the retired men if they could be young again and go to work now whether they would. With few exceptions, the answer was no. They generally felt that they had earned their retirement. As Mr. J. put it:

I enjoy my wife, but you know what I enjoy? I sit down and brag. I worked and lived and tried to take care of my family, but I enjoy my retirement. Since I've retired, God knows I've enjoyed every minute of it. I didn't have to answer a whistle in the morning. I didn't have to get up and go nowhere. I've had a few dollars. So now why couldn't I enjoy that? I should and I have all the way from the first day up until today.

The men of my sample did not seem to feel that making money was unrewarding. In fact, they saw this ability as a paramount virtue in themselves. Job security, adequate pay, and work that was not too physically demanding seemed to them to be a lot. On top of that, there was the opportunity to be with other men. Few of the men felt that most of their close friends were people with whom they worked, but all of them expressed enjoyment in their relationships with their work-mates while on the job.

In their book, HIDDEN INJURIES OF CLASS, Sennett and Cobb discussed the self-estrangement of workers (presumably, mostly white) generated by their relationships with the next generation -- their own children primarily. They told of their sense of betrayal when the sacrifices, which they made for their children, not only left them personally unfulfilled but also diminished their self-images in that it created relational discrepancies and disconnectedness between themselves and their better educated children. Among the black men with whom I talked, not only were their children better educated than they, but often their wives were as well. I asked them, "Does educating children separate them from their parents?" "No." said nine of the retired men. "No." said six of the men still working. Four of the working men felt that children who were educated tend to look down on their parents. Interestingly, however, two of those men have no children, and a third has raised only foster children. The fourth does have children in whom he is disappointed. His children, however, disappoint him because "they don't have any ambition," not because they are educated and look down on him. The retired men appeared extremely proud of their educated children. Mr. Be. whose son holds a Ph.D. in microbiology and was then in H.E.W. as director of the bureau which funds medical school programs, Mr.

109

Ba. whose son is now in college and whose daughter just graduated, Mr. P. whose two children are teachers, Mr. De. whose step-daughter teaches, Mr. T. whose deceased daughter was a teacher, Mr. D. who has one daughter in college and one teaching, Mr. L. whose teen-aged children are college bound, Mr. V. whose oldest son is in college and expects the other three to follow, all strongly approved of education for children as a positive factor in their relationships. The concensus was that rather than making relations worse, it made them better because education made the person better and more appreciative. Mr. Be., whose son holds the Ph.D., was most expressive.

No. I could say that for myself and my friends. We are proud to see these changes come. Where I come from, the white man used to laugh because we couldn't understand his questions, but now they (the children) answer all their questions. The answer is education. But a person can make it on two levels. The first thing is education. With an education you can go a far ways and the religious life is next. It looks like two classes there. . . . The most educated people seem not to want to be associated with the lower class of people. Then next the person (the less fortunates) looks for the church. You see the church people are always collecting for people who don't have things. They get satisfaction doing things for people.

I asked him, "Do you think the educated people are a different kind of people?"

No, not different **kind**, but the educated people think a different way from the religious people. They have a deeper insight on things. . . They want to do for themselves. It's the one's with less education, who live up to their Christian teachings, that the most people (community) depend on and that way they (church people) get just as much respect as the educated people get for being educated. I feel that I have contributed a lot just by talking to different people. You take me and my son. He had the opportunity to get an education (Ph.D.) but I didn't. But right now, we get in conversations, and we think alike yet.

Discussion

Although the men did not seem to see themselves as intrinsically intertwined with their work, it is apparent that their self-concepts are greatly impacted by their work. They appeared to be well-adjusted and content with their lot. It seemed to me, as we talked, that their

110

needs for self-actuation and the order of their priorities in terms of the arena in which that occurs were different, say, than mine or other professional people's. I became more and more convinced that the assumption of work as a "species" need was being brought into question and, therefore, also much of the material which purports to describe the working class, particularly, the black working class. These men saw work as necessary and satisfying, as a means rather than an end. They viewed inter-personal relationships and community involvement as ends, and, therefore, higher in their priorities.

It appeared to me that while these men were imbued with strong values for self-sufficiency , mastery and respectability, they were not inclined to take on the responsibilities of capitalistic economic determinations. They seemed to have a sense of using the system to meet their own needs. In arriving at his conclusions about the effects on the worker by the relations of production in capitalistic working conditions, Marx observed the European workers of his own environment. Subsequently, Western scholars have followed Marx's theoretical framework and assumptions. Black, Chicano, and Southern European workers are often treated parenthetically in these studies and whatever differences are found may either be lost in the statistical weighting of the ethnic majority, explained away or devalued as exceptional. By Marx's definition, the men in my sample may be correctly said to have false consciousness. My own impression is that they are products of a different set of community- and, therefore, occupationally-relevant socialization experiences. Work for them seems not the most essential link between man and nature. The appropriate ends in life seem to have to do with relationship among people for them, and work fits into place as a not unpleasant means for facilitating the achievement of that end.

The already retired men, therefore, did not experience retirement as a void, but as an earned freedom to do those things which were even more personally satisfying. "Does a man get less respect after he retires than he got when he was working?" I asked, and to the man, they answered, "No."

Another factor to be considered in a study of alienation among black workers is discriminatory, racist practices which in terms of status achievement kept the men focused on their communities rather than their jobs. As they said over and over, one gets respect for working and for earning a good living, but one's status in the community is derived from one's own work **within** the community. They perceived both paid and voluntary labor as "work." It was from the latter that

111

they saw gains in recognition and approval. Their sense of well-being and positive self concepts should be related to the fact that while they maintain high status in their communities where it counts to them, they also have approached parity with white workers, in terms of earning power. They are still very aware that status as black men keeps them from attaining many positions within their companies, but at the same time, with the support of government intervention, their incomes in the same jobs are on the same level with whites. Their ability to provide themselves and their families with material comforts is similar, if not identical, with that of white workers, as long as there is prosperity in the system. Perhaps a closer look needs to be taken of the contributions of black community life as an independent variable conditioning how work and retirement is experienced.

In LABOR AND MONOPOLY CAPITALISM, Braverman decries the loss of the craft orientation of labor and the increasing rationalization of the labor process. One factor struck me as I talked with the men. They, rather than having lost something from this process, actually gained. During their working lives, they have been largely excluded from craft labor which is, and has been, the province of higher status groups. It has only been through the rationalization of labor which reached into what Braverman calls "the reserve army of labor" that they have been able to make any gains and to establish a secure footing in the working class. They have not achieved the same social status as whites, but they have advanced in income and, materially, are not obviously different from white workers when their jobs are secure. For most of them, the material comforts which they enjoy in the working class represents achievement and upward mobility.

Accepted analytic insights may decree that alienated working conditions deny man's "species nature", but for the men with whom I talked, the changing of work milieus represented the opening up to black men of an otherwise status determined closure to opportunity for any sort of material achievement through personal effort.

REFERENCES

Robert Blunner
ALIENATION AND FREEDOM: THE FACTORY WORKER AND HIS INDUSTRY (Chicago, 1964).

Harry Braverman,
'LABOR AND MONOPOLY CAPITALISM: THE DEGRADATION OF WORK IN THE TWENTIETH CENTURY. Monthly Review Press (New York and London, 1974).

Karl, Marx
Economic and Philosophic Manuscripts of 1844 in Robert C. Tucker, ed. THE MARX-ENGLES READER. W. W. Norton & Co. (New York, 1972).

Melvin Seeman
On the Meaning of Alienation, AMERICAN SOCIOLOGICAL REVIEW. 1972, 24:783-791.

Richard Sennett and Jonathan Cobb
THE HIDDEN INJURIES OF CLASS. Vintage Books (New Jersey, 1972).

Max Weber
THE PROTESTANT ETHIC AND THE SPIRIT OF CAPITALISM: THE RELATIONSHIP BETWEEN RELIGION AND THE ECONOMIC AND SOCIAL LIFE IN MODERN CULTURE. Charles Scribner's Sons (New York, 1958).

I believed in the higher education of a Talented Tenth who through their knowledge of modern culture could guide the American Negro into a higher civilization. I knew that without this the Negro would have to accept white leadership ...

W. E. B. DuBois
AUTOBIOGRAPHY, 1964

CHAPTER EIGHT

PROBLEMS OF BLACK COMMUNITY LEADERSHIP: A CHALLENGE FOR URBAN EDUCATION

Wornie L. Reed

The current economic crisis and its devastating effects on minority communities has generated many calls for community self-help programs (Williams, 1982). The success of this type of community development will depend to a large extent on the quality of local leadership structures. Leadership, however, is one of the more problematic aspects of the black community (Cox, 1950; Staples, 1976; Hope, 1980). In this paper, I will discuss community leadership, in the context of black urban communities and the system of urban education.

Background

Black America's frustration with the efficacy of federal programs has led to a renewed interest in self-help initiatives. A growing body of literature is developing which outlines some parameters for these endeavors. For example, there have been examinations of traditionally black organizations (Yearwood, 1980), black families (Johnson, 1981), and black fund-raising organizations (Bremond, 1976; Brown, 1977).

Until recently, mutual aid programs in black communities were largely successful (Drake and Cayton, 1945; Kutzik, 1979). In fact, during the mid-1800s blacks in large eastern cities were among the more successful groups in "caring for its own." This, of course, was spurred by the economic and social pressures of this period. However, the

Public Assistance programs initiated in the 1930s with the Social Security Act had the effect of diminishing the strength of these organizations by decreasing the need for them. (Kutzik, 1979). Presently, due to major economic crises and poor race relations, many blacks feel the need for establishing modern mutual aid programs (Norman, 1977), as well as preserving existing self-help organizations (Yearwood, 1980).

A basis argument in this paper is that the eventual success of community self-help efforts will depend upon the quality of community leadership structures. In addition to having capable individuals to take the roles of leaders, a community must have residents involved with the issues and consequently, with these leaders.

While acknowledging the importance of other approaches to black community development, the analysis in this paper addresses the issue from a different viewpoint, albeit a complementary one. In this paper, the community school is examined with special emphasis on the potential role it can play in community development in general and leadership development in particular. In addressing the roles of local organizations and institutions in black community development, local schools should not be overlooked. An urban school may assist leadership development in at least two ways. It may help (1) through an active cooperative relationship with other community organizations and institutions and (2) through relevant civics curricula for students.

Before discussing either of these two methods, it may be instructive to examine the nature of leadership in general and leadership in the black community in particular.

LEADERSHIP IN THE BLACK COMMUNITY

The Nature of Leadership

Burns (1978) defined leadership in the following manner:

> I define leadership as leaders inducing followers to act for certain goals that represent the values and the motivations -- the wants and needs, the aspirations and expectations--of both leaders and followers (p. 19).

Similarly, Holland (1978) defined leadership as:

> A process of influence which involves an ongoing transaction

115

between a leader and followers. The key to effective leadership is in this relationship. Although most attention is given to the leader, leadership depends upon more than a single person to achieve group goals. Therefore, the followers as well as the leader are vital to understanding leadership as a process. Followers support the leadership activities and the leader's position (p. 16).

Thus, leadership, a process, is to be distinguished from "leader," a role in this process. "Leader" and "follower" are roles in a relationship involving a dynamic process which includes two-way influence between leaders and followers. In this view, leadership includes an active role for those who are not leaders (i.e., the followers). At a minimum, followers should be informed. In responding to leaders, followers should have adequate knowledge of alternative leaders and programs and the capacity to choose among those alternatives.

All too often leadership is confused with power. Therefore, it is useful to distinguish between the two concepts. Both are relational: power expresses the relationship where A has control over B. In other words A, the leader, induces B, the follower, to do what A wishes, regardless of B's desires. However, leadership, seen in its proper mature function, expresses the relationship where leaders (A's) induce followers (B's) to act for certain goals that represent the wants, needs, and aspirations of both leaders and followers (See Burns, 1978).

One problem with power relationships is that B's, the followers, can be controlled by persons who have the resources to manipulate the A's. Historically, this has been the perception of the situation in some black communities. Consequently, the term "black leader" occasionally has a pejorative connotation. Educational institutions may be the appropriate arenas to initiate changes in the meaning of leadership in black urban communities.

Black Community Development

During the "War on Poverty" era, begun by the Economic Opportunity Act of 1961, a number of community organizations were charged with the responsibility of developing solutions to some of the problems of poor urban communities. These were the organizations in which -- and with which -- local untrained as well as trained individuals would work and give directions to the organizations' efforts. Many of these efforts failed, not because of the problem of indigenous leadership, but because of a hostile socio-political environment. These processes have been described by Bachrach and Baratz (1970), Rose (1972), and Warren, Rose, and Burgunder (1974).

Each of the above studies suggest that the balance of power lies outside of the indigenous community. The perception by blacks that their communities were little more than domestic colonies in the 1960s effectuated their participation in community-based organizations. However, the studes cited above reveal how these efforts were thwarted. This research underscores the oft repeated claim in poor urban communities that adversarial relationships exist between public service organizations and the public they are designed to serve. Studies on the roles of public school administrators reveals that these policy makers have often been a "part of the problem" (Warren, Rose & Burgunder, 1974).

Characteristics of Black Leadership

Max Weber, the distinguished German sociologist, described three ideal types of authority held by leaders of organizations -- charismatic (religious and political heroes), traditional (kings and queens), and bureaucratic, or rational-legal (officeholders -- i.e. presidents and governors). According to Weber, the authority of a charismatic leader lies in personal qualities like oratorical abilities and physical attractiveness (Gerth and Mills, 1958). This leader mesmerizes his/her followers. Inevitably, charismatic authority becomes unstable and fritters away.

Traditional authority is more permanent and is based on custom. This type of leader exercises authority through inherited status. By justifying their status in terms of traditional authority, leaders may inject arbitrariness into their decisions.

Rational-legal authority is based on impersonal rules that are rationally established by a formal organization. Authority rests in the office, not the person. Persons with rational-legal authority are obeyed because of a general faith in the rationality of the system that gave these people the power to command.

In black community organizations, leadership has tended to be charismatic. In other words, any power exercised by such a leader is the result of his or her personality. Leadership seldom flows from the organization itself. Charismatic leadership may be very effective in the early stages of a movement, but for sustained efforts more institutionalized mechanisms are required.

117

In black community organizations, there is a gradual transition from charismatic leaders to traditional leaders. However, as argued by Hope (1980), that is as far as it usually goes. Seldom is leadership based on legal-bureaucratic authority. According to Hope (1980), if they are to successfully perform their duties in this technical world, black organizations must relinquish authoritarian-traditional leadership roles and adopt more participatory styles of operation. To do this, members of an organization must be educated in terms of their roles and obligations. Out of this type of social environment effective leadership will develop.

URBAN EDUCATION AND COMMUNITY DEVELOPMENT

From the foregoing discussion, we may conclude that there is a great need to develop community "readiness" for leadership. Urban schools may help to accomplish this in two ways. One way is through the classroom. The other way is through a school's community relations. In the classroom, schools may emphasize citizenship issues. This may appear obvious, since "good" citizenship is taught in junior high school civics classes. But seldom is an urban school student able to relate the civics lesson to his or her own community. Yet, according to a traditional definition, the purpose of education is to train individuals to find their places in society and to use these places to better themselves and society. If this objective is to be realized by an urban school, class material must be made relevant to the lives of the students. Such training would be instrumental in helping to develop better citizens while simultaneously promoting participatory schemes of decision-making.

It is beyond the scope of this paper to propose the specific content of "community citizenship" school curricula. However, curricula for citizen education have been established in a number of settings with the goal of preparing "students for current and future responsibilities in their interpersonal, community, and political lives" (Bowers and Root, 1979; Hill, 1978; Presseisen, 1980). A number of citizen education attainment tests are available (Sanders, 1980; Tuckman and Montare, 1975), and although the results are mixed, some studies have found positive relationships between civics curricula and political participation (Lewellen, 1974).

In addition to arranging meaningful curricula that will assist in the development of community leadership, urban school administrators should give attention to the linkages between the local school and the community. In contrast to the suburban situation, many inner

118

city schools have no parent-teacher organizations. Although the parent-teacher groups in suburban communities have been judged to have limited influence and effectiveness, even this structure is missing from many inner city schools (Janowitz, 1969). In addition to the lack of, or the weakness of, parent-teacher organizations, many urban schools have antagonistic relationships with parents and community residents. Although somewhat dated, the observations of Janowitz (1969:102) remain pertinent.

> The typical pattern of contact with an individual family or parent has been essentially negative and on occasion repressive. Direct observation day-to-day underlined the consistent pattern by which the public school in the slum community operated to keep parents from understanding its educational programs. Parents (have) had to live with a lack of adequate information about school procedures and the obligations of the school authorities toward their students.

As Warren et al. (1974) found, urban schools are often guilty of the same types of hostile practices that other community decision organizations exhibit.

A key aspect of this discussion is that the classroom and the school are viewed as existing within a social milieu. The classroom is located within a school, which is within a social milieu, that includes not only the inter-organizational field as discussed by Warren, et al. (1974), but also the informal aspects of the community. Students are members of families which in turn form the community. In the past decade special attention has been devoted to the "ghetto child" because of his problematic social environment. We need to look at this issue from a different perspective.

Since the student in the classroom is part of larger social milieus and since the school is part of more encompassing milieus, the student-classroom situation must be viewed in this wider context. To examine some of the problems in the relationship between urban schools and community residents it is useful to apply concepts related to power relationships. By definition, a school is a people-changing organization, which means, teachers seek to induce their students to attain certain desired goals. This is a non-coercive power relationship in which A, the teacher or administrator, attempts to get B, the student, to comply with A's objectives. Compliance is a central element of organizational structure (See Etzioni, 1977).

119

(Compliance) refers both to a relation in which an actor behaves in accordance with a directive supported by another actor's power, and to the orientation of the subordinated actor to the power applied (Etzioni, 1977:7).

Power differs according to the means used to induce subjects to comply. Thus, a school, which has the objective of transmitting culture -- science and art etc. -- uses normative power to obtain compliance. This kind of power rests on the allocation and manipulation of symbolic rewards and deprivations. Organizations that have cultural goals must rely on normative powers because the realization of these goals requires commitments from the lower participants in the organization -- the students -- to representatives of the organization -- the teachers -- and their objectives.

Coercion or antagonism makes identification with organizational representatives very unlikely. In fact, coercive power, the use of force or the threat of the use of force, is more appropriate for order goals, which are often the objectives of prisons and custodial mental institutions. In a classroom setting, a coercive or antagonistic environment is counterproductive.

In past years, public schools have been hostile to other agencies and institutions such as church groups, community organizations and welfare agencies, that have offered educational programs. Instead of separating themselves from other organizations with educational capacities, public schools should embrace these organizations with gratitude.

Since community leadership has been defined herein as a reciprocal relationship between leaders and followers, leaders should be developed out of what may be called a "ready" community. A ready community is one in which a healthy relationship exists between community agencies and community residents -- a relationship that is supported by a shared belief-value system, or what Warren called the institutionalized thought structure (1974). In this view, an urban school may assist in leadership development by (1) integrating itself with other community educational, recreational, and cultural organizations, and (2) working on the institutionalized thought structure -- through both classroom and community based activities -- to direct it toward community development. These two efforts are not unrelated. When an educational institution becomes accessible to members of the community and more involved in community activities, it will effect positive changes in the general thought structure of the community.

Summary and Conclusion

Increasingly, there are calls for self-help initiatives in black communities. I have argued that to be successful these self-help initiatives require certain community structures -- leadership and community readiness. Leadership has been defined as a reciprocal process of influence between persons occupying the roles of leaders and those occupying the roles of followers. The role of an informed follower is an active one, in that such a person has knowledge of alternative programs, as well as alternative leaders, and possesses the capacity to choose among them. Community readiness describes a community with an abundance of such persons. Urban schools may help to develop community readiness in general and community leadership in particular through its activities in the community as well as through its curricula.

Historically, black community leadership has tended to be charismatic or traditional. Neither type of authority is appropriate for meeting the challenges presented by the technologically-oriented contemporary world. Of course, external forces have affected the processes of black leadership. As Hope (1980) has indicated, and as the studies by Rose (1972), Warren et al. (1974), and Bachrach and Baratz (1970) had demonstrated, the dominant society has tended to limit the development of black organizations and black leaders. In fact, the Warren study showed how community development has been thwarted by white-dominated community agencies, including public school administrations.

This paper has suggested one potential avenue to black community/ leadership development -- the local urban school. The modus operandi for a school's involvement in facilitating black leadership is consistent with the school's traditional role of "training an individual to find his place in society (community) and to use that place to better society."

Perhaps with the realization of its occasional role in the thwarting process, as well as its potential role in the development process, urban schools will help provide appropriate remedies. They may do this in two ways. First, urban schools could come to realize their roles as centers of community education. As such, they must operate in a more cooperative manner with indigenous community institutions, especially those that are involved with educational programs. This cooperation will enhance the local reputation of public school systems. Presently, the adversarial relationship between black community residents and white-dominated organizations fosters a "we-they" conception in the community. Changes must occur in the attitudes and behaviors of all actors or school representatives and community residents will remain worlds apart, in which case, more than black leadership will suffer.

REFERENCES

Bachrach, P., and Baratz, M.S.
POWER AND POVERTY: THEORY AND PRACTICE. New York:
Oxford University Press, 1970.

Bremond, W.
The Black United Fund movement. THE GRANTSMANSHIP
CENTER NEWS. Los Angeles: The Grantsmanship Center, 1976.

Bowers, J. J., and S. Root.
ACTIVITIES AND INTERESTS IN CITIZEN EDUCATION: A TRI-
STATE SURVEY. Philadelphia: Research for Better Schools, Inc.,
1979. (ERIC Document Reproduction Services No. ED 191 776).

Browne, R. S.
Developing Black Foundations; An Economic Response to Black
Community Needs. THE BLACK SCHOLAR, 1977, 9 (4): 25-28.

Burns, J. M.
LEADERSHIP. New York: Harper and Row, 1978.

Cantor, M. H.
The Informal Support System of New York's Inner City Elderly:
Is Ethnicity a Factor? In D. E. Gelfand and A. J. Kutzik (Eds.),
ETHNICITY AND AGING. New York: Springer Publishing Co.,
Inc., 1979.

Cox, O. C.
Leadership Among Negroes in the United States. In A. Gouldner
(Ed.) STUDIES IN LEADERSHIP AND DEMOCRATIC ACTION.
New York: Harper & Row, Publishers, 1950.

Drakes, S. C. and Cayton, H. R.
BLACK METROPOLIS: A STUDY OF NEGRO LIFE IN A NORTH-
ERN CITY. New York: Harper & Row, 1945.

Etzioni, A.
Power, Goals and Organizational Compliance Structures. In R.
G. Leger and J. R. Stratton (Eds.), THE SOCIOLOGY OF CORREC-
TIONS: A BOOK OF READINGS. New York: John Wiley And Sons,
Inc., 1977.

Gerth, H. H., and Mills, C. W.
   MAX WEBER: ESSAYS IN SOCIOLOGY. New York: Oxford University Press, 1958.

Hamilton, C.
   Black Power and Participation. In P. C. Sexton (Ed.), SCHOOL POLICY AND ISSUES IN A CHANGING SOCIETY. Boston: Allyn and Bacon, Inc., 1972.

Hill, R. A.
   A CONCEPTUALIZATION OF CITIZEN EDUCATION. Philadelphia: Research for Better Schools, Inc., 1978.

Hollander, E. P.
   LEADERSHIP DYNAMICS. New York: The Free Press, 1978.

Janowitz, M.
   INSTITUTION BUILDING IN URBAN EDUCATION. New York: Russel Sage Foundation, 1969.

Hope, R. O.
   Patterns of Black Leadership. In L. S. Yearwood (Ed.) BLACK ORGANIZATIONS: ISSUES ON SURVIVAL TECHNIQUES. Lanham, MD.: University Press of America, Inc., 1980.

Johnson, R. C.
   The Black Family and Black Community Development. THE JOURNAL OF BLACK PSYCHOLOGY, 1981, Vol. 8 (1).

Kutzik, A. J.
   American Society Provision for the Aged: An Historical Perspective. In D. E. Gelfand and A. J. Kutzik (Eds.), ETHNICITY AND AGING: THEORY, RESEARCH, AND POLICY. New York: Springer Publishing Co., 1979.

Lewellen, J.R.
   ADOLESCENT POLITICAL EDUCATION AND POLITICAL PARTICIPATION. Philadelphia: St. Joseph's College, 1974. (ERIC Document Reproduction Service No. ED 099 298).

Norman, A. J.
   Mutual Aid: A Key to Survival for Black Americans. THE BLACK SCHOLAR, 1977, 9 (4), 44-49.

Presseisen, B. Z.
   CITIZEN EDUCATION AT RESEARCH FOR BETTER SCHOOLS. Philadelphia: Research for Better Schools, Inc., 1980.

Rose, S.M.
THE BETRAYAL OF THE POOR: THE TRANSFORMATION OF COMMUNITY ACTION. Cambridge, Mass.: Schenkman Publishing Co., 1972.

Sanders, N. M. THE SEARCH FOR CITIZEN EDUCATION MEASURES CONTINUED. Philadelphia: Research for Better Schools, Inc., 1980. (ERIC Document Reproduction Service No. 191 790).

Staples, R.
INTRODUCTION TO BLACK SOCIOLOGY. New York: McGraw-Hill, Inc., 1976.

Tuckman,B. W., and Montare, A. P. S.
EDUCATIONAL GOAL ATTAINMENT TESTS: CIVICS. Bloomington, Indiana: Phi Delta Kappa, 1975.

Warren, R. L., Rose, S.M., and Burgunder, A.F.
THE STRUCTURE OF URBAN REFORM: COMMUNITY DECISION ORGANIZATIONS IN STABILITY AND CHANGE. Lexington, Mass.: D.C. Heath & Co., 1974.

Williams, E.
Perspective. FOCUS, 1982, 10 (4), 2.

Yearwood, L. S. (Ed.).
BLACK ORGANIZATIONS: ISSUES ON SURVIVAL TECHNIQUES. Lanham, MD.: University Press of America, Inc., 1980.

Once the colored child understands the world's attitude and the shameful wrong of it, you have furnished him with a great life motive -- a power and impulse toward good, which is the mightiest thing man has.

W. E. B. DuBois
THE CRISIS, 1912

CHAPTER NINE

BLACK PARENTS AND CHILDREN, AND TEACHERS: PARTNERS IN TEACHING AND LEARNING

Henry E. Hankerson

This essay represents two decades of personal, on-hands experiences in teacher education and research studies. The data obtained through these efforts supported the idea that parents, teachers and teacher aides can work together to improve the lives of educationally and socially disadvantaged Black children. This coupling of significant others I have previously called the "partners" concept (Hankerson, 1972). In this essay I will expand upon the partners concept.

The theoretical frame for this study is based on the action theorists' postulations. Action theorists contend that a child's motivation and achievement performances are influenced by his/her primary interactions with parents and significant others (Mead, 1934; Brookover, 1959; Smith, 1968; Smith and Brache, 1963). Smith (1968) defined significant others as persons (such as teachers, teacher aides, and community members) other than natural parents who are important to an individual. If parents serve as teacher aides, both motivating factors are met.

Black parents participating as teacher aides in their community schools is an educational strategy that provided a promising approach to the enhancement of community development and the improvement of academic achievement. Research studies on teacher aides and parent involvement in early childhood and elementary education programs showed that with Black parents and teachers operating as partners, children made significant cognitive gains. Both personal experiences and similar research studies showed that these children continued to sustain improved academic achievement as they continued in school (Hankerson, 1972, 1980; Hogan, 1978).

The year 1986 finds us, like the 1970's, with a scarcity of dollars for hiring teachers on the one hand and the increased specialization of teaching on the other. Therefore, a cadre of non-professional assistants, as in the case of these Black parents, should be employed to aid the teacher. Other factors that have produced a need for additional help to teachers in urban schools at a reduced cost for services are: (1) larger class sizes, (2) lengthening of teacher preparation periods, (3) development of technical support devices and computers, and (4) today's teachers' greater challenge to educate--since the many needs, misconceptions, and misunderstandings that confront the Black child are brought into the classroom. With parents as teacher aides, -- participating in the learning process, taking care of the nonteaching duties to which teachers normally attend -- the teacher can devote more time to actual instruction. Simultaneously, pupils are not neglected to any great degree in areas related to human growth and development.

Gratifyingly, a viable carryover from school to home via parents as partners in this teaching-learning process was that of parents' seeing and understanding the impact of mutual support of the children's school experiences through home and school cooperation. Smith and Brache's study (1963) showed that parents and significant others were vital to education growth, not as the primary teacher, but as the prime figure in the children's development as persons. Some of the tasks performed by parents and significant others that resulted in educational growth included (1) providing quiet study areas for the children at home; (2) monitoring study time; (3) regulating bedtime; (4) making sure the children ate breakfast before going to school; (5) reading to the children daily; (6) listening to the children read -- either words or pictures; (7) asking the children questions; (8) praising their achievement; and (9) making sure that the children had pencils, paper, notebooks, and dictionaries. Thus, it is hypothesized that the participation of parents as teacher aides in urban schools will provide a "ripple" effect that enables teachers to provide more services to a greater number of pupils, give parents an opportunity to increase their levels of knowledge, attitudes, and skills in the home-school-community relationship; provide an economic alternative to the increasing cost of education; and bring about a positive investment in community improvement through establishment of new careers.

Prominent professionals in the social sciences have described the paraprofessional approach as an innovation in career development. The projected increases in services by professionals have generated a great need for support from the helping professions, especially in the areas of education, health, recreation, and business (London, 1970; Gartner, 1971; Gartner & Riessman, 1974). Since the service professions require many hundreds of thousands of additional personnel, the potential for new kinds of careers is tremendous. Also, since more than 20 percent of the people in the United States can be classified as socially and educationally disadvantaged, and the number is increasing in 1986, a serious moral, economic, health, and educational problem exists. Recognition has been given to these problems, and several efforts have been launched to ameliorate the conditions which are at the base of problems. Obviously, the first step toward a solution is to provide employment in order to help the disadvantaged raise their standards of living. This has not been a reality in the 1980's. Teaching, training, learning, socialization, and political influences must be utilized to deal positively with the process of urbanization, technological revolution, population mobility, and other ills that have contributed significantly to the creation and maintenance of the disadvantaged conditions that characterize Blacks and others in urban environments (Totten, 1970; Sumption and Engstrom, 1966; Gartner and Riessman, 1974). Expansion and provision in paraprofessional careers will provide economic and social opportunities that can also be related to community development needs (Aker, Kidd, and Smith, 1970; Hankerson, 1980; 1984).

As a career category, teacher aide is one of the types of paraprofessionals that have been established during the past two and a half decades. While college is a prerequisite for most careers in human service fields, new careers like teacher aides emerged which allowed persons with limited but specialized education to work under the supervision of professionals. The establishment of paraprofessional corps comprised a strategy that incorporated adult education as a key element in launching this career category as a major segment in the job force (Gartner, 1971). Black parents working in schools in their communities as teacher aides represent an important concept for initiating cooperative working relations and collaboration of intellectual pursuits in social, economic, and educational interventions. Shank and McElroy (1970) predicted that this trend would continue as the pressure of new knowledge and an ever-increasing pupil enrollment would force schools to seek maximum service from fully prepared and certified teachers. This development has occurred parallel to the growth of educational technology aimed at improving public education by increasing teacher efficiency, as well as by involving parents as partners in the education of their children. At present the career endeavor of teacher aides is more visible in urban schools that serve a high number of underachieving pupils who are associated with compensatory education. However, the size of these programs has diminished due mainly to a reduction of federal, state, and local funds, increased academic improvements of children in some programs, and because of a lack of program appraisal in view of strategies that work. Education systems are faced with the growing demands of the taxpayer for increased productivity and assurance that the quality of education will improve. With the present crisis in millage passages, the cutbacks in congressional appropriations for education, and the great need for both qualitative and quantitative returns for tax dollars in terms of student achievement, pressure has been placed upon the schools and their instructional programs to obtain greater services from classroom teachers, who are the greatest single investment in public education (Benson, 1961). The increased clusters of disadvantaged children in urban areas, and inadequate school aid, presently, challenge urban schools to provide the most economically feasible alternatives in staffing for the instructional program ("Teacher Aides in Public Schools," 1970). In reviewing the status of Blacks in America today (1986), this same dilemma is present. A viable alternative is the "parents as partners" concept. It is therefore suggested that a revisitation of such can be beneficial to the educational system in fulfilling its mission and obligation to Blacks.

A further look at the continuation of parents as teacher aides and teacher aides as paraprofessionals (in reference to new careers and economic implications) shows other provisions germane to the positive effects of implementing this concept, e.g.: (1) alleviating the strain created by taking children out of the inner city for a few hours each day and teaching them how to adapt to a middle-class learning pattern entirely different from the skills they need to survive in the matrix of their urban home environment (Usdan and Bertolaet, 1966); (2) helping to provide a middle-class person with the insights required to identify with and be less judgmental about the various worlds perceived by educationally disadvantaged adults and their children (Frost and Hawkes, 1966); (3) incorporating additional human services occupations in the field of education like those provided in other professions (Aker et al., 1970); and (4) emphasizing the division-of-labor factor in group efforts toward lowering pupil/adult ratios at a minimal cost to the schools. These provisions are linked to the proper utilization of supplementals (human and mechanical), since teacher aides are sure ways of utilization, unlike machines that can easily serve as

129

dust catchers. Also, educationally disadvantaged children perform better in their cognitive arenas -- as implied by the action theorists' postulations -- with "parental and significant other" influences, not machinery. This signifies the need to restudy and survey the budgetary costs and the possibility of over-utilization of hardware and computers in urban schools. Parents as teacher aides, coupled with the teacher, bring about the possibility of greater productivity in team teaching concepts with a low cost to the operational budget (Kerber and Bommarito, 1965; Hankerson, 1972). Since teacher aides have emerged as a job classification, and many are already employed, a need exists to provide clearly defined tasks in terms of hours, skills, human interaction patterns, and desired productive endeavors (a clearly defined role of the paraprofessional corps) (Shank and McElroy, 1970). These conceptualizations set the base for studying the implications of analyzing paraprofessional intervention in urban school communities that have large numbers of educationally disadvantaged Black children and disenchanted Black parents. A most recent research update and account of this conceptualization was published in THE URBAN RE-VIEW (Hankerson, 1983) and serves as the basis for this analysis.

Purpose of Study

The study focused on two aspects of the significance of parents as teacher aides as related to (1) the problem of satisfying the educational requirements in communities having large numbers of educationally and socially disadvantaged underachieving children, and (2) the approach of new career innovations to improve the community through the incorporation of paraprofessional corps (Hankerson, 1972). The theoretical implications of the action theorists (Mead, Smith, Brookover, et al.) were prevalent, as the teacher aides in the study were Black parents for the most part, from urban school communities.

Research questions specifying the expectations and behaviors for the several roles interacting in the classroom, and in certain community school context, were formulated, and statistical evidence (.05 significance level) was provided upon analyzing the problem in terms of these hypotheses: (1) There would be greater academic gains in reading and mathematics, but the gains would be more significant in mathematics for children in classrooms with both a teacher and a teacher aide than for children in classrooms with just a teacher; (2) There would be more time spent in individual and small-group instruction by teachers who had teacher aides than by teachers who did not have teacher aides; (3) There would be a high degree of correlation among three groups of participants (teachers, teacher aides, and administrators) on the postulation that the establishment of paraprofessional corps in urban schools would result in a valuable educational strategy for improving academic attainment and for improving the community.

METHOD OF THE STUDY

The study was conducted in a large midwestern urban community (Flint, Michigan) with a large population of socially and educationally disadvantaged children in the public schools.

It was conducted in two phases. **Phase 1** examined pupils' academic achievement in reading and in mathematics and utilization of the instructional time of classroom teacher with and without teacher aides. This phase was conducted through pre- and post-test results and classroom observations. **Phase 2** investigated the roles and utilization of paraprofessionals in personal, social, school, and community involvements. This phase was conducted through a written survey and an interview-type evaluation.

Subjects

One hundred twenty-five pupils (third- and fourth-graders) in 15 self-contained classrooms constituted the subjects for the first phase of the study. These pupils were selected from Title I and Section III schools that provided federal and state compensatory programs. All the subjects had scored below the 15th percentile in reading and mathematics, and were predominantly Black children.

With reference to type of instructional staff, the 15 classrooms to which these pupils were normally assigned were as follows: 10 had full-time teachers plus full-time teacher aides (5 were model teacher aides with training, and 5 were average teacher aides with no training; all 10 were residents of the school community and had children attending the schools where they worked); 5 classrooms had a full-time teacher and no teacher aides. Thus, three groups were formulated for study: Group Z consisted of students (N=55) in classrooms with no teacher aides, and Groups X and Y were the experimental groups.

The subjects in Phase 2 of the study, which employed the completion of a survey instrument and some personal interviews, were as follows: 21 teachers in grades K-6 (inclusive of the 15 teachers used in Phase 1), 138 teacher aides (including the 10 aides used in Phase 1), and 20 elementary school principals from schools in the inner-city area of the Flint Community School District. All subjects responded to the questionnaires (100%).

Instruments

Pupil attainment was measured by the Science Research Associates (SRA Achievement Test) in reading and mathematics. The pretests were given in September, and the posttests were given in May. The results of the tests were classified in terms of mean differences of pupils in classrooms with full-time teacher aides as compared with those of pupils in classrooms without teacher aides.

Two instruments were used to collect data to substantiate the hypotheses of the study. In order to examine the utilization of instructional time of the classroom teachers with and without full-time teacher aides, Instrument 1 (an observation instrument) was used (adapted from Miller (1970) and Hagstrom (1962)). This instrument (used in Phase 1 of the study) was characterized by the following: (1) The trained observer wrote down briefly the activities (instructional, routine, and/or clerical) as performed by the teacher and the teacher aide; (2) the time used for each activity was recorded by using a stopwatch taped to a clipboard; (3) in order that a record could be kept of the teacher's and the teacher aide's behaviors with an individual child, a small group of children (less than seven), or a whole group of children, the observer checked alongside the written activity the column headed "I" (individual), "S" (small group) or "W" (whole group). The second instrument developed was a questionnaire survey called a Paraprofessional Rating Scale. It was used in Phase 2 of the study to gather information on paraprofessional intervention in view of what happens in classrooms with and without full-time teacher aides, and to help evaluate these findings with respect to pupil needs and the role of the school and community in providing ways of meeting them. There were seven parts to this instrument. Six of the parts were quintuple and multiple-choice. One part required "yes" or "no" answers and was open-ended in order to provide for collecting information that forced answers might not provide. This instrument represented adaptations of work done by Nelson and McDonald (1954) and the Paraprofessional Training Project of the Wayne County Intermediate School District (1969).

ANALYSIS OF DATA

Phase 1 of the study sought to find two things. First, the study sought to find out if, following pre- and posttests, students in classrooms with full-time teacher aides would show significantly greater gains in reading and mathematics scores than students in classrooms with no teacher aides. Analysis of variance, using a one-way covariance model, was conducted with this phase of Phase 1.

A second concern of Phase 1 was the utilization of instructional time by teachers with and without full-time teacher aides. It was hypothesized that teachers with full-time teacher aides would devote less time to noninstructional activities than would teachers without teacher aides. Analysis of variance for individual, small-group, and whole-group instruction was done for the three groups -- X, Y, and Z. The differences in time spent in each type of instruction by each group were determined to show the attained significance.

Phase 2 of the study, which dealt with the roles and utilization of paraprofessionals in personal, social, and community involvements, dealt with several hypotheses: (1) that paraprofessional corps are valuable components of the community and schools in regard to both academic achievement of pupils and community improvement; (2) that teacher aides from the school-community intervention would serve to alter the participants' socioeconomic aspirations and conditions through new career innovations, more educational training, and as more conscientious advocates of education for their children; and (3) that teacher aides improve their personal involvement in school and community endeavors, improve their self-concepts, and serve as catalysts for bridging the gaps between the home, school, and community. The questionnaire survey was complemented by data from classroom teachers, the teacher aides themselves, and the administrators regarding the roles, expectations, aspirations, and conceptualizations of the establishment and utilization of paraprofessionals in urban schools and communities. A comparative analysis of the groups (teacher, teacher aides (who for the most part were Black parents), and administrators) was done in reference to factors that were extremely important, very important, important, could be important, and not important.

RESULTS OF THE STUDY

The results of the academic attainment in reading and mathematics were significant (see Tables 1-7). Thus, hypothesis 1 was not rejected. More significant difference was shown in the mathematics scores than in the reading scores.

Table 1 summarized the analysis of variance for the mathematics difference. A summary of mean differences for the three groups in mathematics is presented in Table 2. Table 3 summarizes an analysis of variance for the reading difference, while a summary of mean differences for the three groups in reading is presented in Table 4. Table 5 shows a comparison of the mathematics and reading intercepts.

133

TABLE 1.

Summary of Analysis of Variance for Mathematics Differences Among Groups

Source	DF	Sum of Squares	Mean Square	F	Statistical Significance
Zero slope	1	384.62	384.621	12.548	.0006
Error	121	3708.8	30.651	- - -	- -

TABLE 2.

Results of Mean Differences of Groups in Mathematics[a]

Stratum	(1) = X	(2) = Y	(3) = Z
Mean	12.618	5.6111	5.8000
Adjusted mean	13.156	5.4772	5.5545
Sample size	34	36	55

[a]Group X had a mean score higher than those of Groups Y and Z. Groups Y and Z were almost the same, having no significant difference in means.

TABLE 3.

Summary of Analysis of Variance for Reading Differences Among Groups

Source	DF	Sum of Squares	Mean Square	F	Statistical Significance
Zero slope	1	492.83	492.82	12.731	.0005
Error	122	4684.1	38.711	- - -	- -

TABLE 4.

Results of Mean Differences of Groups in Reading[a]

Stratum	(1) = X	(2) = Y	(3) = Z
Mean	.3824	5.2500	4.8727
Adjusted mean	8.0747	4.1172	5.1862
Sample size	34	36	55

[a]Group X had a mean score higher than those of Groups Y and Z. Group Z's mean was slightly higher than Group Y's.

TABLE 5.

A Comparison of the Mathematics and Reading Intercepts Among Groups

Stratum		(1) = X	(2) = Y	(3) = Z
Intercept	(math)	17.254	9.5745	9.6518
Intercept	(reading)	13.847	9.8898	10.959

TABLE 6.

Summary of Analysis of Variance for Individual Instruction Time[a]

Source	Sum of Squares	DF	Mean Square
Between strata	43800	92	21900.
Within strata	38444	12	3202.7
Total	92244	14	- - -

[a]The F statistic is 5.8360 with attained significance (.0104).

TABLE 7.

Summary of Analysis of Variance for Small-Group Instruction Time[a]

Source	Sum of Squares	DF	Mean Square
Between strata	0.10610 D 07	2	0.53033 D 06
Within strata	0.15776 D 06	12	13146
Total	0.12188 D 07	14	

[a]The F statistic is 40.353 with attained significance (0.000004).

134

The second part of Phase 1 of the study was interpreted through the results of an analysis of variance for individual and small group instructional time spent by teachers with and without full-time teacher aides. Table 6 shows an analysis of variance for individual instruction time, while Table 7 presents an analysis of variance for small-group instruction time. The results of mean differences in time spent in individual instruction show Bartlett's chi square is .80257 with 2 df and attained significance (.6695); mean differences in time spent in small-group instruction resulted in Bartlett's chi square (1.7619) with 2 df and attained significance (.4144). These results indicated that the teachers in Group X (with experienced and well-trained teacher aides) spent significantly more time in individual and small-group instruction than the teachers in Group Z (without teacher aides). Teachers in Groups X and Y were relieved of certain noninstructional activities such as collecting monies, fixing bulletin boards, escorting children to toilets, duplicating materials, checking papers, assisting pupils in personal matters, gathering and preparing curricula materials, reinforcing lessons and providing tutorial services, and several other routine and clerical activities. Because teachers in Group Z had to perform the aforementioned activities themselves, they spent less time in instructional activities directly related to teaching subject matter. The data as presented strongly support the hypothesis.

The results of the questionnaire survey administered to teachers, teacher aides and administrators who participated in the second phase of the study were congruent with the hypotheses. There was a high degree of positive agreement among the participants regarding the establishment of paraprofessional corps to take action in the educational system as a valuable program component of school and community development. Factors considered "extremely important" to a successful teacher aide program by teachers, teacher aides, and administrators were: (1) one aide is needed for one teacher; (2) aides are needed in schools; (3) roles of aides need to be clearly delineated; (4) aides should live in the school community; (5) aides should be supervised by the teacher; (6) aides should assist with group instruction; (7) aides should alert teachers to special pupil needs; (8) aides should encourage and praise pupils; (9) aides should serve as home-school liaisons; (10) aides should demand respect from pupils; and (11) aides should reinforce lessons.

The role of the teacher aides as depicted by the teachers and the teacher aides, but not by the administrators, as "extremely important" were: (1) aides should interact in pupil-oriented activities because these are more important than task-oriented ones; (2) aides should escort the children to the toilet, bus, and playground; and (3) aides should perform monitorial and clerical duties. The role of the teacher aides rated as "could be important" as depicted by the teachers and the administrators, but not the teacher aides themselves, included the following: (1) aides should fix and prepare bulletin boards; (2) aides should check papers; and (3) aides should record grades. The teachers rated "aides should participate in lesson planning" as "very important." The administrators rated as "very important" the idea that pupil-oriented activities are more important than task-oriented ones," and they rated as "could be important" the following: (1) aides should escort children to the toilet, bus, and playground; (2) aides should perform monitorial and clerical duties; and (3) aides should prepare and fix bulletin boards. The three groups rated the following as "not important" in delineating the roles of teacher aides: (1) aides should arrange the classroom; and (2) aides should be certified.

Information was gathered on the idea of whether teacher aides (already working) have been motivated to alter their socioeconomic aspirations and to continue their education either at the high school or at the college level. Of the 121 respondents, 65 (54%) identified with the job as teacher aides and were interested in remaining at that career level; 28, or 23 percent saw the job as teacher aide as a step toward becoming a teacher; 18, or 15 percent were interested in self-improvement in order to become better teacher aides; 7, or 6 percent, were chiefly interested in self-help, and 3, or 2 percent, had no definite plans for continuing their education.

The teacher aides were asked to comment on how they felt their jobs might have influenced their behavior. The following is a summary of their responses. The teacher aides felt that they (1) had received more knowledge, (2) had taken more initiative, (3) were less confused about their roles, (4) tended to read more material, (5) used better grammar, (6) were more sensitive to the feelings of others, (7) respected the opinions of others more readily, (8) had increased their ability to understand pupils' behaviors, (9) had improved academically and socially as exemplified by their being better able to help the teachers in instructionally related activities by exploring and transmitting more and better ideas and being more patient, confident, and happy in the school environment, and (10) were better able to communicate with the total community.

CONCLUSIONS, RECOMMENDATIONS, AND IMPLICATIONS

Phase 1 of the study generated information and ideas germane to controversy in research conducted with disadvantaged subjects. Since little significance was shown as the result of the standardized tests in reading and mathematics, researchers might agree that the tests of significance for subjects typical of the ones used in this study present a criterion that is much too strict (Peters and Van Voorhis, 1940). Stephens (1967) contended that "it is true that tests of wider aspects of growth may show the results pedagogical innovations even when no difference appears in the narrower field of scholastic growth." Therefore, this study utilized a variety of instruments (standardized tests, surveys, questionnaires), procedures (interviews, observations), and innovations (parents as teacher aides) to show more sensitive analyses toward a comprehensive assessment of the marked differences yielded by this humanistic approach to academic achievement and community improvement.

The observational procedure of the second part of Phase 1 utilized the technique of interactional analysis. Nevertheless, the results were not collected, compiled, or interpreted in the true sense of Flander's (1961) analysis. However, the results in amount of time spent in individual and small-group instruction are indicative of teacher-pupil interactions in the classroom with the teacher aide as an added dimension in the process. Whereas the approach provided an objective account of instructional and noninstructional activities, many subjective, crucial requirements of teaching and learning were operating. Teacher attitudes and expectations for the disadvantaged (Rosenthal and Jacobson, 1968) were being tested, adapted, and revised; and socialization, motivation, and industry were being reconsidered and/or revised (White, 1958) by the parents who served as teacher aides. Both teachers and teacher aides (parents) represented the implementation of the action theorists' postulation that "children will become more academically minded, more social and more positive attitudinally toward self-improvement when they observe parents and significant others actively involved in the business of education -- at home, at school, and in the community" (Smith's speech to class-room teachers in Flint, Michigan, 1972). This sets the premise that "Black parents as partners" is the basis for improving the educational, social, personal, and emotional climate for Black children and their parents in our American society.

Increased academic and social successes as seen through direct observation and participation and research have led administrators, teachers, parents, and pupils to gain faith in the paraprofessional corps as one of the few remaining successful strategies for enhancing achievement in urban schools. However, with the greatest majority

137

of financial aid to support this effort coming from compensatory subsidiaries, there is much uncertainty from year to year about the possibility of using this cadre of assistants. Therefore, school districts must weight the significance of this educational strategy in view of (1) research, (2) prior experiences, (3) responsibilities for educating its pupils and parents, and (4) establishing this concept as a standard part of their labor force.

These promising approaches and reorganizational recommendations are typical of roles and responsibilities that can be affected by well-trained paraprofessionals. Urban programmers should, therefore, reexamine their priorities and consider these approaches and others in view of the team teaching concept in an effort to yield high productivity in educational achievement at an inexpensive rate to the budget. By the same token, the investigator in the empirical study (Hankerson, 1972) discovered and heard through personal interviews and working relationships with other educators, children, and lay citizenry, that the use of parents as teacher aides was a most valuable strategy in helping to solve the community's problem of cultural assimilation on a large scale in view of their assistance in helping children to adjust to a middle-class school orientation. Too, an informal survey concerning paraprofessionals that was conducted recently (Hankerson, 1980, 1984) revealed that parents as teacher aides (1) assist in easing the children's degree of emotional disruptions and frustrations in school, (2) aid the children in developing good feelings about themselves and others, (3) attempt to strengthen pupil-teacher relationships, and (4) arouse the children's appreciation of various cultural traits and differences. These paraprofessionals became functional participants in the dynamics of human organization, which helped them in acquiring new social values and enhancing their own positive self-images.

The status of Blacks in America in the 1980's is similar to the conditions of the 1970's. Moreover, it is not far-fetched to even say that the 1980's find Blacks in the educational arena in worse shape than in the 1970's for the aforementioned reasons, as well as a reshaping of the federal support to education. Historically, it is known that states have not fulfilled their responsibilities to educating all on the same basis. Being Black for many years and experiencing the inequalities in education have suggested to me that a "revisitation" of the "parents as partners" concept is a viable one for the 1980's. Blacks must play a vital role in the education of our children and the improvement of self and our communities. Tried and proven strategies are what Blacks need to implement and support. Such dynamic changes indicate that public school systems should incorporate "parents as partners" (teacher aides) as a regular and integral part of the school's organization, such as other already functioning career-type components (janitors, secretaries, community counselors, etc.) (Shank and McElroy, 1970). This career-type institutionalization will help to improve the status of Blacks in America. Such a commitment of "home-school partnership" can be long-lasting and beneficial to both the Black child and his parents, as well as to the educational system. In a nut shell, the words of Reverend Jesse Jackson, "A school system without parents at its foundation is just like a bucket with a hole in it," (Nedler and McAfee, 1979) are very appropriate to the message conveyed in this chapter.

REFERENCES

Aker, G., Kidd, J.R., and Smith, R. (Eds.)
HANDBOOK OF ADULT EDUCATION. New York: Macmillan, 1970.

Amidon, E., and Hough, J.R.
INTERACTION ANALYSIS: THEORY, RESEARCH AND APPLICA-
TION. Reading, Mass.: Addison-Wesley, 1967.

Benson, C.S.
THE ECONOMICS OF PUBLIC EDUCATION. Boston: Houghton
Mifflin, 1961.

Brookover, W.B.
"Some social psychological conceptions of classroom learning."
SCHOOL AND SOCIETY, 1959, 84.

Flanders, N. A.
"Interaction analysis: A technique for quantifying teacher influence." Paper read at the annual meeting of The American Educational Research Association, Illinois, 1961.

Frost, J., and Hawkes, G.
THE DISADVANTAGED CHILD: ISSUES AND INNOVATIONS.
Boston: Houghton Mifflin, 1966.

Gartner, A.
PARA-PROFESSIONALS AND THEIR PERFORMANCE. A SURVEY
OF EDUCATION AND SOCIAL SERVICE PROGRAMS. New York:
Praeger, 1971.

Gartner, A., and Riessman, F.
THE SERVICE SOCIETY AND THE CONSUMER VANGUARD.
New York: Harper and Row, 1974.

Hagstrom, E.A.
"The Teacher's Day." THE ELEMENTARY SCHOOL JOURNAL,
1962, 62, 422-431.

Hankerson, H.E.
"A Study On An Educational Strategy For Community Development: The Role of Para-professional Corps for Socially Disadvantaged Children" (Doctoral dissertation, University of Michigan, Ann Arbor, 1972.

Hankerson, H.E.
"How Do You Feel About Teacher Aides" (Published survey, Howard University, Washington, D.C., 1980, 1984).

Hankerson, H.E.
"Utilizing Parents for Para-professional Intervention," THE URBAN REVIEW, 1983, Volume 15, Number 2, 75-88.

Hogan, J.
"Getting Parents involved in their children's education." (NEWS, NOTES, AND QUOTES -- Newsletter of Phi Delta Kappan), 1978, 22 (6).

Kerber, A. and Bommarito, B.
THE SCHOOLS AND THE URBAN CRISIS. New York: Holt, Rinehart, Winston, 1965.

London, J.
in Aker, C., Kidd, J.R., and Smith, R., HANDBOOK OF ADULT EDUCATION. New York: MacMillan, 1970, pp. 17-18.

Mead, G.H.
MIND, SELF AND SOCIETY. Chicago: University of Chicago Press, 1934.

Miller, J.
"A Comparison of How First Grade Classroom Teachers with and without Full-Time Aides Utilize Instructional Time and the Effects of Aide Utilization Upon Academic Performance of Children (Doctoral dissertation, University of Maryland, College Park, 1970).

NEA Research Bulletin, March, 1970.

Nedler, Shari E. and Oralie E. McAfee.
WORKING WITH PARENTS (Guidelines for Early Childhood and Elementary Teachers). Belmont, California: Wadsworth Publishing Company, 1979.

Nelson, L., and McDonald, B.
GUIDE TO STUDENT TEACHING. Dubuque, Iowa: Wm. C. Brown Company, 1954.

News Notes, PHI DELTA KAPPAN, June, 1978.

Paraprofessional training project, Wayne County Intermediate School district, 1500 Guardian Building, Detroit, Michigan, 1969.

Peters, C., and Von Voorhis, R.
STATISTICAL PROCEDURES AND THEIR MATHEMATICAL BASES. Westport, Ct.: Greenwood Press, 1940. (Reprinted in 1972).

Rosenthal, R. and Jacobson, L.R.
"Teacher expectations for the disadvantaged." SCIENTIFIC AMERICAN, 1968, 218 (4).

Shank, P.C., and McElroy, W.R.
THE PARA-PROFESSIONALS OR TEACHER AIDES: SELECTION, PREPARATION AND ASSIGNMENT. Midland, Mich.: Pendell, 1970.

Smith, M.B., and Brache, C.I.
"When School and Home Focus on Achievement." EDUCATIONAL LEADERSHIP, 1963, 20, (5).

Smith, M.B.
"Home and School: Focus on Achievement." In A. H. Passow, (Ed.), DEVELOPING PROGRAMS FOR THE EDUCATIONALLY DISADVANTAGED, New York: Teachers College Press, 1968.

Stephens, J.M.
THE PROCESS OF SCHOOLING: A PSYCHOLOGICAL EXAMINATION. New York: Holt, Rinehart, Winston, 1967.

Sumption, M., and Engstrom, Y.
SCHOOL-COMMUNITY RELATIONS: A NEW APPROACH. New York: McGraw-Hill, 1966.

Teacher Aides in the Public Schools. NEA RESEARCH BULLETIN, October 1970.

Totten, F.
THE POWER OF COMMUNITY EDUCATION. Midland, Mich.: Pendell, 1970.

Usdan, M., and Bertolaet, F.
TEACHERS FOR THE DISADVANTAGED. Chicago: Follett, 1966.

White, R.
"Motivation Reconsidered: The Concept of Competence." In S. Cohen, and D. J. Delaney (Eds.), READINGS IN PERSONALITY AND SOCIAL DEVELOPMENT. New York: Selected Academic Readings, 1968.

As I look about me today in this veiled world of mine, despite the noisier and more spectacular advance of my brothers, I instinctively feel and know that it is the five million women of my race who really count.

W. E. B. DuBois
DARKWATER, 1920

CHAPTER TEN

BLACK WOMEN: STANDING TALL IN EDUCATION

Lorene Barnes Holmes

Black women educators have made and are continuing to make significant contributions to American society. One paper in an anthology is inadequate to highlight the noble deeds, sacrifices, and contributions of these women. Women cited in this paper are but a few of the growing number of professionals who have made their marks in the field of education during the last decade.

According to Naisbitt (1982:249), "We are living in the 'time of parenthesis,' the time between eras. It is as though we have bracketed off the present from both the past and the future, for we are neither here nor there." Naisbitt's words accurately describe the present status of Black women. Even if women were to achieve equality with men tomorrow, Black women would continue to carry the entire array of oppression and handicaps associated with race. Racial oppression of Black people in America did what neither class oppression nor sexual oppression, with all of their perniciousness, have ever done: destroy an entire people and their culture (BLACK WOMAN'S VOICE, 1980:7). Yet, Black women have made significant contributions to American culture. According to Davis (1981:315):

The Black women born into the twentieth century America have continued the tradition of their pioneering predecessors. They are teachers, builders, and molders of character in the tradition of Lucy Craft Laney, Janie Porter Barrett, and Mary McLeod Bethune. They are community developers in the tradition of Cornelia Bowen and Christine Benton Cash. They are activists in the tradition of Ida Wells Barnett and scholars in the tradition of Josephine A. Silone Yates. They continue to break down the barriers of race and sex, and set examples worthy of emulation by women of all races.

143

The former United States Representative, Barbara Jordan summarizes the aspirations of Black women:

> . . .the women of this world . . . must exercise a leadership quality, dedication, a concern and commitment which is not going to be shattered by inanities and ignorance and idiots, who would view our cause as one which somehow is violative of the American dream of equal rights for everybody. All we are trying to do is to make this government of the United States of America honest. We only want, we only ask, that when we stand up and talk about one nation under God, liberty, justice for everybody; we only want to look at the flag, put our right hand over our hearts, repeat those words, and know that they are true (Radin, 1976:11).

Black Women In Education In The Federal Government

Traditionally, the federal government has been less hostile to the aspirations of Blacks than have state, county and city governments. Civil Rights laws, those with "teeth," are initiated at the federal level and the federal government has afforded Blacks their highest positions of authority. It is not surprising that many Black women have made their marks at the federal level, especially in education departments.

The Developing Institutions Programs of Title III of the Higher Education Act of 1965 was established to aid Black colleges by Willa Beatrice Player, a Black administrator. Perhaps her most notable accomplishment was to divide the Developing Institutions Program into the Advanced Institutional Program (AIDP) and the Basic Institutional Development Program (BISD). Other Black women who distinguished themselves at the federal level were: Anita F. Allen, former President of the School Board of the District of Columbia, who later became chief of the Advanced Development Branch; Audrey Dickerson who headed the Basic Institutional Development Program; and, Mary Frances Berry, a powerful orator, who served as Assistant Secretary for Education, Department of Health, Education and Welfare from 1977-1979. Another pioneer was Deborah Partridge Wolfe who served as Education Chief with the Committee on Education and Labor of the United States House of Representatives. Thirty-five public laws affecting education and labor were passed during her tenure (Davis, 1981: 318-319).

The first Black woman to serve in two federal cabinet posts was

Patricia Roberts Harris. After resigning as Secretary of Housing and Urban Development, Harris became the Secretary of Health, Education and Welfare (HEW). When the American people, primarily Whites, became disenchanted with President Carter's performance few could find fault with Harris' stewardship.

Black Women In Education In State Government

State governments, especially those in southern and border states, have often initiated and/or encouraged discriminatory practices against Blacks and other racial minorities. During the height of the Civil Rights struggle it was not uncommon for governors and other state officials to oppose social equality for Blacks; candidates from both major political parties, and a host of minor political organizations, campaigned on the platform of keeping "nigras" in their places. Given these occurrences, it is amazing that Black women educators, in less than two decades, hold positions of authority in every state.

A representative sample of Black women educators who held state-wide positions would include Ruth E. Dixon, who served as Supervisor of the New Jersey State Department of Education for two years, and Ruth Mitchell Laws, State Supervisor of Research and Planning in Vocational Education and State Director of Adult and Continuing Education in the Delaware State Department of Public Instruction. Both women served with distinction.

Black women have also made tremendous strides in states which were once bastions of racial hatred. For example, Marianna Davis was the first Black and first woman appointed to the South Carolina Commission on Higher Education (Davis, 1981:316). Another Black woman of note is Willie Lee Campbell Glass of Tyler, Texas, who served as consultant for Vocational Homemaking Education for the state of Texas for approximately twenty-four years. The Willie Lee Glass Homemaking Building at Texas College in Tyler, Texas, is named in her honor (Holmes, 1984).

Black Women Superintendents

The local education-related position invested with the most authority is the superintendent. These "politicians" enjoy influence far beyond the schoolyard -- as community leaders, they influence public policy and help shape community folkways and mores. Traditionally, superintendents (and other gatekeepers) have been White males, but this situation is slowly changing.

145

In 1973, for example, Blacks headed only 43 of the nation's then 17,500 public school districts and, according to the American Association of School Administrators in Arlington, Virginia, not one among the group was a woman. Five years later, the number of Black women superintendents had risen to five, a mere drop in the bucket. Today, there are 15 Black women superintendents, still a minuscule number. Even so, Black women manage some of the largest public school systems in the country (EBONY, 1983:88).

The superintendent of the nation's third largest school system, Ruth Love, is a Black woman. Prior to her appointment as superintendent of the Chicago Public School System in 1981, Love served as superintendent of the Oakland (California) Unified School District. She is an articulate and dynamic leader in a city often torn by racial strife. In 1982 Constance Clayton was appointed superintendent of the huge Philadelphia Public School System. Among her achievements was the installment of standardized curricula at each grade level, and she balanced the system's budget -- it had not been balanced in 18 years. As testimony to her achievements, the Philadelphia School Board recently extended her contract for another five years (EBONY, 1983:88-89; Bullock, 1985:46). Black women are also superintendents in Lowndes County (Alabama), Wellston (Missouri), Linwood (California), Nyack (New York), Ewing (New Jersey), and Plainsfield (New Jersey).

Black Women Presidents of Colleges and National Associations

Although Black women have served in various capacities in historically Black institutions of higher education, their roles have been limited -- professors, chairpersons, and deans. Except in very rare instances, Black women have been clustered in positions below the level of president. Over approximately 145 years of existence, there have been only several exceptions -- Mary McLeod Bethune, founder of Bethune-Cookman College; Willa Player, President of Bennett College; and Mable McLean, president of Barber Scotia College (Nyangoni, 1981:3). Of the 42 new presidents of Black colleges since 1980, only one, Yvonne Walker-Taylor, who took office in 1984 as the first woman president of Wilberforce is a Black woman (EBONY, 1984:73).

Black women presidential aspirants have fared even worse at historically White universities. Two notable exceptions are Jewell Plummer Cobb and Mary Francis Berry. In 1981 Cobb became President of California State University at Fullerton. She became the first Black woman to head a major public university on the West Coast (EBONY, 1982:97). Berry, a prominent Civil Rights spokesperson, served as Chancellor of the University of Colorado in the 1970s.

Because of their large numbers in the teaching profession, secondary and primary schools, many Black women have held high-ranking positions in national education associations (JET, 1984:22). For example, Mary Harwood Futrell is head of the 1.7 million member National Education Association. A staunch supporter of her fellow teachers, Futrell has initiated reforms to improve the work-environment of teachers -- higher salaries, better benefits, and more autonomy.

According to Davis (1981:319-321), a number of other Black women have held positions of leadership in national educational and education-related associations. These include Evangeline Jones Ward, who served as President of the National Association for Education of the Young Child from 1970 - 1974; and, Clara Stanton Jones, who in 1976 became the first Black President of the American Library Association. During the same year, Marianna W. Davis was elected the first Black President of the Conference on College Composition and Communication. Women who served or are serving in similar capacities are Anna Daniels Reuben, President of the Southern Conference of Deans, Faculties and Academic Vice Presidents; Nellie Quamder served as President of the National Association of Elementary School Principals; and, Dorothy S. Strickland who served as President of the International Reading Association (Davis, 1981:319-321).

Conclusion

In modern America, Black women are confronted by three obstacles: race, gender and poverty. Despite these problems, Black women continue to contribute to American culture, this is especially true of Black women educators. Over the past few years, there has been an increased interest in and awareness of the Black woman in education and other areas of life. Since the feminist movement in the 1960s, resources relative to the study of Black women have become more available. Scholars, more than ever before, are researching (through oral history and holdings in various libraries and archives) the history and status of Black women. For example, more subject entries relating to Black women are being added to general card catalogs in libraries. In some libraries, special files devoted to Black women are being developed (Harley, 1978:vii). A number of research centers are being established to document the historical contributions of Black women.

Finally, Black women are receiving their "just due." John H. Johnson, publisher, sums up the plight and promise of Black women in this way:

> The Black woman of this generation . . . is not defined by calendars or clocks. She is creating -- in the home, factory and office -- a new image of woman. Life for her -- and for us -- "ain't been no crystal stair." But she, like her forebears, is still "a-climbin' and turning corners and goin' in the dark" (EBONY, 1983:33).

REFERENCES

BLACK WOMAN'S VOICE
1980   "The Black Family: An Appraisal." April:6-7.

Brignano, Russel C.
1974   BLACK AMERICANS IN AUTOBIOGRAPHY. North Carolina:
Duke University Press.

Bullock, Celeste
1985   "The Grapevine: Essence Women." ESSENCE 15:46.

Chanbers, Frederick
1978   BLACK HIGHER EDUCATION IN THE UNITED STATES.
Connecticut: Greenwood Press.

Davis, Marianna W., Ed.
1981   CONTRIBUTIONS OF BLACK WOMEN TO AMERICA,
Volume II. South Carolina: Kenday Press, Inc.

EBONY
1984   "A New Generation of Black College Presidents." Decem-
ber:73-77.

EBONY
1982   "A Shaper of Young Minds." August:97-100.

EBONY
1977   "Publisher's Statement." August:28.

EBONY
1982   "Publisher's Statement." August:33.

EBONY
1983   "Superwomen of Public Education." June:88-94.

EBONY
1982   "Women at the Top." August:146-148.

EBONY
1982   "Women to Watch." August:52-56.

Harley, Sharon and Rosalyn Terborg-Penn
    1978   THE   AFRO-AMERICAN   WOMAN: STRUGGLES   AND
            IMAGES. New York: Kennikat Publishers.

Holmes, Lorene Barnes
    1984   Information obtained from personal conversation with Willie
            Lee Glass and vita.

Gite, Lloyd
    1984   "Work Style: Another Country." ESSENCE 15:28-30.

JET
    1984   "Education." September 10:26.

Jet
    1984   "Education." September 17:22.

Ladner, Joyce A.
    1977   "The Black Woman Today." EBONY 32:33-42.

Lawson, Don, Editor-in-Chief
    1980   WORLD TOPICS YEARBOOK. Illinois: Tangley Oaks Educa-
            tional Center.

Naisbitt, John
    1982   MEGATRENDS: NEW   DIRECTIONS   TRANSFORMING
            OUR LIVES. New York: Warner Books.

Nyangoni, Betty
    1981   "Reflections on the Status of Black Women as College
            and University Presidents in Historically Black Institutions
            of Higher Education," BLACK WOMEN'S EDUCATIONAL
            POLICY   AND   RESEARCH   NETWORK   NEWSLETTER.
            September: 3,5.

Radin, Beryl and Hoyt H. Pervis, Editors
    1976   "The American Woman in a Changing World." Women in
            Public Life: Report of a Conference. Texas: The University
            of Texas at Austin.

CHAPTER ELEVEN

ON BEING GODS: A SOCIAL SCIENTIFIC CRITIQUE OF REV. IKE'S UNITED CHURCH AND SCIENCE OF LIVING INSTITUTE

David Pilgrim

The majority of black Christians are affiliated with the Baptist and Methodist denominations. The largest black segments of these denominations are as follows: the National Baptist Convention U.S.A. Inc., with 6.8 million members; the National Baptist Convention of America, with 3.5 million members; the Progressive National Baptist Convention, Inc., with 1.1 million members; and, the African Methodist Episcopal Church, the African Methodist Episcopal Zion Church, the Christian Methodist Episcopal Church, and the United Methodist Church which have a combined membership of approximately 6 million (Blackwell, 1985:28). These impressive numbers mask a significant trend, namely, the defection of blacks to "peripheral" religious groups like the Jehovah's Witnesses, Seventh Day Adventists, Pentecostals, and Positive Thinking cults.

This paper purports to analyze the history, theology, and social implications of Rev. Ike's United Church and Science of Living Institute, a positive thinking cult. The data used in this paper were obtained with document analysis of newspapers, magazines, and Rev. Ike's sermons.

History

Rev. Ike was born Frederick J. Eikerenkoetter II, on June 1, 1935, in Ridgeland, South Carolina. His father was a Pentecostal minister and the younger Eikerenkoetter received his "calling" at the age of

151

fourteen (Blau, 1972:75). In his own words: "But mine had always been a sort of natural ministry; even when I was a young child, the other kids came to me to solve their problems. So at a very early age, I sensed my calling, even before it actually came, you see, I have always had to devise answers for other people" (Riley, 1975:26).

After receiving a Bachelor in Theology from American Bible College in 1956, Rev. Eikerenkoetter enrolled for a two-year stint in the Air Force Chaplain Service (Malney, 1977:266). In 1958 he returned to Ridgeland to form the United Church of Jesus Christ for All People. During this period, the young clergyman's theology was a mixture of civil rights advocacy and southern Pentecostalism. The charismatic and attractive preacher enjoyed considerable popularity among the local glossolalia-speaking and Holy Ghost seeking Christians but he had a thirst for national prominence and Ridgeland was too small.

In the summer of 1964 he took his show on the road and established the Miracle Temple, his new headquarters, in Boston. The competition for souls was stiffer in the North but the opportunistic preacher accepted the gauntlet. Later, he reflected: "Faith healing was the big thing at the time, and I was just about the best in Boston, snatching people out of wheelchairs and off their crutches, pouring some oil over them while I commanded them to walk or see or hear. I don't know if I cured many folks but its a wonder I didn't kill somebody though" (Riley, 1975:28).

In 1966, Rev. Eikerenkoetter, recognizing the limited opportunities for a black Messiah in Boston, moved his organization to Harlem, New York. Housed in a dilapidated movie theater, the Sunset, on 125th Street, Rev. Eikerenkoetter eagerly entered the world of sects, cults and the occult. He "specialized" in prophesy, discernment of spirits, glossolalia and faith-healing. To promote his services he changed the name on the marquee from Rev. Eikerenkoetter to "Rev. Ike Every Sun" (Riley, 1975:28). The new name was flashy and easy to pronounce and aided the meteoric rise of Rev. Ike.

In the late sixties, Harlem was a hotbed of religious wares. Rev. Ike, recognizing the community's spiritual and financial potential, began selling prayer cloths. These divine hankerchiefs, blessed by Rev. Ike, were advertised as "cures" for asthma, cancer, rheumatism, marital problems, financial worries, and a host of other maladies and stresses. Between 1966-1969, Rev. Ike and his prayer cloths became household words in Harlem. Despite increasing criticism from civic and religious leaders that he was too flamboyant, the once-country preacher was now an affluent businessman with a rapidly growing following.

In 1969, Rev. Ike changed his location and his theology. He paid $600,000 for the Loews building on 175th and Broadway. More importantly, he recanted his former beliefs in Biblical inerrancy, the virgin birth and resurrection of Jesus, and the existence of God, Satan, heaven, hell and sin. It is not known if Rev. Ike's change in theological orientation was influenced by his graduate studies -- he claims to have received a Ph.D. in psychiatry in 1969 -- (Marquis, 1978:943); interestingly, the identity of the conferring university remains a mystery. In the same year, he founded the United Church and Science of Living Institute, which remains the headquarters of Rev. Ike's organization.

Theology

Rev. Ike's theology is a hodgepodge of psycho-dynamics, humanism, positive thinking, Epicureanism, and the Protestant work ethic. Although undoubtedly influenced by numerous persons, it appears that three individuals played significant roles in his development, they were, Norman Vincent Peale, Father Divine, and Sigmund Freud. Rev. Ike, borrowing liberally from the ideas of these notables, developed the theological orientation that he calls "The Science of Living" (Giovanni, 1975:22).

Rev. Ike adamantly denies that The Science of Living is a church doctrine, cultist dogma, or personal theology. Instead, he claims: "It is the teaching of how a person may live a positive, dynamic, healthy, happy, successful, prosperous life through the consciousness of the Presence of God -- Infinite Good -- already within everyone" (Giovanni, 1975:22).

The most salient concept in The Science of Living is the "cosmic law of mind." This concept, derived from Rev. Ike's interpretation of psycho-dynamics, is the route to spiritual enlightenment and material prosperity. According to Rev. Ike, the cosmic law of mind "directs the human mind to concentrate its energies and assert the will toward bringing about the materialization of subjective desires. . . I teach people to put themselves in touch with that higher consciousness that enables them to control their lives by controlling their minds. I teach them to focus individual attention on positive forces in the universe, the forces that make good things happen" (Riley, 1975:30).

153

Implicit in the concept of the cosmic law of mind is the negation of the God of traditional Christianity. Rev. Ike and his followers reject the notion of an omnipotent, omnipresent, and omniscient God separate from humanity. Instead, God is seen as the recognition and utilization of the cosmic law of mind. In Rev. Ike's words: "There are no outer saviours, each man is taught how to save himself by coming to know himself and to know the mastery of his own mind and his own affairs" (Lucas, 1973:58).

For Rev. Ike, there are as many Gods as there are people who recognize their innate divinity. A frequent feature of his radio broadcasts is a spiel on the divinity of humanity. For example, "I am God. You are God. There is no God sitting on a fancy throne somewhere in heaven. God is here, within each of you. I am free from the God of depression, the God of blind allegiance. Praise God, praise me" (WMOO, April 1978).

After discovering his own divinity, a revelation undoubtedly influenced by Father Divine the Harlem based "God" of the 1930's, Rev. Ike began a wholesale dissection of his former Pentecostalism. For instance, the traditional conception of sin was incompatible with the notion of positive thinking inherent in the cosmic law of mind; therefore it had to be reconceptualized. According to Rev. Ike: "Sin is the refusal to walk faithfully with the God in you. Sin is guilt, depression, and negative thoughts" (WMOO, April 1978). Some observers contend that Rev. Ike's rejection of the Christian conception of sin is a reaction against his Pentecostal background (See, Allen, 1972:1). In a related vein, Rev. Ike's conception of Satan departs from his former Pentecostalism. "You are God, but the God in you may lay dormant. The Devil is your ignorance of your individual possibilities" (WMOO, May 1978).

Although he regularly cites passages from the Christian Bible, Rev. Ike views the Bible as only "interesting" literature. The "real" Bible is written daily by proponents of the cosmic law of mind. "The Word of God is what I say and believe about myself" (Chandler, 1976:24). While many Christians probe the Bible for answers to the "ultimate" questions, Rev. Ike's Science of Living theology provides his followers with these answers. For example, regarding the question of death and dying, Rev. Ike teaches his followers that death is inconsequential. "Heaven and hell are only states of the mind. I have no conception of death or the hereafter. I have a concept only of life. There is only now" (NEW YORK AMSTERDAM NEWS, 1978:15).

Rev. Ike also opposes prayer, meditation and fasting. These religious

154

practices are seen as remnants of a lower state of consciousness. "Awaken to the truths of the cosmic law. I don't waste my psychic energies practicing superstitious mumbo jumbo. Get off your knees, when you pray you're in perfect position to get kicked in the butt" (WMOO, May 1978). His view of fasting is equally adamant: "Fast, why should I fast? I want the world and the fullness therein. Poor folks been praying and fasting too long. I don't want to fast, I want a nice, big juicy steak. Fasting is for people who deny their divinity" (WMOO, May 1978).

Although Rev. Ike's theology is diametrically opposed to the Pentecostalism of his youth, his Sunday church services exploit the orthodox backgrounds of his audience. For example, his choir sings Gospel music and Black Spirituals. In addition, Bibles are present and Rev. Ike uses terms like Jesus, God, salvation, grace, holy and rebirth -- of course, his use of these terms is not consistent with their usage in orthodox or conservative camps. It should be mentioned that Rev. Ike, although exploiting the symbolic meanings attached to his ministerial title, does not claim to be a "reverend": "No, I am not a man-of-God, not in the way that others are. I am a preacher of positive thinking, of faith in the God within each of us. I am not a 'reverend,' I'm not sure what that is. I have a new ministry" (WMOO, April 1978).

Epicureanism

The most controversial aspect of Rev. Ike's theology is the blatant emphasis on the accumulation of wealth. An unabashed epicurean, Rev. Ike flaunts opulence. For example, in 1976 his evangelistic empire included twenty-four automobiles, six mansions, several hundred finely tailored suits, and a fortune in jewelry (See, Sanders, 1976:151; Robinson, 1977:26). In recent years he has added several Rolls Royces, mansions, and real estate holdings to his ever-growing affluence. According to Rev. Ike: "Money serves me, money loves me, I see myself having money, making money. God blessed me with money. God is interested in my prosperity" (WMOO, April 1978).

Rev. Ike's voluminous wealth came from the monetary contributions of his members and followers. These persons respond to Rev. Ike's "need" for money. To his audiences, Rev. Ike says: "It's time for you to give me some money. Now you do want to do that, don't you? Well, I ask only one thing as the sisters come among you with the buckets we use here to collect money when my cup runneth over ... I ask you not to put change in our envelopes. Change makes your minister nervous in the service" (Riley, 1975:30).

Apparently, the followers of Rev. Ike believe that their monetary contributions are consistent with the principles of the Science of Living. They are taught that giving him money is a prerequisite for exploiting the cosmic law of mind in their own lives. Explaining why he requests his parishioners and other followers, many of whom are impoverished, to give large donations, Rev. Ike responded: "When people learn to give, they have the experience of money. Giving presupposes that I have and brings to pass that which it presupposes" (Blau, 1972:75). This is consistent with Freud's idea that people appreciate "guidance" only when it has a price tag.

While simultaneously seeking their money, Rev. Ike admonishes his listeners to exploit the capital-producing potentials of positive thinking -- a technique borrowed from Norman Vincent Peale. His approach takes two shapes. First, he appeals to their intellects: "I teach people to recognize the cosmic law of mind as the crystallization and the real meaning of terms like Jesus Christ and the Lord. When people know this, the true forces in their lives can be centralized, focused into a dynamic, powerful agency capable of bringing about those things they truly need and desire. Each man thus becomes the cause and power that make what should happen to him actually happen" (Riley, 1975:32). After employing the intellectual approach, Rev. Ike appeals to the greed of his listeners: "Close your eyes and see green. Money up to your armpits, a roomful of money. And there you are, just tossing around in it like a swimming pool" (Blau, 1972:75).

To reinforce the idea that immense wealth is readily accessible to Science of Living practitioners, Rev. Ike conducts his Church services in a magnificent facility. The walls of the United Church are made of gold filigree, the columns and ceiling are covered with intricate, handpainted designs, the entire stage is on an elevator, and its 5,000 seats are upholstered with scarlet velvet plush to match the carpet throughout the facility (Sanders, 1976:151). To further substantiate the reality of wealth, Rev. Ike's midtown Manhatten office is filled with authentic French rococo furniture, antique chandeliers, candelabra and expensive wall hangings (Keerdoja, 1982:16).

Many of his contributors were introduced to Rev. Ike through ACTION, the official publication of the United Church and Science of Living Institute. This magazine, issued quarterly, has become the catalyst and conduit for a regular cash flow between Rev. Ike and seven million contributors around the world (Keerdoja, 1982:16). The magazine is a glossy, multi-colored extravaganza filled with accounts of successful followers of Rev. Ike. Typically, a welfare mother is shown receiving an unexpected fortune. The inference is clear: irrespective of your social status, if you follow Rev. Ike you will receive a material blessing.

In ACTION, Rev. Ike claims that all people can receive cars, homes, jewelry, furs, and money by applying the principles of the cosmic law of mind (Martin, 1979:189). The "blessing" process begins when people communicate with Rev. Ike. According to Rev. Ike when an individual reads ACTION she receives "psychic contact" with him (Blau, 1972:75). After establishing psychic contact, Rev. Ike solicits money. His success ratio is evident when one considers that almost all the correspondences that he receives contain contributions, ranging from $5 to $5,000.

Not only does Rev. Ike market his success idea, but he sells more blatant indulgences like red prayer cloths. He promotes these items on his weekly radio and television broadcasts which are aired in at least thirty states. These prayer cloths, originated in his early years in Harlem, also help the recipients to obtain psychic contact with their leader. By 1982, over 70 million individuals had purchased a prayer cloth. Rev. Ike claims that the prayer cloths are free of charge but he strongly encourages the recipients to "contribute to the ministry -- as much as possible" (Keerdoja, 1982:16).

In one issue of ACTION it was stated that the prayer cloth caused miracles of healing, blessing and deliverance. According to Rev. Ike the cloth is a reminder not a major healer (Blau, 1972:75). In his own words: "I am a healer only insomuch as I bring people to realize that health is within you. Some faith healers try to work some kind of hocus-pocus on you, try to make you believe they have some special gift of God. Everyone has this gift within themselves" (Blau, 1972:39). Despite these claims, Rev. Ike periodically hosts healing and blessing crusades (Brown, 1979:18). These crusades produce a great deal of wealth for Rev. Ike and his United Church and Science of Living Institute.

At various times, Rev. Ike has experimented with a Blessing Plan. Participants pay a fixed amount for monthly literature and "prayers" from Rev. Ike. The more money they invest the greater the blessing they receive. Some observers claim that the psychology of the Blessing Plan is similar not only to that of chain letters and the numbers game, but to the statement of Freud that patients had to be charged what they thought the psychoanalyst was worth, or they wouldn't think he was worth it (Allen, 1972:k9).

Through one ruse or another, Rev. Ike has become the most affluent black minister in the history of America. Although claiming an annual salary between $32,000 and $75,000, Rev. Ike has access to tens of millions. When asked about his income, Rev. Ike responded: "It's whatever I need. Money is issued to me by check by the organization, according to my request" (Keerdoja, 1982:16). The United Church and Science of Living Institute is probably worth in excess of $100 million and Rev. Ike has mechanisms in place to increase this sum.

Criticisms of Rev. Ike

It is not surprising that the flamboyant and outspoken Rev. Ike would be the recipient of harsh and continued criticism from observers. The most popular criticism is that he is engaged in a rip-off of the black community -- over ninety percent of his followers are black and usually they are below or near the poverty line. After a healing and blessing crusade in Chicago, Rev. Ike was confronted by a group of blacks led by a local radio commentator, Lu Palmer. Palmer, his remarks punctuated with a shaking fist, yelled at Rev. Ike: "You've got no business ever coming back to Chicago. You take money from blacks and give it to honkies. All your aides and workers are whites. You're stealing from us to make yourself acceptable to them" (Riley, 1975:28).

In many quarters of the black community, Rev. Ike's name is synonymous with greed and corruption. Black politicians, teachers, and ministers who are suspected of graft or self-aggrandizement are categorically labeled "Rev. Ikes." His negative image is reinforced by several highly-publicized remarks attributed to him. For example, "Don't give me black power, I can't buy anything with it" (Allen, 1972:k9). Also, "I use to be black myself then I went green" (Chandler, 1976:24). These statements, and others too numerous to cite here, have earned Rev. Ike the reputation of being callous toward the plight of poor blacks.

Rev. Ike rejects the claim that he exploits blacks. When asked what he was doing for blacks, Rev. Ike responded: "The same thing I'm doing for white people. Trying to give them a positive self-image and bring out that ability in them to have a healthy, prosperous life" (Blau, 1972:75). He contends that the criticisms against his ministry are misguided. "Many people are alive and doing well because I am alive and doing very well, and for that, like any sensible person, I expect to be made prosperous" (Riley, 1975:36).

To address his critics, Rev. Ike attacks federal programs designed to assist poor blacks. "All these people's crawl-ins, and poverty-council beg-ins, are used as part of the negative self-image psychology that is the real oppressor of black people in this country, because it keeps black people turned against themselves for needing help so much" (Riley, 1975:35). He also demeans the role of the traditional Church in the Black community. "Jealous preachers belittle me because I teach the depressed soul how to recognize the God within. Self-pity is the religion of the masses. Now, I come along and try to change this and my lot is criticism" (WMOO, April 1978).

"Envious" ministers are not the only observers who question Rev. Ike's motivation and methods. James Cone, a sociologist of religion, remarked: "Rev. Ike is just like many other popular 'messiahs': he's a slick talker like any good salesman of vacuum cleaners or anything else and he can appeal to what is absent in people's experience" (Sanders, 1975:152). Henry Allen, a noted journalist remarked: "It's like Dale Carnegie or Norman Vincent Peale or Barry Goldwater doing their smile, hope and free enterprise numbers to a heavy gospel shuffle" (Allen, 1972:k9). A disgruntled former aid to Rev. Ike stated: "The money seems to overwhelm him, which is understandable because the contributions are incredible at times, hundreds of thousands of dollars" (Riley, 1975:38). In addition, many local black newspapers have labeled him a charlatan (See, NORFOLK JOURNAL AND GUIDE, 1978:8).

Rev. Ike insists that some of his leading critics, especially ministers, secretly agree with his theology and methods. "The ministers will come up here quietly and say, 'We know you're right, but we just can't change our preachments and our practices" (Keerdoja, 1982:16). His final defense is that his ministry is unique but not harmful. "I am the first black man in America to preach positive self-image psychology to the black masses within a church setting" (Riley, 1975:12).

Social Implications

From at least the time of the Great Awakening, blacks have been active participants in religious cults in America as evidenced in such distinctive examples as Father Divine's Peace Mission, the Black Church of God, the United House of Prayer for All People, and Jonestown, where in the latter instance better than 80% of the members were black (Soles, 1979:54). This paper adopts the stance that Rev. Ike's United Church and Science of Living Institute constitutes a religious cult.

Milton J. Yinger, a prominent sociologist of religion, defines cults as the "growth of alienation from the traditional religious system as well as of alienation from society" (Yinger, 1970:279). Yinger suggests that cults are generally small in size, weak in structure, and under the leadership of a charismatic individual. The manifest goals of cults are three-fold: (1) the importance of the individual; (2) personal peace of mind; and (3) setting the individual in tune with the supernatural (Johnstone, 1975:127). Generally, the latent goals of cults differ from the manifest goals: (1) financial stability for the leader if not all the members; (2) separation from the mainstream of society; and (3) a rather rigorous re-socialization process for those being inducted into the cult (Pilgrim and Morgan, 1979:47).

The manifest goals of the United Church and Science of Living are consistent with the definition of cults suggested by Yinger. For example, Rev. Ike stresses individual achievements, spiritual and material. Each individual is believed to possess an innate divinity and thus are theoretically equal to their earthly leader. Each individual, through recognizing and using the cosmic law of mind, is expected to heal, improve and "save" herself. Regarding peace of mind, Rev. Ike teaches that poverty is the barrier to contentment. If individuals are financially secure then they will have peace of mind. "I teach poor folks to get out of the ghetto and into the get-mo. The love of money is not the root of evil, the lack of money is the root of evil. You feel good about yourself when you've got a fistful of dollars" (WMOO, April 1978). To Rev. Ike, only the poor lack personal contentment.

Like most cults, the United Church and Science of Living Institute stresses the supernatural. However, as aforementioned, Rev. Ike has transplanted the God of Christianity into the awakened consciousnesses of his followers. The cosmic law of mind is seen as the spiritual and material equivalent of the Christian God. However, Rev. Ike does place strict parameters around the use of the "Gods" within his followers. "But I also tell the people not to try and use the cosmic law of mind to bring about so-called miracles, magic and superstitious nonsense. Some folks should concentrate their wills on acquiring a pair of warm gloves or decent shoes before they try using mind science to acquire yachts and Cadillacs" (Riley, 1975:30).

Interestingly, the pursuit of material wealth, which is a latent goal for most cults, is a manifest goal of the United Church and Science of Living Institute. Rev. Ike makes no pretense of economic modesty, rather, opulence is viewed as outward manifestations of the divinity within him and his followers. Contributors donate more than $25 million to Rev. Ike each year and he is expected to flaunt the wealth of his organization.

In psychological terms, Rev. Ike's contributors, the majority of whom are poor, derive pleasure from contributing to his riches. This phenomena is best described as vicarious affluence -- even though the individual members of the cult are not financially secure and certainly do not exemplify economic advancement, nevertheless, they participate in the flagrant and conspicuous consumptive lifestyle of their religious leader (Pilgrim and Morgan, 1979:51). Not only are they collectively enriched psychologically but there is always the outside chance that the immense wealth will trickle down.

It should be mentioned that Rev. Ike's followers, unlike the constituencies of Dr. Sun Myung Moon, Maharaj-Ji, and His Divine Grace A. C. Bhaktivedanta Swami Prabuhpada, are not coerced into withdrawing from society. Rev. Ike's followers also do not undergo a rigorous resocialization process. These cultist features would necessitate the assuming of responsibility by Rev. Ike for the lives of his followers; he wants their money not their souls! Rev. Ike tells his followers: "You don't need heroes. I'm not your hero. I'm not your God. Stop looking for saviors and messiahs. You are God, each of you is God. Your fate is your own. God will take care of you. The God in you will take care of you. The God in me is busy making me prosperous" (WMOO, April 1978).

The extremism of cults makes them potentially dangerous and Rev. Ike's cult is no exception. The dangers inherent in this cult are illustrated by the following statements from a former aide to Rev. Ike:

"But what he's dealing with is not about money, but about the application of basic metaphysical principles based on universal laws that operate on this planet. Treated casually, these things can be very dangerous. He's giving people small parts of some extremely important truths, which can be explosive if he's not careful. Right now, his advocates are getting from him about as much as they can handle, but ten years from now, if they grow and continue to learn, he'll have to be far past where he is now in order to maintain sufficient influence to prevent thousands of them from suffering terrible emotional collapse" (Rile, 1975:38).

The meteoric growth of Rev. Ike's United Church and Science of Living Institute may be partially explained by the disenchantment of many blacks with the theologically and politically conservative black Church. Blacks, faced with numerous problems, most notably economic woes, are turning to religious organizations with a more this-worldly orientation. These persons may be drawn into "Social Gospel" and "Economic Gospel" churches. For these people, Rev. Ike's cult is a viable alternative to the fundamentalist Christianity that has has so long been associated with American blacks. In the words of Rev. Ike: "Why wait for the pie-in-the-sky when you can have it on earth with a cherry too" (WMOO, April 1978). This is generally sound advice, but Rev. Ike is more concerned about his piece of the pie than the comfort of his followers. For now, Rev. Ike is a **black** problem, but when his message becomes more palatable to whites he will be placed under national scrutiny.

REFERENCES

Allen, Henry
    1972   He Offers Heaven, and A Cadillac Too." WASHINGTON
            POST. 11 June, section K, p. 1.

Anonymous
    1956   "Dr. Peale's Reply." NEWSWEEK. (Jan 2), Vol. XLVII
            No. 1, p. 39.

Anonymous
    1978   "Rev. Ike Movement Grows." NEW YORK AMSTERDAM
            NEWS. 25 March, section B, p. 15.

Anonymous
    1978   "Editorial on Rev. Ike." NORFOLK JOURNAL AND GUIDE.
            18 January, section A, p. 8.

Blackwell, James E.
    1985   THE BLACK COMMUNITY: DIVERSITY AND UNITY.
            New York: Harper & Row.

Blau, Eleanor
    1972   "Harlem Preacher Stresses Power of Money and Prayer."
            NEW YORK TIMES, 26 July, p. 39.

Browne, J. Jamsba
    1979   "Rev. Ike Visits Brooklyn." NEW YORK AMSTERDAM
            NEWS. 26 May, p. 18.

Chandler, Russell
    1976   "Rev. Ike: 'You Can't Lose With The Stuff I Use,' He Tells
            Poor." LOS ANGELES TIMES, 27 February, section 1,
            p. 3.

Eikerenkoetter, Frederick J.
    1978   Sermon delivered in April and presented on WMOO in
            Mobile, Alabama. Was untitled, about thirty minutes
            in duration.

Eikerenkoetter, Frederick J.
1978   Sermon delivered in May and presented on WMOO in Mobile, Alabama. Testimonies of members dominated the untitled broadcast. About thirty-five minutes in duration.

Giovanni, Nikki
1975   "You Can't Lose With The Stuff I Use." ENCORE, (March), pp. 21-22.

Johnstone, Ronald L.
1975   RELIGION AND SOCIETY IN INTERACTION: THE SOCIOLOGY OF RELIGION. Englewood Cliffs, New Jersey: Prentice-Hall.

Keerdoja, Eileen, et al.,
1982   "Rev. Ike Preaches About the Profits." NEWSWEEK, Vol. 100, (December 20), p. 16.

Liddick, Betty
1972   "A Positive Preacher In A Pink Suit." LOS ANGELES TIMES. 3 November, p. 1.

Lucas, Bob
1973   "Church of Here, Not the Hereafter." SEPIA (January), pp. 54-58.

Malney, Albert Nelson
1977   WHO'S WHO AMONG BLACK AMERICANS 1977-78. Northbrook, Illinois; WHO'S WHO AMONG BLACK AMERICANS, INC. p. 266.

Marquis, Albert Nelson
1978   WHO'S WHO IN AMERICA. Chicago: Marquis Who's Who, Inc., p. 943.

Martin, William C.
1979   "The God-Hucksters of Radio." In, MODERN SOCIOLOGICAL ISSUES. Edited by Barry J. Wishart. New York: Macmillan Publishing Co.

Pilgrim, David and John Morgan
1979   "Cultus Mystique: Black Vulnerability in Profile." INTERNATIONAL BEHAVIOURAL SCIENTIST. Vol. XI, (Sept.), pp. 45-56.

Riley, Clayton
1975   "Golden Gospel of Reverend Ike." NEW YORK TIMES. (May), pp. 12-13.

Robinson, James
    1977   "Praise the Lord and Pass the Contributions." CHICAGO
            TRIBUNE, 4 December, section 1, p. 12.

Sanders, C.L.
    1976   "Gospel According to Rev. Ike." EBONY (December),
            pp. 148-52.

Soles, Henry
    1979   "Churchmen Hunt Clues on Cult's Lure for Blacks."
            CHRISTIANITY TODAY, 12 (March), p. 54.

Yinger, Milton J.
    1970   THE SCIENTIFIC STUDY OF RELIGION. London: Collier-
            Macmillan, Ltd.

> *We want the laws enforced against*
> *rich as well as poor; against capitalist*
> *as well as laborer; against white as*
> *well as black.*
>
> W. E. B. DuBois
> *RESOLUTIONS NIAGARA MOVEMENT, 1906*

CHAPTER TWELVE

BLACK FEDERAL JUDGES: FROM FDR TO RONALD REAGAN

Abraham L. Davis

Historically, the scarcity of black judges is as American as apple pie. Integration of the third branch of the Federal Government has been painfully slow. In 1963, twenty-six years after William Hastie was appointed as the first black federal judge by FDR, only 1% of the nation's judges were black. Seven years later (1970), the percentage remained the same although blacks comprised 11% of the population.[1] Several months before President Carter took office, the WASHINGTON POST reported on the status of blacks in the judiciary in the nation's Capital in these words:

> After decades in which Washington's courts had no more than one black judge, there are now 15 black men and women among D.C. superior court's 44 judges, two blacks on the nine judge D.C. Court of Appeals, four black judges among a total of 15 on the U.S. district court bench and one black judge among the nine on the U.S. Court of Appeals. Most of these black judges reached the bench in the last decade.[2]

On April 17, 1978, President Carter appointed Paul Simmons to the U.S. District Court for the Western District of Pennsylvania. This appointment was the first of forty-one that he would make at all levels of the federal judicial hierarchy. Thirty-one were appointed to the District Courts, but only twenty-nine were confirmed. Ten

---

[1]Beverly Blair Cook, "Black Representation in the Third Branch," THE BLACK LAW JOURNAL, Volume 1, 1971, p. 260.

[2]WASHINGTON POST, April 15, 1976, p. A14.

were appointed to the circuit courts of appeals, but only nine were confirmed. These thirty-eight appointments more than doubled the number of black federal judges that had been appointed by all other American presidents combined. Indeed, only sixteen black Americans were federal judges at the time of President Carter's election. Fred Gray (Alabama) and James Sheffield (Virginia) were not confirmed for different reasons. Gray who was nominated for a position on the district court (Alabama) was vehemently opposed by the American Bar Association's (ABA) standing committee on the Federal Judiciary. Attorney Gray made it clear that he would withdraw if another black was nominated in his place. Myron Thompson, a black graduate of the Yale Law School was nominated and confirmed. Nine days after President Carter submitted his name to the Senate, Judge U. W. Clemon became the first black to sit on the federal bench in Alabama and Judge Thompson became only the second black federal judge in Alabama's history.

James Sheffield was a victim of poor timing and allegations made by the Senate Judiciary Committee's investigatory staff. When Sheffield asked for time to prepare a defense to the allegations little did he know that the "extra" time would cost him the appointment. Because of the Reagan-Carter presidential campaign, Sheffield's nomination along with fifteen others ran into stiff Republican opposition.[3] The Republicans wanted the next president to fill these positions. Thus, Reagan's victory prevented Virginia from having its first black U.S. District Court Judge. The unfortunate thing about Sheffield's situation was that the Department of Justice had already cleared him of the allegations and the ABA had rated him Qualified. Senator Kennedy's cavilous investigatory staff had reduced by one the number of qualified blacks Carter had intended to serve in the federal judicial hierarchy. In addition, Andrew Jefferson was nominated by President Carter to the Court of Appeals for the 9th Circuit but was never confirmed. Despite these setbacks, the legacy that President Carter left becomes more apparent when one compares his record with that of his predecessors.

Historical Appointments

On March 26, 1937, William Hastie, a distinguished attorney was confirmed as a federal judge for the Virgin Islands. Franklin Roosevelt

---

[3]Sheldon Goldman, "Carter's Judicial Appointments: A Lasting Legacy," JUDICATURE, Vol. 64, No. 8, March 1981, p. 353.

appointed him upon the recommendation of Harold Ickes, Secretary of the Interior. At 32, Hastie became the first black American to be named to the federal bench and one of the youngest American jurists. He had graduated first in his class from Amherst College in 1925, and by 1932, this Phi Beta Kappa graduate had obtained the LL.B and J.D. degrees from the Harvard Law School. He had become the fourth United States judge for the Virgin Islands in a period of nineteen months. The NEW YORK AGE summed up the significance of this historic appointment succinctly in these words:

Former judges and governors there have been the butt of much criticism and turmoil both by the islanders and Americans on the mainland interested in the natives. It may be however, that being white, these administrators of law and justice have been unable to act and work with the natives with the sympathy and harmony that would guide a member of their own group.[4]

Two years after having been appointed a federal judge, Hastie returned to Washington, D.C., where he served as Dean of the Howard University School of Law. In 1940, he served in FDR's black cabinet as a civilian aide to the Secretary of War. However, he resigned approximately three years later in protest over the War Department's failure to act against segregation in the armed services. His efforts to secure equal treatment for black Americans in uniform were repeatedly frustrated. Hostility to his policies was intense. Judge Hastie explained the impossible position in which he found himself that led to his resignation in these words:

When I took office, the Secretary of War directed that all questions of policy and important proposals relating to Negroes should be referred to my office for comment or approval before final action. In December, 1940, the Air Force referred to me a plan for a segregated training center for Negro pursuit pilots at Tuskegee. I expressed my entire disagreement with the plan giving my reasons in detail. My views were disregarded. Since then the Air Command has never on its own initiative submitted any plan or project to me for comment or recommendation.[5]

---

[4]NEW YORK AGE, Vol. 51, No. 31, April 3, 1937, p. 6.

[5]Leslie H. Fishel, Jr., and Benjamin Quarles, THE BLACK AMERICAN: A DOCUMENTARY HISTORY (Glenview, Illinois: Scott Foresman and Company, 1970), p. 474.

In fact, the segregated Tuskegee Air Force Flying and Training Center was established, and as late as 1942, not one officer and very few instructors were black. The office of Civilian Aide was regarded as insignificant by influential members of the War Department but the black community viewed it as a symbol of progress. Historians agree that Hastie achieved significant breakthroughs in race relations in the military because of his efforts. Blacks were admitted to specialized training programs and officer candidate schools. Recreational facilities at some military bases were integrated and black physicians were commissioned in the reserve. Moreover, black pilots were trained as heavy bombardment fliers and both the Army and Navy started experimenting with units that were racially mixed.[6] An armed force that was totally segregated in 1943, was ninety-five percent desegregated by 1953.

In 1943, Judge Hastie received the Spingarn Medal from the NAACP because of his efforts to eradicate racial bigotry and discrimination from the military. A genuine respect for every individual's human dignity was at the top of his priority list.[7] Despite his resignation from FDR's black cabinet, the distinguished career of this public servant was not over. On May 1, 1946, he was confirmed as Governor of the Virgin Islands. President Truman had given him the opportunity to be the only black American to govern an American territory since Reconstruction. Governors would later be appointed from among the islanders themselves.

In 1945, Truman appointed Irvin Mollison, a black man, to the Customs Court and on October 15, 1949,[8] he appointed FDR's choice, William Hastie, to the U.S. Circuit Court for the Third Circuit. Judge Hastie had enthusiastically supported Truman in 1948. This was the highest legal post ever attained by a black American up to this point in American history. He served on the appellate court for approximately twenty-one years, three as chief judge. On his retirement in 1971, he assumed

---

[6]See Phillip McGuire, "Judge William H. Hastie: Civilian Aide to the Secretary of War, 1940-1943," NEGRO HISTORY BULLETIN, Vol. 40, No. 3, May-June 1977, p. 713.

[7]See Phillip McGuire, "Judge Hastie, World War II, and the Army Air Corps," PHYLON, Vol. XLII, No. 2, June 1981, p. 165.

[8]Alton Hornsby, THE BLACK ALMANAC: FROM INVOLUNTARY SERVITUDE 1619-1860. (New York: Barron's Educational Series, Inc., 1977), p. 98.

the title of senior judge. Thurgood Marshall was appointed to the circuit court of appeals by President John F. Kennedy in 1961. In 1965, he resigned and became Solicitor General of the United States and in 1967 President Lyndon Johnson appointed him to the United States Supreme Court.

In 1939, FDR appointed Herman Moore to a federal judgeship in the Virgin Islands. His appointment of two blacks to the federal judicial hierarchy was matched by Truman and ethnic diversity in the third branch of Federal government had become a reality. Black Americans had been given a glimpse of hope. President Eisenhower did not appoint any blacks to the U.S. District Courts or the U.S. Circuit Courts of Appeals, during his eight years. However, on April 18, 1957, he appointed Scovel Richardson to the U.S. Customs Court. Approximately one year later, he appointed Walter Gordon to a federal judgeship in the Virgin Islands. President Kennedy appointed five black Americans to the federal courts. James Parson, Wade McCree, Spottswood Robinson and A. Leon Higginbotham were appointed to the U.S. District Courts while Thurgood Marshall was appointed to the U.S. Court of Appeals for the Second Circuit. President Lyndon Johnson appointed eight blacks. Thurgood Marshall was elevated to the United States Supreme Court while Wade McCree and Spottswood Robinson were elevated to the U.S. Courts of Appeals for the Sixth and D.C. Circuit, respectively. Johnson also appointed William Bryant, Aubrey Robinson, Joseph Waddy, Damon Keith and Constance Motley, to the U.S. District Courts. He also appointed James Watson to the Customs Court. President Nixon appointed six blacks to the federal district courts. They were David Williams, Barrington Parker, Lawrence W. Pierce, Clifford Green, Robert Carter and Robert Duncan. President Ford appointed three blacks to the U.S. District Courts. They were Henry Bramwell, Cecil Poole and George Leighton. He also appointed Matthew Perry to the Military Court of Appeals. Approximately three years into Reagan's first term, he had appointed only two blacks to the federal judicial hierarchy. Judge Lawrence Pierce was elevated to the Second Circuit Court of Appeals from a federal district court position to which he had been appointed by President Nixon in 1971. Reginald Gibson, a black American, was also appointed to the U.S. Court of Claims by Reagan in 1983. President Carter's appointment of thirty-eight black Americans to the federal judicial hierarchy stands like a shining beacon compared to the record of other presidents. He emphasized his accomplishments in many of his campaign appearances for re-election, especially among predominantly black audiences. In a speech at the Annual Hubert H. Humphrey Award Dinner on January 17, 1980, he remarked:

In the last three years, we haven't done very much, but we've begun, again to realize the dreams of Hubert Humphrey, George Meany, Clarence Mitchell and others. . . . More women, more blacks, more Hispanics have been appointed to the federal courts than in all previous administrations in the history of our country. Of the 32 women who now serve on the federal courts, 28 of them were appointed in the last 3 years. But the point is, that's still just a beginning.[9]

Black District and Appeals Court Judges Appointed by Carter: Age, Sex, and Prior Experience

The black federal judges appointed by former President Carter ranged in age from thirty-seven to sixty-five at the federal district court level and from forty-three to sixty-nine at the federal circuit court level. The average age of the black federal district court judges at the time of appointment was fifty-eight. The average age of the appeals court judges was fifty-six.

Six of the twenty-nine black district court judges are females. They range in age from forty-one to fifty-nine. Three (50 percent) had prior judicial experience and the remaining three had prior experience, respectively, as a prosecutor, a lawyer and a lawyer associated with a law firm. Significantly, prosecutorial experience was not a very important career trait of the Carter appointed federal judges compared to those of previous administrations. Thirteen of the twenty-three black male district judges (57 percent) had prior judicial experience. The choice of appointing a significant number of state judges to serve as federal judges is probably due to former President Carter's campaign pledge to appoint all federal judges strictly on the basis of merit. Sheldon Goldman spoke to this point when he wrote about President Carter's judicial nominees. He observed that "state judges picked for advancement presumably have already demonstrated their judicial abilities thereby taking some of the guesswork from the selection process."[10] Some previous administrations also placed emphasis on appointing sitting judges. More than fifty percent of the appoint-

---

[9]Weekly Compilation of Presidential Documents, Volume 16, Number 5, February 4, 1980, pp. 222-223.

[10]Sheldon Goodman, "A Profile of Carter's Judicial Nominees," JUDICATURE, Vol. 62, No. 5, November, 1978, pp. 249.

BLACK FEDERAL JUDGES APPOINTED TO THE SUPREME COURT, THE U.S. COURTS OF APPEALS AND THE
U.S. DISTRICT COURTS

NAMES	COURT		APPOINTED BY	STATE
William Hastie	Federal Court	-- 1937	Franklin D. Roosevelt	Virgin Islands
William Hastie	U.S. Court of Appeals	-- 1949	Harry S. Truman	District of Columbia
James Benton Parson	U.S. District Court	-- 1961	John F. Kennedy	Illinois
Wade H. McCree, Jr.	U.S. District Court	-- 1961	John F. Kennedy	Michigan
	U.S. Court of Appeals	-- 1966	Lyndon B. Johnson	
	(6th Circuit)			
Thurgood Marshall	U.S. Court of Appeals	-- 1961	John F. Kennedy	District of Columbia
	Supreme Court	-- 1967	Lyndon B. Johnson	
Spottswood W. Robinson	U.S. District Court	-- 1963	John F. Kennedy	District of Columbia
	U.S. Court of Appeals	-- 1966	Lyndon B. Johnson	
	(D.C. Circuit)			
A. Leon Higginbotham, Jr.	U.S. District Court	-- 1963	John F. Kennedy	Pennsylvania
	U.S. Court of Appeals	-- 1977	Jimmy Carter	
	(3rd Circuit)			
William Benson Bryant	U.S. District Court	-- 1965	Lyndon B. Johnson	District of Columbia
Constance Baker Motley	U.S. District Court	-- 1966	Lyndon B. Johnson	District of Columbia
Aubrey Eugene Robinson, Jr.	U.S. District Court	-- 1966	Lyndon B. Johnson	District of Columbia
Joseph C. Waddy	U.S. District Court	-- 1967	Lyndon B. Johnson	District of Columbia
Damon Jerome Keith	U.S. District Court	-- 1967	Lyndon B. Johnson	Michigan
	U.S. Court of Appeals	-- 1977	Jimmy Carter	
	(6th Circuit)			
David W. Williams	U.S. District Court	-- 1969	Richard Nixon	California
Barrington Daniel Parker	U.S. District Court	-- 1969	Richard Nixon	District of Columbia
Warren Lawrence Pierce	U.S. District Court	-- 1971	Richard Nixon	New York

172

BLACK FEDERAL JUDGES APPOINTED TO THE SUPREME COURT, THE U.S. COURTS OF APPEAL AND THE
U.S. DISTRICT COURTS

NAMES	COURT	APPOINTED BY	STATE
Clifford Scott Green	U.S. District Court --- 1971	Richard Nixon	Pennsylvania
Robert Lee Carter	U.S. District Court -- 1972	Richard Nixon	New York
Robert Duncan	U.S. District Court -- 1974	Richard Nixon	Ohio
Henry Bramwell	U.S. District Court -- 1974	Gerald Ford	New York
Cecil Poole	U.S. District Court -- 1976	Gerald Ford	California
George Leighton	U.S. District Court -- 1976	Gerald Ford	Illinois
Julian Cooke	U.S. District Court -- 1977	Jimmy Carter	Michigan
Robert Collins	U.S. District Court -- 1978	Jimmy Carter	Louisiana
Jack Tanner	U.S. District Court -- 1978	Jimmy Carter	Washington
Theodore McMillian	U.S. Court of Appeals -- 1978 (8th Circuit)	Jimmy Carter	Missouri
Mary Johnson Lowe	U.S. District Court -- 1978	Jimmy Carter	New York
Paul Simmons	U.S. District Court -- 1978	Jimmy Carter	Pennsylvania
John Penn	U.S. District Court -- 1979	Jimmy Carter	District of Columbia
David Nelson	U.S. District Court -- 1979	Jimmy Carter	Massachusetts
Gabrielle McDonald	U.S. District Court -- 1979	Jimmy Carter	Texas
Clyde Cahill	U.S. District Court -- 1980	Jimmy Carter	Missouri
Almeric Christian	U.S. District Court -- 1978	Jimmy Carter	Virgin Islands
U. W. Clemon	U.S. District Court -- 1980	Jimmy Carter	Alabama

BLACK FEDERAL JUDGES APPOINTED TO THE SUPREME COURT, THE U.S. COURTS OF APPEALS AND THE U.S. DISTRICT COURTS

NAMES	COURT	APPOINTED BY		STATE
Richard C. Erwin	U.S. District Court	---1980	Jimmy Carter	North Carolina
Benjamin Gibson	U.S. District Court	-- 1979	Jimmy Carter	Michigan
James Giles	U.S. District Court	-- 1979	Jimmy Carter	Pennsylvania
Earl B. Gilliam	U.S. District Court	-- 1980	Jimmy Carter	California
Alcee Hastings	U.S. District Court	-- 1979	Jimmy Carter	Florida
Terry Hatter	U.S. District Court	-- 1979	Jimmy Carter	California
Thelton Henderson	U.S. District Court	-- 1980	Jimmy Carter	California
Odell Horton	U.S. District Court	-- 1980	Jimmy Carter	Tennessee
George Howard	U.S. District Court	-- 1980	Jimmy Carter	Arkansas
Joseph Howard	U.S. District Court	-- 1979	Jimmy Carter	Maryland
Norma Johnson	U.S. District Court	-- 1980	Jimmy Carter	District of Columbia
Consuelo Marshall	U.S. District Court	-- 1980	Jimmy Carter	California
Matthew Perry	U.S. District Court	-- 1979	Jimmy Carter	South Carolina
Anna Taylor	U.S. District Court	-- 1979	Jimmy Carter	Michigan
Anne Thompson	U.S. District Court	-- 1979	Jimmy Carter	New Jersey
Myron Thompson	U.S. District Court	-- 1980	Jimmy Carter	Alabama
Horace Ward	U.S. District Court	-- 1979	Jimmy Carter	Georgia
George White	U.S. District Court	-- 1980	Jimmy Carter	Ohio

BLACK FEDERAL JUDGES APPOINTED TO THE SUPREME COURT, THE U.S. COURTS OF APPEALS AND THE
U.S. DISTRICT COURTS

NAMES	COURT		APPOINTED BY	STATE
Analya Kearse	U.S. Court of Appeals (2nd Circuit)	-- 1979	Jimmy Carter	New York
Joseph Hatchett	U.S. Court of Appeals (5th Circuit)	-- 1979	Jimmy Carter	Florida
Nathaniel Jones	U.S. Court of Appeals (6th Circuit)	-- 1979	Jimmy Carter	Ohio
J. Jerome Farris	U.S. Court of Appeals (9th Circuit)	-- 1979	Jimmy Carter	Washington
Cecil F. Poole	U.S. Court of Appeals (9th Circuit)	-- 1979	Jimmy Carter	California
Harry Edwards	U.S. Court of Appeals (D.C. Circuit)	-- 1980	Jimmy Carter	Michigan
Warren Lawrence Pierce	U.S. District Court	-- 1971	Richard Nixon	New York
	U.S. Court of Appeals (2nd Circuit)	-- 1981	Ronald Reagan	New York

ments made by President Nixon and Johnson came from the judiciary. Approximately seventy-five percent of Ford's appointments had been sitting judges.[11]

Only one of the twenty-three black male federal judges had experience in public life at the time of his appointment. U.W. Clemon was a state senator in Alabama prior to his appointment to a district judgeship. None of the black district or appeals court judges held governmental posts at the time of their appointment. The remaining district court judges were practicing lawyers (1), lawyers in law firms (5), and professors (3).

Former President Carter appointed nine blacks to the U.S. Circuit Courts of Appeals. Two of the nine (Higginbotham and Keith), were elevated to the third and sixth circuits respectively from the district court level on October 11, 1977. Amalya Kearse, a brilliant lawyer, was the only female.

Six of the nine appeals court judges had prior judicial experience. The remaining judges were a lawyer in a law firm, a lawyer in private practice and a law professor.

The Appointment of Other Minorities

The term minority is not limited to black Americans. It also encompasses other ethnic groups and some academicians would include women also. Carter emphasized during his campaign for the presidency that in addition to blacks he intended to appoint more women and Hispanics to the federal courts. He pinpointed what he was trying to accomplish through these appointments in a speech to southern black leaders in Atlanta on September 16, 1980:

> I see a Federal Court System that's filled not only with a desire for justice but a desire for understanding of the special deprivation of justice that still prevails in this country against those who are poor or inarticulate or not well organized or not well educated. We've got a long way to go in the Federal Courts where, still, money available to have competent lawyers is an obstacle to true justice. But whenever I appoint a black judge or Hispanic

---

[11]See Elaine Martin, "Women on the Federal Bench: A Comparative Profile," JUDICATURE, Vol. 65, No. 6, December-January, 1982, p. 310.

CARTER APPOINTED BLACK U.S. DISTRICT COURT JUDGES: AGE, SEX, EDUCATION
AND PRIOR EXPERIENCE
Educational Institutions Attended

Name	Undergraduate School Attended	Law School Attended	Experience Prior to Appointment	Age	Sex
Cahill, Clyde	St. Louis University	St. Louis University	Missouri Circuit Judge	60	M
Christian, Almeric (Virgin Islands)	Columbia College	Columbia Law School	Lawyer	64	M
Clemon, U.W.	Morehouse College	Columbia Law School	Alabama State Senator	40	M
Collins, Robert F.	Dillard University	Louisiana State University	Collins, Douglas & Elie	53	M
Cooke, Julian A.	Pennsylvania State	Georgetown	Cook & Curry, Pontiac	53	M
Erwin, Richard C.	Johnson C. Smith Univeristy	Howard University	Court of Appeals Judge	60	M
Gibson, Benjamin	Wayne State University	Detroit College of Law	Professor, Thomas Cooley Law School	52	M
Giles, James	Amherst College	Yale Law School	Pepper, Hamilton and Scheetz	41	M
Gilliam, Earl B.	San Diego State College	Hastings College of Law	Western State University College of Law Part-time Faculty	51	M
Hastings, Alcee	Fisk University	Flordia A&M University	Judge Seventeenth Judicial Court, Broward County, Fla.	47	M
Hatter, Terry	Wesleyan University	University of Chicago Law School	Judge, California Superior Court, Los Angeles	51	M
Henderson, Thelton	University of California	Boalt Hall School of Law	Golden State University	50	M
Horton, Odell	Morehouse College	Howard University Law School	Referee-in-Bankruptcy	54	M
Howard, George	University of Arkansas	University of Arkansas	Court of Appeals Judge	59	M

177

CARTER APPOINTED BLACK U.S. DISTRICT COURT JUDGES: AGE, SEX, EDUCATION
AND PRIOR EXPERIENCE

Educational Institutions Attended

Name	Undergraduate School Attended	Law School Attended	Experience Prior to Appointment	Age	Sex
Howard, Joseph	University of Iowa	Drake University	Associate Judge on the Supreme Bench of Baltimore City	61	M
Johnson, Norma	District of Columbia Teachers College	Georgetown University	Associate Judge Superior Court	51	F
Lowe, Mary Johnson	Hunter College	Brooklyn Law School	Justice, New York Supreme Court, First Judicial District	59	F
Marshall, Consuelo	Howard University	Howard University	Superior Court Judge	47	F
McDonald, Gabrielle	Boston University	Harvard Law School	McDonald & McDonald	41	F
Nelson, David S.	Boston College	Boston College Law School	Assoc. Justice, Superior Court of Mass. (Boston)	50	M
Penn, John G.	University of Massachusetts	Boston University School of Law	Judge, Superior Court of the District of Columbia	51	M
Perry, Matthew	South Carolina State College, Orangeburg	South Carolina State College	U.S. Court of of Military Appeals, Washington, D.C.	62	M
Simmons, Paul A.	University of Pittsburgh	Harvard University	Judge, Common Pleas	62	M
Tanner, Jack E.	University of Puget Sound	University of Washington Law School	Tanner, McGavick, Felker, Fleming, Burges & Lazares	65	M
Taylor, Anna	Barnard College	Yale Law School	Law Dept., City of Detroit, Supervising Asst. Corp. Counsel	51	F

178

CARTER APPOINTED BLACK U.S. DISTRICT COURT JUDGES: AGE, SEX, EDUCATION
AND PRIOR EXPERIENCE

Educational Institutions Attended

Name	Undergraduate School Attended	Law School Attended	Experience Prior to Appointment	Age	Sex
Thompson, Anne	Howard University	Howard University School of Law	Prosecutor, Mercer County	49	F
Thompson, Myron	Yale University	Yale University	Thompson & Faulk, Partner	37	M
Ward, Horace	Morehouse College	Northwestern University	Judge, Superior Court, Judicial Circuit (Atlanta)	56	M
White, George	Baldwin Wallace College	Cleveland Marshall Law School	Judge, Court of Common Pleas	52	M

179

judge or even a woman judge, I know that they not only have committed in their own hearts a vision of what this nation ought to be but a special knowledge of the effects of past discrimination that are still there as a means to prevent equality of opportunity.[12]

Carter's campaign promise became a reality after he took office. By appointing forty women to the federal courts (29 to U.S. District Courts and 11 to the Appeals Courts), he offset the traditional white male bias of the federal judicial hierarchy and exceeded the efforts of all previous presidents combined.[13] Thus, approximately 15.3 percent of the 262 judges that Carter appointed to the federal judicial hierarchy during his presidency were women. Blacks and Hispanics constituted 14.5 and 6.1 percent of his appointments, respectively.[14] In addition, he appointed one woman to an Article I legislative court. Between 1949, when President Truman appointed Burnita Matthews as the first woman to ever serve on a U.S. District Court and the emergence of the Carter era, only nineteen women were appointed to the federal bench.

The first black woman to be appointed to a judgeship in this country was Jane Matilda Bolin. Mayor LaGuardia appointed her to the New York Family Court in 1939.[15] The first black woman to be appointed to a U.S. District Court was Constance Motley. President Lyndon Johnson appointed her in 1966, one year before he appointed Thurgood Marshall to the U.S. Supreme Court.

In 1934, President Franklin Roosevelt appointed Florence Allen to a federal appeals court. This first was followed by Lyndon Johnson's appointment of Shirley Hufstedler to a court of appeals. President Carter appointed eleven women to the appeals courts. This number

---

[12]Weekly Compilation of Presidential Documents, Vol. 16, No. 38, September 22, 1980, p. 1753.

[13]For an excellent article on women in the federal judicial hierarchy see, Elaine Martin, "Women on the Federal Bench: A Comparative Profile," JUDICATURE, Vol. 65, No. 6, December-January, 1982.

[14]Bennett H. Beach, "The Reagan Brand on the Judiciary," TIME, Vol. 121, No. 9, February 28, 1983, p. 74.

[15]Beverly Blair Cook, "Black Representation in the Third Branch," p. 260.

is significant when one considers that as late as 1969, Judge Hufstedler was the only woman serving at this level of the federal judicial hierarchy. Presidents Nixon and Ford appointed no women to the appellate courts. However, each of them saw fit to appoint one woman to a U.S. District Court. One percent of their appointments were women compared to fifteen percent of President Carter's appointments. Carter also appointed fourteen Hispanics to the U.S. District Courts and two Hispanics and one Asian American to the U.S. Circuit Courts of Appeals.[16]

Ronald Reagan's record of appointing women, blacks and Hispanics to the federal judicial hierarchy during his first three years in office is dismal compared to President Carter's record. In three years, he had appointed two blacks, two Hispanics, and four women including Associate Justice Sandra Day O'Connor to the federal judicial hierarchy. Moreover, three additional women and two Hispanics from among twenty-one nominees were awaiting confirmation by the Senate. Of eighty-eight judges appointed by Reagan to life tenure (excluding Justice O'Connor) only seven were black, Hispanic or women. It is important to emphasize that the two Hispanics were appointed to the federal court in Puerto Rico.

President Reagan emphasized during the 1980 Presidential campaign that the most qualified women he could find would be appointed to the U.S. Supreme Court if and when a vacancy occurred. He kept his promise and appointed Sandra Day O'Connor, an Arizona Appeals Court Judge, to replace Potter Stewart who retired. She was confirmed on September 21, 1981, by the U.S. Senate by a vote of 99-0.

Carter appointed approximately forty percent of the judges on the entire federal bench during his four-year term of office. These appointments were possible because of the passage of the Omnibus Judgeship Act of 1978 which created 117 new seats for the federal district courts and thirty-five new seats for the Circuit Courts of Appeals. Sheldon Goldman pinpointed the likely results of a judiciary composed of members from different ethnic groups in these words:

> Diversity of backgrounds is likely to produce some diversity of views and perspectives, and that should be welcomed, particularly when our courts are being called upon to respond to difficult

---

[16]Sheldon Goldman, "Carter's Judicial Appointments: A Lasting Legacy," pp. 349-351.

issues that at best can be dealt with by judicial art and not science.[17]

Carter transcended the tokenism that had pervaded the federal courts and succeeded in his goal of bringing diversity to this traditionally nearly all white male club. His sensitivity to ensuring greater ethnic diversity is only one aspect of the legacy that he left. It is perhaps ironic that a southerner took such a giant step since the south has always carried the stigma of being more racist towards black Americans compared with other sections of the country. Carter's legacy can be viewed as a model for future presidents to follow if the egalitarian principle is to have real meaning within the American polity. Reagan's performance thus far indicates that he will not follow the example set by President Carter. The two men seem to differ vastly in their list of priorities and in their understanding of, and sensitivity to, harsh historical realities. This view is shared by Arnold Torres, Executive Director of the League of United Latin American Citizens and Judge Gladys Kessler of the District of Columbia Superior Court. Referring to Reagan's appointment of minorities and women to the federal bench Torres said: "We knew darn well they weren't going to be appointing Hispanics in this Administration."[18] Judge Kessler shared Torres' view. She remarked, "We have some grave concerns about whether this Administration is really looking for women candidates."[19]

---

[17]Sheldon Goldman, "A Profile of Carter's Judicial Nominees," p. 253.

[18]Bennett Beach, p. 74.

[19]Bennett Beach, p. 74.

The white man, as well as the Negro,
is bound and barred by the color-line.

W. E. B. DuBois
THE SOULS OF BLACK FOLK, 1903

CHAPTER THIRTEEN

BLACKS AND COALITION POLITICS:
POISON OR PANACEA

Ronnie Stewart

The role of Blacks in biracial coalitions has long been a topic of vigorous debate in the Black community. As far back as the 1890's, in the Populist Movement, Blacks were divided on the merits of aligning themselves with groups seeking political power. Almost a century later the debate continues. In the mid-1980's, The Reverend Jesse Jackson attempted to recruit poor Whites, Hispanics, Blacks, women and other minorities into a "Rainbow Coalition." The inability of the charismatic preacher-politician to forge meaningful coalitions between these groups suggests that Blacks must remain prepared to effectuate social change without the aid of other groups -- this is especially true when non-Black groups are not the obvious or primary beneficiaries of the coalition.

The purpose of this paper is to present the different views about biracial coalitions that have been articulated by Black scholars, politicians, and civil rights activists. Since this controversy reached its height in the 1960's, most of the classical arguments may be located in the published rhetoric of this tumultuous decade -- twenty years later these arguments are presented with only slight variations. After I have presented these arguments I will offer an answer to the question of whether biracial coalitions are poison or panacea for Blacks.

Arguments In Favor Of Biracial Coalitions

One of the most consistent proponents of biracial coalition politics is Bayard Rustin, pacifist and civil rights leader. For Rustin, the key to greater life's chances for Blacks is not uniracial organizations, but multiracial organizations -- with all Americans working together for a common goal. The crux of his argument is that all of the victories obtained by the Civil Rights Movement occurred when Blacks coalesced with other groups. For example, he cites the alliance Rev. Martin Luther King had in Chicago with the Industrial Union Department of the AFL-CIO and with various religious groups which led to the weakening of the Daley-Dawson political juggernaut (Nelson, 1983:2). He also contends that a liberal-labor-civil rights coalition played a significant role in making the Democratic party more responsive to the aspirations and needs of all poor people. Further, Rustin attributes the success of the March on Washington, passage of the Civil Rights Act of 1964, and President Johnson's landslide victory to coalitions formed by Blacks, trade unionists, White liberals, and religious groups (Rustin, 1964:25-31). Rustin's position is clear in the following excerpt.

"But we must remember that the effectiveness of a swing vote depends solely on 'other' votes. It derives its power from them. In that sense, it can never be 'independent,' but must opt for one candidate or the other, even if by default. Thus coalitions are inescapable, however tentative they may be. . . The issue is which coalition to join and how to make it responsive to your program. Necessarily there will be compromise" (Rustin, 1964:29).

Another notable advocate of biracial coalitions is former Massachusetts Senator Edward W. Brooke. As a Congressman, Brooke deemphasized race; he once remarked, "I do not intend to become a national leader of the Negro people; I intend to do my job as a Senator from Massachusetts" (Littleton and Burger, 1971:246). He observed that Blacks in the past had taken too narrow a view of coalitions, regarding them as permanent and as a threat to Black identity. Rejecting that view, he urged Blacks to form "free-floating coalitions across racial lines. ... these coalitions must be based on specific and pragmatic issues of common interest" (Morris, 1975:298). Brooke's position is summarized below:

"The American Negro must win allies, not conquer adversaries. For the harsh reality is that we are a small minority. . . And we need all of the moral, legal, economic and political assistance that allies can offer. To those who oppose us, our strategy must be based on influence and inducement, on altering thought patterns and old standards -- on appeals to hearts and minds. For the best way to defeat an enemy is to make of him a friend. Not the sword, but persuasion" (Littleton and Burger, 1971:248).

The list of notable Blacks who supported (or who still supports) biracial coalitions is impressive -- Rev. Martin Luther King, Sterling Tucker, Rev. Ralph Albernathy, A. Philip Randolph, and Whitney M. Young all supported Black-White coalitions. The arguments in this section may be summarized in the following manner. Biracial coalitions are essential if Blacks are to acquire real power and influence in the larger society. Blacks share many problems with other groups, and these problems may serve as a basis for coalition building. The Black-White coalition is not necessarily synonymous with assimilation. In some instances, assimilation may be the goal of the union, but often the alliance has more limited goals. In any event, Blacks need sympathetic Whites.

Arguments Which Oppose Biracial Coalitions

The leading statement against the forming of coalitions by Blacks was written by Carmichael and Hamilton, BLACK POWER. Their chapter entitled "The Myths of Coalition" debunks several misconceptions held by protagonists of coalition politics. These myths may be summarized as follows: (1) the belief that in the context of present-day America, the interests of Black people are identical with the interests of White liberal, labor and other reform groups; (2) the assumption that a politically and economically insecure group can collaborate with a politically and economically secure group without being exploited; and (3) the idea that political coalitions can be sustained on a moral, friendly, sentimental basis; by appeals to conscience. (Carmichael and Hamilton, 1967:60).

Karenga (1982:59-60) states in regards to the first misconception that there is some confusion among blacks between alliance and coalition. Alliance is a long-term ongoing unity based on common interests and common basic principles, whereas a coalition is a short-term working association based on specific short-term goals. Failure to make and observe this basic distinction has created situations in which Blacks have assumed too much about their relationship with their more powerful coalition partners and left themselves vulnerable to joint actions not mutually beneficial and to withdrawal of expected support at crucial times. Simply because Blacks and Whites march together, or picket together, does not mean that they have formed an alliance.

In reference to the second myth, dealing with relations between super-ordinate and subordinate groups, Karenga argues that these arrangements constitute patronage politics. He cites the problems that Blacks encountered with Jewish and Democratic coalitions; coalitions which Blacks sought. The problem is, that by depending on patrons, Blacks cannot effectively penalize or reward these partners (Jews/Democrats) in any significant way to compel compliance. The Jewish withdrawal of support from SNCC and CORE as they transformed into Black power structures and their opposition to affirmative action are examples of the disenchantment and disengagement without penalty from coalition partners. So is the Democratic Party's unwillingness to support fully Black social justice and social welfare goals under Carter and their unwillingness and inability to produce under Reagan (Karenga, 1982:255).

Regarding the idea that meaningful coalitions may be formed out of altruistic motivations, Carmichael and Hamilton adamantly reject any selfless pretensions by dominant groups. These authors, following the lead of Hobbs, see individuals and groups as power seekers. Their position is summarized below:

We believe that political relations are based on self-interest; benefits to be gained and losses to be avoided. For the most part, man's politics is determined by his evaluation of material good and evil. Politics results from a conflict of interests, not of consciences. (Carmichael and Hamilton, 1967:75).

Another Black scholar who is skeptical of biracial coalitions involving Blacks and Whites is Manning Marable, a widely read political activist. Marable sees coalitions as detrimental to the Black masses; he states, "In almost every instance in Afro-American history, black-white coalitions evolved gradually into entities which expressed the central concerns of the white majority, abandoning the needs of the black masses and leadership" (Marable, 1981:178). Although he opposes biracial coalitions, he does support "common programs." His views are articulated below:

"What we must do in the 1980s is struggle together, along parallel lines of development, finding those points within our own agendas that promote common work across the barriers of race, ethnicity, sexuality and income groups, and have the courage to enter into joint work, without illusions, without false promises, and without immediate revolutionary expectations" (Manning, 1981:178).

Critics of Black-White coalitions suggest that White Americans can not truely emphathize with the plight of the Black masses. These critics wonder if Whites can be trusted to assume an egalitarian stance toward Blacks -- few Americans transcend our racist socialization process. The pervasiveness of structural and individual racism makes it difficult for Whites to see Blacks as equals -- this is as true of White progressives as it is of White conservatives!

Poison Or Panacea?

Historically, Blacks have formed coalitions with Whites for less than ideal reasons. Ideally, comparable groups with complimentary interests would coalesce; the union would be mutually beneficial -- this is a rarity in Black-White coalitions. American Blacks have always lacked real political and economic power, therefore their coalitions with Whites have resulted in a pattern of superordination and subordination, with Blacks occupying the inferior role. In these cases, Blacks must sacrifice too much. When the dominant group exploits its superior position, under the guise of improving the status of the minority group, coalitions are poison.

Senator Brooke was wrong, Afro-Americans should not spend their time, energies, and monies trying to befriend Whites; we have more important tasks. Blacks must address the problems that confront our communities -- unwanted teenage pregnancies, Black-on-Black crime, drug abuse, school truancy, and rising suicide rates. We have already invested too much time in trying to cultivate friendships with White Americans. We do not need "buddies" we need jobs, and this will only be accomplished through concerted protest by a united Black community. First, we unite to solve our problems, then we must maintain this unity and address broader, but equally important issues such as the systematic denial of economic and legal rights to Blacks.

It matters little that coalitions have led to the democratization of the Democratic Party (and I am not certain that this is true) when the White House is controlled by a clone of Woodrow Wilson. The pendulum has swung, the nation embraces the worst kind of conservatism. Is this a good time to form coalitions? In the past, when Blacks faced hostile federal administrations and naive average White Americans, we started, in fits of desperation, searching for White allies. In these cases, coalitions were poison.

Coalitions should be categorically avoided in favor of Common Programs. Blacks should only consider short-term relations with Whites; long-term alliances are impractical because Afro-Americans have

187

a unique history, and unique goals and needs. Whites must be screened to make sure that common programs are not infested by well-meaning but plastic liberals. Black interests are often the antithesis of White interests, therefore Blacks who share a common program with Whites must demand parity, if not superiority, in leadership positions. In many instances, we do not need assistance from Whites, and we do not need Blacks who think we do. Whites must understand that their assistance is not a godsend -- indeed, patronizing Whites are as detrimental to our needs as are rednecks from southern Indiana.

Many Blacks have viewed biracial coalitions as a panacea, because they saw integration as a panacea. Integration has created more problems than it solved. Our children are not being educated. We can not afford to eat in integrated restaurants. Besides, only welfare lines, unemployment lines, and prisons are integrated. We bought the idea of integration, and we made a mistake. The mistakes must stop. The Black community must be organized, and the pathologies which dominate our communities must be addressed; we can do this ourselves. The only panacea that we have ever known is self-help.

REFERENCES

Carmichael, Stokely and Charles V. Hamilton
   1967   BLACK POWER. New York: Vintage Books.

Karenga, M.
   1982   INTRODUCTION TO BLACK STUDIES. Inglewood, California.

Littleton, Arthur C. and Mary W. Burger
   1971   BLACK VIEWPOINTS. New York: New American Library.

Marable, Manning
   1981   BLACKWATER, Dayton, Ohio: Black Praxis Press.

Morris, M.D.
   1975   THE POLITICS OF BLACK AMERICA. New York: Harper & Row Publishers.

Nelson, Willie
   1983   "Blacks In Coalition Politics," Unpublished classroom lecture at The Ohio State University, Columbus, Ohio.

Rustin, Bayard
   1964   "From Protest to Politics: The Future of the Civil Rights Movement." COMMENTARY. (February). XXXIX, pp. 25-31.

I became painfully aware that merely being born in a group, does not necessarily make one possessed of complete knowledge concerning it.

W. E. B. DuBois
AUTOBIOGRAPHY, 1964

CHAPTER FOURTEEN

AN ANALYSIS OF TRENDS IN BLACK POLITICS: THE SEARCH FOR AN ACCEPTABLE FRAMEWORK

James F. Barnes and James N. Upton

The purpose of this paper is to provide a brief analysis of the current condition, or status, of black politics, and to suggest some areas of concern for further research and evaluation. Our thesis is that black political strength can only be understood and improved within the context of the heterogeneous black community. In order to provide a framework for our analysis, we have constructed three categories of black political activity. We do not presume that these categories are exclusive or absolute. We have found them helpful to us in giving some conceptual order and clarity to our interest in black politics and our effort to formulate our ideas about basic political relationships:

Category #1: **Electoral Politics**

  a) electing mayors, councils, congressmen, judges (state and local)

  b) influencing party platforms, conventions, caucuses, etc.

  c) third party candidatures, Mississippi Freedom Party

  d) Black Panther Party

Category #2: **Civil Rights and/or Civic Organizations**

  a) Niagara Movement, NAACP

  b) Garvey Movement

  c) Urban League

190

d) CORE, SNCC, SCLC

e) Black Muslims

f) Churches, Masons, Fraternal, Sororal groups

Category #3: **Policy Process Orientation**

a) efforts to influence executive policy process (local, state, national)

b) legislative lobbying (local, state, national)

c) federal court system: appointments, bringing of cases (NAACP)

Collectively, these categories represent the sum total of black politics, from a historical and contemporary point of view. Individually, each category represents a different emphasis and strategy for the achievement of black political goals. It is obvious that there is a substantial degree of overlapping among the categories. For example, the NAACP is involved in both voter registration projects and court cases involving a broad range of "legal" issues. Was the Black Panther Party a political party in the traditional sense? Are the Black Muslims a political or a-political group? These are not questions that should be ignored, but our purpose is to demonstrate a point, and the further refinement of these categories is not essential to that task.

An analysis of these categories reveals that black politics has, from the beginning, reflected an extensive range of organizational forms, outlooks and strategies. The celebrated "debate" between Booker T. Washington and W.E.B. DuBois demonstrates this fact. Further, in the ante-bellum period, debates among emigrationists and "citizens" reflected a basic difference in attitude and strategy within black communities.[1] The recent ideological clashes between black nationalists and black Reaganites suggests the continuation of diverse philosophies and political strategies in the heterogeneous black community.

Each of the categories of black political activity have explicit, and, perhaps, inherent limitations. In part, these limitations derive from the character of American politics and from a number of historical factors that have shaped the contemporary black community.

It is often noted that American politics are centrist, i.e., pressures exist within the political system that tend to force issues and personalities toward the middle of the ideological spectrum. That American

191

politics are centrist is not accidental; electoral laws favor the dominant two-party division and quite clearly penalize and discourage splinter third pary candidatures. For example, the winner take-all requirement in most national, state and local elections impedes the ability of non-centrist candidates to achieve broad-based electoral support. While a system of proportional representation would offset this tendency, the emphasis on stability in American politics has been the historical winner.[2]

One consequence of this facet of the electoral system has been the development of highly pragmatic political parties, exceptionally willing and able to absorb ideas and personalities into the pattern of two-party politics and rejecting those issues and personalities perceived as constituting a threat to the rules of the game, or the game itself. "McCarthyism" speaks to this point, and it is conventional wisdom in American politics that the losses of Barry Goldwater and George McGovern exemplify the rule of thumb that candidates must at least appear to be of the middle if electoral victory is the goal.

If the centrist description of American politics is accurate, there are significant consequences for black communities that we feel require prolonged thought and discussion.

It is noteworthy that the majority of elected politicians, including those elected by many black communities, differ little in outlook and perception on the major substantive issues of American politics. Whether this is good or bad is not the critical point. What is important is an assessment of whether or not this pattern of legislative behavior is in fact, representative and reflective of the interests and needs of black constituents and, more fundamentally, if any other pattern of voting behavior could be reasonably expected given the constricted ideological parameters that influence the conduct of American politics. Those politicians who aspire to party support must respond to organizational pressures; most who pass the litmus test of the party primary will themselves reflect the centrist pressures.

As there are rules in the electoral game, there are formal and informal norms which apply to organizational politics and efforts to influence the policy process. Lobbying requires money and a persistence that derives from stable organizational and community support. It is, in the legislative arena, for example, difficult for black organizations to compete with the larger nationally funded lobbies which dominate the congressional discussions on domestic spending, taxes, health care and military spending. Moreover, the courts, historically pivotal in the Civil Rights battles, can change dramatically as the personnel and philosophies of the legal system change in response to shifting economic and political moods. The "liberalism" of the Warren Court has been edged aside by the weight of Nixon and Reagan appointees on the Supreme Court. At one level of analysis, these situations are simply reflections of the minority status of blacks in American society. It may also speak to the inability of the black community to focus its energies and imagination on the development of a stronger basis for political influence.

In this sense, there is pressure on the structure and policy process activities of black organizations similar to that which operates in the electoral system. The substance and tone of politics is established by the dominant political groups, and as a minority, blacks must become attuned or suffer the drastic consequences of intellectual and political inflexibility.

It should be understood that black Americans are clearly handicapped in exerting political pressures by being a large population that is geographically and ideologically dispersed. The black community is not a monolith; in fact, it has many, often conflicting, interests and rarely reflects common goals or consensus on a range of major issues. Blacks are Maoists, nationalists, Republicans, Democrats, Socialists, proletarians and aspiring members of the bourgeoisie. One result of these differences has been a propensity for intra-community conflict, and the absence of a broad-based structure of support for candidates or issues. While this fact distresses many, our position is that it is merely a sign of diversity and, perhaps, a source of potential strength. It is unreasonable to expect that a minority as large and diverse as the black population would share a common outlook; it is more fruitful to view black communities as a plurality of views and outlooks, which, if channeled toward proximate solutions, might provide a framework for communal action.

It is from this background of reflections that we propose to discuss the idea of participation, or citizen action, as a significant and often overlooked dimension of black politics.

Participation has long been regarded as a basic component of democratic ideals. Indeed, recent commitments on the part of the federal government (OEO Maximum Feasible Participation, Title I Advisory Councils, Early Childhood Education Councils, Mandated Court Councils, Blue Ribbon Advisory and Study Commissions, Neighborhood Planning Units, etc.) to study and promote organizational participation seems to imply that participation is something desirable and valued. The Civil Rights Movement, the Womens Movement and the labor movement have served to heighten public consciousness about sectors of our society traditionally excluded from institutionalized participatory channels. In a broad sense, the rise of these social movements have had an impact on the entire process of social scientific inquiry. The upheavals of the 1960's and 1970's set in motion a reexamination of existing social science paradigms that focused on questions of order, stability, and consensus. In the wake of political assassinations, urban riots, and student protests, social scientists could no longer afford to take for granted models of social reality that excluded the dynamics of conflict, power and change. Indeed, today it is impossible to escape noticing aspects of social reality that were invisible to social scientists decades ago.[3]

Our assumptions about the significance of the participation model of political activity are the result of both its theoretical and "practical" attractiveness. Democracy, as both Plato and Montesquieu have reminded us, is a difficult proposition in large, complex heterogeneous societies. We know, often instinctively, that human existence assumes meaningful and manageable proportions within relatively small social units. A major contemporary issue is the impersonality and engendered hostilities of large bureaucratically controlled cities as opposed to the intimacy of smaller communities. It is the neighborhood community that should loom large in any analysis of future political alternatives. In addition to the theoretical attractiveness of specifying the community as our organizational model, the idea of practicality makes a compelling companion.

People **exist** at the level of local neighborhoods and communities. State and national residence is, after all, an abstraction. While it is apparent that we share local, state and national citizenship, our daily lives are essentially local and are, in many ways, the totality of existence. One's daily life is bound primarily to an array of local experiences which are the most common source of one's habitual joys and frustrations. It is imperative that we approach the effort to strengthen the basic structure of communal relationships as the central focus of black politics. Community organization and participation are too often described as something to do when all else has failed. This is a fundamental error. Political power is a consequence of community strength, not its source. To the extent that black neighborhoods and communities have been crippled by the pathologies of urban life and victimized by the policy-makers who have favored suburban over urban interests, the **basis** of political power and the potential for political influence and effectiveness have been eroded.

To focus on neighborhoods and communities also brings conceptual and ideological clarity. Blacks must dominate their local communities before they seek macro level change. This is not, as critics might suggest, setting one's sights too low. It is, rather, an effort to promote the realization that democracy is ultimately a bottoms-up process; its fulfillment requires the creation or revitalization of social units whose health and vitality lead to influence and change.

Our image of participation is effectively presented in this passage from Richard Harris:

> ...In New York City today, for example, there are more than ten thousand block associations run by local residents, and there are hundreds of other community self-help organizations. There are auxiliary fire and police departments, ambulance corps, school-crossing guards, senior-citizen "helpers," night-school tutors, musicians performing in settlement houses, English-and-Spanish-speaking teachers helping Hispanic newcomers learn enough English to find jobs and enroll in schools, "block-watchers" who report trouble to local police precincts, "green guerillas" who plant and care for trees and gardens on their blocks, "foster-grand-parents" who serve as babysitters at nonprofit daycare centers, and a multitude of other kinds of volunteers ... [4]

To recognize that community vitality is the key to political influence is not to suggest that efforts to influence the policy process or engage in the electoral process are futile or undesirable. One is dependent on the other. Legislators must be elected to secure the funds and assistance required for community enhancement -- education, day care facilities, employment -- and should be evaluated on their records and not on their campaign rhetoric. The legal struggles must be continued and a wide, disparate range of "ideologies" should be accommodated and judged on the basis of their contribution to the development of stable, healthy communities.

It is also clear that the participatory base must be broadened to include a wider range of national and international issues and concerns; the conflict about economic development and conservation is one that should engage black attention. Blacks must again confront the issue of alliances and coalitions. Many problems are too often perceived as of little interest to black people. For example, the rising tide of tax reduction leading inevitably to reductions in essential community services must be carefully examined and discussed by those who publish newspapers, by the neighborhood clubs and organizations, teachers, union members, etc.

It is clear that there is a crisis of community in American life, this is especially true regarding the black community. The rapid pace of industrialization and urbanization have produced intense stresses and strains within traditional social units. The cohesiveness of communities and neighborhoods has been jeopardized by both the rapidity and scope of social change.[5] It is within this context that participation assumes its importance and significance. Communal institutions are the bases for positive social changes. While institutions must themselves change, they must evolve in a manner that promotes continuity and cohesion. The rapid deterioration of America's major cities is, quite fundamentally, a result of the erosion of viable communities. The pathologies of urban life -- crime, drugs, etc. -- are the consequences of deterioration, not its cause. A renewal of focus on the importance of community and community participation is both a prerequisite for black politics and its most significant goal.

Our three descriptive categories now become mutually supportive strategies. None is better than the others. What becomes critical are measures of performance, development of strategies, and the sophistication of those who seek to influence the allocation of rewards. This will enable scholars to compare and contrast the strategies of black Reaganites and black Nationalists as they vie for dominance in the black community.

Throughout the political and economic debates of the 19th and 20th centuries, black Americans have often maintained a skeptical distance; often wishing that the world around them would disappear. This is a viewpoint that is understandable, yet clearly not conducive to the obtainment of collective and individual goals. Despite the persistence of individual and institutional racism, the black community must continue to lead the struggle for the political, economic, and social equality of its members.

To focus on community development and strength is the only future for black politics; and one should not need to be reminded that this is in the tradition of **both** Washington and DuBois.

FOOTNOTES

1. See discussion in Howard Brotz, editor, NEGRO SOCIAL AND POLITICAL THOUGHT 1850-1920 (New York: Basic Books, 1966) pp. 1-37.

2. This issue is throughly discussed in Piven and Cloward, POOR PEOPLE'S MOVEMENTS (New York: Pantheon Books, 1977).

3. The extensive literature on Urban Violence is illustrative; e.g., Michael Lipsky, "Protest as a Political Resource," APSR. vol. 62, No. 1, pp. 1145-58; Bachrach and Baratz, POWER AND POVERTY: THEORY AND PRACTICE (New York: Oxford, 1970).

4. Richard Harris, "A Nice Place To Live," THE NEW YORKER, April 25, 1977.

5. An excellent analysis is provided by Kenneth Clark's DARK GHETTO: DILEMMAS OF SOCIAL POWER (New York: Harper and Row, 1965).

We have seen -- Merciful God! in these wild days and in the name of civilization, justice, and motherhood -- what have we not seen, right here in America, of orgy, cruelty, barbarism, and murder done to men and women of Negro descent.

W. E. B. DuBois
DARKWATER, 1920

CHAPTER FIFTEEN

ON THE RESURGENCE OF THE KU KLUX KLAN: A THEORY OF SCHADENFREUDEN SOCIALIZATION

David Pilgrim

Most Americans regard the Ku Klux Klan as a nuisance -- a pesky relic of racial bigotry and jingoism. Klansmen are viewed as illiterate, rural rednecks who are trapped in a time warp -- unable and unwilling to embrace the social changes wrought by the turbulence of the last two decades. Implicit in this characterization is the dangerous assumption that the Klan is an insignificant body which can and should be ignored. An analysis of the life-cycle of this organization reveals periods of widespread popularity followed by a general decline and then a period of resurgence. The dominance of conservative ideologies at the national level, the abandonment of affirmative action programs at the state and county levels, and the general belief among many whites that too much time, energy, and money have been devoted to civil rights, suggests that the conditions are ripe for a resurgence of the Ku Klux Klan.

The purpose of this paper is two-fold: to analyze the history of the Klan in America, and to present an original theoreticai framework to account for their existence and persistence.

The data used in this paper were derived from newspapers, magazines, pamphlets, brochures, and historical documents. These data, used to analyze the Klan's membership rates, organizational formats, recruitment techniques, political tactics, and racial ideologies, are presented in four periods: 1865-1871, 1915-1930, 1954-1974, and 1975-present.

1865-1871

On Christmas Eve 1865, in Pulaski, Tennessee, six bored ex-Confederate officers formed a fraternity. For a title, they took the Greek word for cycle, **kyklos,** appended the word **klan** for the Scottish clans from which they were descended, and derived Ku Klux Klan (King, 1980:38). For a symbol, they chose the burning cross.

Armed with mystical pretensions and youthful tomfoolery, they created an "Invisible Empire," populated with Halloweenish characters: wizards, dragons, hydras, furies, goblins, and so forth. After developing an elaborate initiation rite, the newly formed Klan celebrated with midnight gallops through Pulaski. During these late night escapades, the youths and their horses were adorned with robes and hoods made from bedsheets and pillowcases. Alcohol, homemade and store-bought, was a regular companion on these joyrides.

Most historians claim that the Klan's progression from a rowdy collegiate-like fraternity to a white supremacist vigilante organization was accelerated by a serendipitous finding: their ghastly appearance frightened superstitious blacks (Chalmers, 1965:9; Johnsen, 1923:20; King, 1980;38). It should be mentioned that white historians overestimated the presence of superstitious fears in the black community. Granted, the Klan, in an effort to frighten blacks, carried human and animal skulls with coals of fire for eyes and they rattled sacks of animal bones, but the fear experienced by blacks had its roots in objective reality.

Within a few months, racial violence replaced youthful pranks as the Klan's raison d'etre. Drunken night riders threatened, raped, flogged, mutilated, shot, stabbed, burned, and lynched blacks. In most instances, the victims were chosen at random -- all blacks that crossed the paths of roving Klansmen were fair game. Scores of whites, anxious to join the fun, established Klan chapters throughout the South.

Klan membership increased drastically but many of the later chapters (klaverns) were undisciplined and only loosely aligned with the mother-klan in Pulaski (Chalmers, 1965:6). Mobs of whites, representing a cross section of the white southern population, engaged in wanton violence against the freedmen and whites from the North. In theory, individual klaverns were governed by rigid rules but in practice each was an autonomous body, thus, bands of whites, all claiming to be Klansmen, were free to administer justice in any way they deemed proper. To rectify this situation, a Klan Continental Congress convened in April of 1867 in Nashville, Tennessee.

The delegates, drawn from southern and border states, created a constitution, a more sophisticated organizational format, and a political platform. With much discussion of unity of purpose, concert of action, proper limits, and authority to the prudent, the delegates laid the foundations for a century of organized terrorism.

The first constitution of the Klan, similar in form and content to those of the White Camelia, the White Brotherhood, the Pale Faces, and other white supremacist organizations, stressed religious fundamentalism, political conservatism, and blatant racism. Walter Fleming, a Vanderbilt University historian who sympathized with the goals and methods of the Klan, summarized their constitution as follows:

> To protect and succor the weak and unfortunate, especially the widows and orphans of Confederate soldiers; to protect members of the white race in life, honor and property from the encroachment of the blacks; to oppose the Radical Republican Party and the Union League; to defend constitutional liberty, to prevent usurpation, to emancipate the whites, maintain peace and order, the laws of God, the principles of 1776 and the political and social supremacy of the white race -- in short, to oppose African influence in government and society and to prevent any intermingling of the races (Lester and Wilson, 1905:198).

The delegates selected ex-Confederate General Nathan Bedford Forrest as the first Imperial Wizard (sometimes called Grand Wizard). Forrest ruled the Invisible Empire which consisted of all southern states. A Grand Dragon presided over each state (realm), and each county (province) was under the leadership of a Grand Giant. The Grand Titan ruled a group of counties (dominion), and local chapters (dens) were headed by Grand Cyclops. Staff officers included Genies, Furies, Magi, Hydras, Goblins, Night Hawks, Turks and Monks. Fittingly, individual Klansmen were labeled Ghouls (Johnsen, 1923:21).

Under the guidance of Imperial Wizard Forrest, wanton violence was replaced by instrumental aggression -- that is, behaviors that are intended to injure others also produces real benefits to the offender (Blalock, 1982:52). Fearing the loss of white supremacy, Klansmen terrorized black people who attempted to exercise their rights as citizens. The Klan's DEAD BOOKS were "hit lists" which contained the names of blacks and whites (usually Radical Republicans) who opposed white supremacy. Black community and civic leaders and white school teachers figured prominently in these "death catalogues." The Klan beat and killed blacks who gained land and prospered, or made speeches, or talked about social and political equality. It was not uncommon for klansmen to march in public with coffins marked for their enemies (Johnson: 1968:127). Further, it was not rare for these coffins to be filled soon after the demonstrations.

By 1868 Klan membership exceeded 550,000 but internal strife and negative publicity threatened the stability of the organization. The widespread beatings, lynchings and mutilations of black militiamen, civic leaders, and white Radical Republicans, earned the Klan notoriety and considerable condemnation (Halsey, 1984:2). In January of 1869, Imperial Wizard Forrest, fearing anarchy within the Invisible Empire, ordered the dissolution of the Klan and the destruction of its records. Most Klan chapters obeyed their "national" leader but a few local dens refused to follow his instructions. This situation was addressed by the United States Congress in 1871-1872. The congressmen passed several laws intended to abolish the Klan; several hundred arrests were made and several convictions of influential Klansmen followed, thus, the Klan was forced underground.

1915-1930

The Klan lay dormant for four decades. The Reconstruction era had failed and whites were confident that the racial caste system would endure (Stampp, 1965:214). The Klan was not needed because the Klan mentality permeated every American institution. Blacks, already a propertyless peasantry, were subjected to de facto and de jure segregation; social and economic segregation gave them inferior schools and jobs; political disenfranchisement kept blacks out of political offices and polling booths; and a pattern of race etiquette made **all** blacks subordinate to **all** whites. To support this apartheid system, whites employed systematic and random violence against blacks. For example, in the decade 1890-1899 an average of two blacks a week were lynched in America. From 1882 to 1938 the number of black lynchings totaled 3,397 (Lincoln, 1968:139). The robes and hoods were in the cleaners, but the Klan mentality was in the streets.

The Klan's rebirth was paved by Thomas Dixon, Jr.'s book, THE CLANS-MAN, which romanticized the Klan as a Christian crusade led by noble gentlemen (TIME, 1965:24), and D. W. Griffith's 1914 film, THE BIRTH OF A NATION, a racist movie which received national legitimacy when President Woodrow Wilson forced his cabinet to view the film. The film, which sold out theaters in every state, glorified the Klan and exacerbated racial problems.

William Joseph Simmons, an itinerant Methodist preacher who watched the film a dozen times, felt divinely inspired to resurrect the Klan. After Simmons was dismissed from the Methodist Church, because he was "mentally inefficient and morally delinquent" (Fuller, 1925:26), he became a fraternalist. The opportunistic ex-preacher recognized the financial possibilities inherent in a revival of the Klan. Copying liberally from the rituals of the original Klan, he produced a 54-page pamphlet "Holy Book," the KLORAN. He then copyrighted the KLORAN and therefore established himself as the lawful owner of the Klan (Jackson, 1967:6). In his own words: "I was its sole parent, author and founder; it was my creation -- my child, if you please, my first born (Simmons, 1926:66).

Simmons' "first born", chartered as a legitimate fraternal organization by the state of Georgia, was purposely similar to the original Klan in terms of objectives and tactics. This fact is evident by the following excerpt from an Imperial Proclamation signed by the Imperial Wizard:

> In this we invite all men who can qualify to become citizens of the Invisible Empire to approach the portal of our beneficent domain and join us in our noble work of extending its boundaries; in disseminating the gospel of "Klankraft," thereby encouraging, conserving, protecting and making vital the fraternal human relationship in the practice of a wholesome clanishness; to share with us the glory of performing the sacred duty of protecting womanhood; to maintain forever white supremacy in all things; to commemorate the holy and chivalric achievements of our fathers; to safeguard the sacred rights, exalted privileges and distinctive institutions of our Civil Government; to bless mankind, and to keep eternally ablaze the sacred fire of a fervent devotion to a pure Americanism (A B C OF THE KNIGHTS OF THE KU KLUX KLAN, 1916:8).

Simmons, in an effort to insure his permanent control of the organization, endowed his position with tremendous authority. He was responsible for the hiring and firing of national officers, the issuing and revoking of klavern charters, and, more importantly, the formulating of rituals and dogma. He divided his kingdom into eight domains, each consisting of a group of states. These domains were each governed by a grand goblin who, in reality, had only minimal power (Jackson, 1967:7). Simmons' reorganization of the Klan amounted to a dictatorship but it did not seem fatal in 1919 -- the Klan only had 3,000 members and appeared to be just another fraternity (U.S. Senate Committee on Privileges and Elections, 1924:422).

The Klan remained a small, relatively insignificant organization until 1920 when two enterprising promoters, Edward Young Clarke and Elizabeth Tyler, joined the fold. Sensing its financial as well as patriotic potentialities, they helped the Klan evolve into a multi-xenophobic organization in which southern and eastern European Catholics and Jews, Orientals, as well as Blacks, were seen as threats to the American character (Parrillo, 1985:324). The American public was fertile ground for a "100 percent American" movement as evidenced by the meteoric growth of the Klan after it adopted the violent anti-alien stance.

By 1921 the Klan had grown to over five hundred thousand paid members and each week thousands of new members and klaverns were added to the Invisible Empire. Much of the growth resulted from the presence of two hundred zealous kleagles, (recruiters) who were paid on a commission basis. Individual kleagles, motivated by the four dollars of each recruit's ten-dollar initiation fee (klectoken) that was their reward for signing new members, accepted all white, Protestant native-born Americans including politicians, ministers, sociopaths, and terrorists.

Usually, kleagles approached local Protestant ministers and offered them free memberships and positions of authority in the organization -- often as kludds (chaplains). Thousands of ministers accepted the offer and thereby transformed segments of the Protestant Church into an arm of the Invisible Empire (Jackson, 1967:10). Most of the lecturers on the Klan circuit were ministers; indeed, hundreds of ministers left their churches for the "wider Klan calling" (Chalmers, 1965:35).

By 1922 the Klan had grown so rapidly that it dominated the politics in Atlanta, Dallas, Memphis, Knoxville, Tulsa, Mobile, Detroit and Indianapolis. In addition, the Klan had made a significant attempt to undermine the democratic process in Chicago, San Francisco, Los Angeles, Louisville, Denver, Portland, Cincinnati, Dayton, and Columbus, Ohio. In these major urban areas Klan membership consisted of governors, state education officials, mayors, state and national congressmen, councilmen, police, and judges at every level (TIME, 1965:25). There is considerable evidence that Woodrow Wilson, Harry S. Truman, Warren G. Harding, Hugo Black, and Robert C. Byrd were all members of the Klan (King, 1980:38).

During its heyday, the Klan completely dominated the state governments in Ohio and Indiana (Taylor, 1927:329-331; Howson; 1951).
Indiana Grand Dragon David S. Stephenson, a fiery orator, made Indiana
the bastion of Klan activity in the nation. Stephenson, who claimed
to be the law in Indiana, was instrumental in the election of all winning
local candidates in the 1924 Indianapolis political campaign. His
bubble was burst in the spring of 1925 when he was arrested for the
rape and murder of his secretary (Chalmers, 1965:172). Before his
demise, Stephenson had expanded his klannishness into Ohio where
the state eventually reached an excess of two hundred thousand Klansmen (Jackson, 1967:164). His arrest and subsequent conviction undermined Klan morale in both states.

Between 1921 and 1924 "The Invisible Empire, Knights of the Ku
Klux Klan" was responsible for thousands of murders, beatings, burnings,
bombings, and rapes throughout the United States (Myers, 1943:230-33).
These terrorist acts were in stark contrast to the claims of moral
superiority emanating from the nation's klaverns (Kent, 1923:279).
For example, the following incidents represent only a fraction of
the violence meted out by Texas Klansmen during a four month period:

> March 15 -- J. Lafayette Cockrell, Houston, black dentist,
> "punished" by Klan for alleged association with white women.
> April 1 -- Alexander Johnson, Dallas, black bellboy, whipped
> and branded for alleged association with white women. May
> 21 -- Joseph J. Devere, Justice of the Peace, tarred and feathered
> for being lenient on blacks. June 17 -- James Collins, black
> vagabond, whipped and branded after grand jury had failed to
> indict him for annoying white women. July 16 -- Beulah Johnson,
> white woman, stripped, tarred and feathered for "looking" at
> black men (Shepherd, 1921:329-31).

The violence which occurred in Dallas was not atypical. Klan floggings
exceeded 2,500 in 1923 in Oklahoma, Indiana, and Georgia (Katz,
1967:397). The Klan had grown to a membership of five million and
these eager knights were wrecking havoc in Black, Jewish, and Catholic
communities.

The Klan's growth and popularity was halted in 1924 when it became
apparent that Klan leaders were guilty of graft and other corruption.
Simmons, discovered as a chronic alcoholic and poor administrator,
had been replaced by Hiram Wesley Evans, the Exalted Cyclops of
the Dallas Klan. Simmons, desiring his former authority, began an
infelicitous campaign against the new Imperial Wizard. The internal

strife resulted in organizational anomie and the loss of members. In addition, public sentiment turned against Klan violence and most cities passed anti-Klan laws. Remarkably, membership had plummeted to no more than 30,000 by 1930 (King, 1980:38). Sporadic Klan violence continued into the 1940's but the glory days were over.

1954-1974

On May 17, 1954, the Supreme Court, in the case of BROWN V. BOARD OF EDUCATION OF TOPEKA, KANSAS, ruled that segregated schools were unconstitutional. The following year the Supreme Court handed down its implementing decree and panic swept the nation, especially in southern and border states. Racial violence occurred each time blacks arrived at "white" schools. In some cases, state governments orchestrated the resistance to the court order thereby inviting government intervention. Race relations between blacks and whites retrogressed from a veneer of peaceful coexistence to blatant and vicious antagonism and conflict. It is an understatement that the climate of mounting tension and mass hysteria was conducive to a resurgence of the Ku Klux Klan.

Unlike its predecessors, the new Klan was not a monolithic organization, rather, it consisted of at least twenty splinter groups each claiming to be the heir apparent to the Klans of Forrest and Simmons. The proliferation of independent Klans led W. J. Griffin, the self-proclaimed Grand Dragon of the Associated Florida Ku Klux Klan, to complain: "We have too many chiefs and not enough Indians to stage a war dance. The old countersign and password won't work because klansmen are strangers to each other" (Vander Zanden, 1973:292).

In 1961 many of these splinter organizations merged and formed the United Klans of America. Robert Shelton, a friend of Alabama governors John Patterson and George Wallace, was selected to serve as Imperial Wizard. Under his governance, the Klan exceeded the violence of their forefathers. The major tactical change was the emphasis placed on gorilla warfare.

Between 1954 and 1967, Klansmen were suspected of over 200 separate bombings. Favorite targets for "bomb parties" were black churches and schools, and the homes and offices of civil rights workers. There were at least 60 black churches bombed in Mississippi and Alabama during this period; the bombings were sanctioned by the Imperial Wizard (Patterson, 1963:8-11). Shelton applauded the murders of

205

three civil rights workers in Mississippi, the assassinations of Medgar Evers and Viola Liuzzo, and the bomding murders of four black girls in a Birmingham church. He held parades, rallies, and banquets to honor the assailants and raise funds for their legal expenses (Upton, 1983:12).

During the height of the Civil Rights Movement membership in the Klan soared. In 1967 the Anti-Defamation League of B'nai B'rith reported that Klan membership reached 55,000 nationwide and was growing at a rate of 5,000 - 10,000 annually. The states with the largest concentrations of Klansmen were: Georgia, 16,280; Alabama, 12,400; North Carolina, 9,800; Virginia, 5,000; Mississippi, 3,090; Louisiana and South Carolina, 1,600 each (CHRISTIAN CENTURY, 1967:1484).

In the mid-sixties the Klan enjoyed widespread public support; conserva- tively, an estimated 6 million Americans sympathized with the goals of the Klan and many gave financial support to the organization (Upton, 1983:3). In addition, the Klan numbered mayors, police sheriffs, judges, ministers, education officials, business leaders and congressmen among its members and supporters. Apparently, many white gate-keepers found the goals of the Klan palatable; these objectives are summarized below:

> To maintain white supremacy by any means necessary; to protect the purity of white women from raping blacks; to rid the nation of aliens, especially demonic Jews and Communist atheists; to fight integration and other communist plots against 100 percent Americans; to defend the principles of the Constitution against agitators within and without; and to make sure that America remains a God-fearing and God-directed nation (Klan handout, 1968).

In the late sixties and early seventies the Klan's popularity began to diminish. This decline was prompted by several Federal investiga- tions and mass media portrayals of blacks being beaten by policemen and attacked by their dogs. Klan members, fearful of imprisonment, left the ghoulish fold. And for a brief period, the nation's white major- ity sympathized with the plight of Black Americans. By 1974 the F.B.I. estimated the active Klan membership at 1,500, it was probably an inaccurate assessment but the Klan was decreasing each week (King, 1980:38).

1975 - Present

Since the late seventies the Klan has made a modest comeback. Spurred by the white backlash against affirmative action and bussing, the Klan has seized the moment and awakened from its short hibernation. Like their immediate predecessors, the modern Klan consists of numerous distinct organizations, and the vast majority were founded after 1975. These new Klan organizations have added several wrinkles to the gospel of bigotry.

David Duke, a graduate of Louisiana State University, founded the Knights of the Ku Klux Klan in 1975. Publicized as the "Klansman in the three-piece suit", the charismatic Duke claims to have made more than 200 appearances on college campuses and on radio and television talk shows. His Ivy League image is attractive to middle class professionals. His former faculty adviser stated: "I used to dismiss the Klan as a bunch of service station dropouts. I take it seriously now. Duke is giving the Klan a white-shirt-and-tie image. He's appealing to the middle class and tapping their frustrations" (Williams, et al., 1977:45). Duke, who has taken his racist gospel to several foreign countries, stated: "White people today are facing more massive racial discrimination than the blacks ever faced. We are the only group standing up for whites in this country" (Upton, 1983:13).

Duke left the organization after a rival Klan leader, Bill Wilkinson, photographed and tape recorded him trying to sell his membership lists. Undaunted, Duke left the Klan and created the National Association for the Advancement of White People, a racist organization modeled after the Third Reich (King, 1980:39-40).

Wilkinson, national leader of the Invisible Empire, Knights of the Ku Klux Klan, ascended to the Klan throne after Duke retreated. Wilkinson's Klan is regarded by the F.B.I. as the most militaristic and violence-prone of the "national" Klans. According to Wilkinson: "Niggers are the dregs of society, lacking any culture, history and purpose. Niggers are parasites sucking the blood of God-fearing white folks" (Upton, 1983:7). He attracted national attention by attending President's Carter's home church dressed in Klan regalia; he has maintained his national image by advocating the killing of black "agitators".

The F.B.I. tabulates fourteen separate klans but some observers claim as many as forty-two. James Venable claims to have over 250,000 members in his National Knights of the Ku Klux Klan. The F.B.I.

refutes this claim but concedes that Klan membership is increasing, and the new converts are inclined to use violence. In addition, Nazi organizations are flourishing in Michigan, Indiana, California, Connecticut, Missouri, and Colorado.

Today, Klan violence falls into four categories: campaigns of terror, episodic group terrorism, episodic individual terrorism, and random individual terrorism. The first situation occurs when Klansmen attempt to dominate an entire community. For example, for two weeks in 1979, Klansmen patrolled the streets of Decatur, Alabama abducting and beating blacks. Throughout the nightmare local police officials refused to intervene. Many of the participants in this reign of terror were "soldiers" at a nearby Klan paramilitary camp. The camp, tacklessly named, My Lai, is supervised by former Green Berets like "Toney" who remarked: "I'd gladly kill blacks, police or the Army because I believe in the white race and this is the way it's going to be before it's all over" (Williams and Dunnavant, 1980:52).

Episodic group terrorism occurs when a large number of Klansmen and their supporters commit isolated acts of violence. For example, in May 1981, in Nashville, Tennessee, a group of Klansmen were arrested before they could bomb a Jewish synagogue. A similar situation occurred in December 1984 in Montgomery, Alabama. Between 15-20 youthful Klansmen were arrested for conspiracy to bomb black protesters (Harmon, 1984:2A).

The most common form of Klan violence is episodic individual terrorism. In these instances Klansmen, with or without permission from their superiors, engage in isolated acts of violence. For example, in Michigan, a Klan leader was arrested after bombing school buses in Pontiac (Upton, 1983:12). Klan psychopaths who shoot into the homes of interracial couples, black politicians and others fit into this category.

The most appalling and irrational of all Klan violence is random individual terrorism. In these cases Klansmen search the streets for a black person and brutally beat, disfigure, or kill the unfortunate victim. For example, in March 1981, two Klansmen randomly chose a young black male to kill in Mobile, Alabama. They beat, castrated, strangled, and hung him from a tree. Neither Klansmen knew the victim (NEWSWEEK, 1984:30).

The new Klansmen are extremely violent and their venom is being spread into new horizons. Klansmen have created youth camps to socialize their offspring into the cult of hate. In addition, women are taking a more active role in Klan rallies, parades, meetings, and paramilitary camps. In addition, the new Klan has lifted its ban on Catholics and immigrants from the eastern and southern parts of Europe, it is moving toward a "united white front" (Morganthau, 1980:32; Keerdoja, 1980:12).

Sociological Theories

Much social scientific ink has been spilled debating the causes of the Klan's existence and persistence. These debates have produced numerous theories and pseudo-theories, namely, authoritarian personality, social change, social disorganization, frustration-aggression, projection, and economic exploitation (Kitano 1974:20-36; Blalock, 1982:10-24). While it is beyond the scope of this paper to critique these theories, it is the contention of this writer that a new theoretical framework is necessary to explain the Klan mentality. The rudiments of this theory, presented for the first time, are discussed at this juncture.

Schadenfreuden Socialization

A clue to the Klan's existence and persistence is found in the following social situations: unemployed steelworkers pay for the privilege of ridiculing human oddities employed as sideshow "freaks;" a dozen males watch as a terrified female is raped on a pool, table; a large crowd encourages a potential suicide victim to leap from a skyscraper; a crowd gathers to watch the victims removed from a burning house; and, thousands of persons, many of whom had just left Sunday morning services at their respective churches, assembles to watch the lynching of a black man accused of "disturbing" white women. The common thread that characterizes these social situations involves the theory of schadenfreuden socialization.

The basic assumption of this theory is that individuals derive pleasure from the misfortunes of others. The word **schadenfreuden** is derived from the German word **schaden** which means damaged or injured, and the Old High German word **frewida** which means happiness or pleasure. Therefore, schadenfreuden refers to the enjoyment obtained from the mishaps of others (WEBSTER'S THIRD NEW INTERNATIONAL DICTIONARY, 1966:2028). The offending party can either cause the mishap or just receive pleasure from its causation.

One simple explanation (maybe too unpretentious for academicians)

209

for the Klan mentality is that Klansmen are socialized to receive certain psychological gains from hating blacks, chief among these is the "pleasure" derived from "injuring" blacks. While it is widely believed that Klansmen gain feelings of superiority and enhanced status through their Klan membership, little sociological attention has been devoted to the mundane pleasure derived from participating, either actively or passively, in terrorist acts.

This oversight on the part of social scientists is puzzling given the voluminous amount of heinous crimes committed by Klansmen and their sympathizers. As shown in this paper, the Klan, since its inception in 1865, has advocated the brutal murder and dismemberment of blacks and other "aliens." The "personable" nature of Klan violence suggests that the perpetrators derived pleasure from their acts. Stated differently, sadistic acts like castrations, human burnings, lynchings, and "tar and feather parties," all require the offending party to witness the agony of the victim. Klansmen and others with the Klan mentality cheered when their executioners lynched or burned blacks. In the past, it was not uncommon for fundamentalist churches to shorten their weekly services so that the membership could "enjoy" lynchings.

The theory of schadenfreuden socialization explains the reluctance of arrested Klansmen to express remorse for their deeds. As children, Klansmen are taught that blacks are aliens who are deserving of pain and agony. Thus, the Klansman does not conceptualize violence against blacks as immoral, rather, these acts are seen as consistent with the laws of God. Addressing the issue of interracial marriages, a leader in a Klan paramilitary camp, remarked, "The Bible says that the penalty for a black and a white mating is death for both of them. We're going to put these people on a lifeboat and send'em back from where they came, and it's gonna be on a lifeboat because if they're not on it they're gonna be six feet under" (Halsey, 1984:2). Klansmen, young and old, are taught that racial violence and the "will of God" are synonymous.

The notion that Klansmen derive pleasure from their acts of terrorism is supported by the Klan's fascination with weapons. Klansmen rank as the most heavily-armed citizens in this country. They stockpile everything from small handguns to grenades to commercial versions of the Army's M-16 assault rifle (Morganthau and McGuire, 1980:32). One Klansman volunteered, "I've got a .22 over the door to my bedroom, a shotgun under the mattress, a .357 Magnum under the toilet bowl, a .44 under the sink and I've got 12 rifles in the trunk of my car. It seats six people, and there's six pistols under the seats" (Halsey, 1984:2).

Another Klansman remarked, "This rifle holds nine hollowpoint .357 Magnum rounds. A hollow-point hits you, it leaves a hole this big on the way out" (Halsey, 1984:2).

The Klan, recognizing the importance of the socialization process, distributes racist brochures and booklets to high school students which advocate a "get tough" policy against arrogant non-whites (Keerdoja, 1982:12). This literature graphically illustrates the ways that pencils, ink pens, and other school supplies may be used as weapons. The Klan has also begun recruiting a "tinymite" corps consisting of grade schoolers. Seven and eight year olds are taught the pleasures of hating blacks.

In recent years the Klan has become a family affair. Klansmen are encouraged to initiate their spouses and children into the organization. The participation of their parents in the Klan obviously impacts on the racial beliefs and attitudes of youths. A female Klansman remarked, "My children are proud of the fact that I'm out here (in a paramilitary camp), that I'm in the Klan. They think it's great." (Williams and Dunnavant, 1980:52). A Klansman who is proudly anti-semitic stated, "I'm educating my four kids. When they see a Jew on television, they remember him" (Halsey, 1984:2). A female Klansman stated, "I'm bringing up my kids in a Christian way. We don't associate with nigger children because I don't want my sons and daughters raped" (Upton, 1983:11).

It should be mentioned that many non-Klan families transmit racist values to their children. Children observe their parents interacting with minorities and model themselves after their interpretation of the nature of these interactions (Parrillo, 1985:68; Henslin, 1983:275-76). If their parents derive pleasure from oppressing blacks, children learn to dislike blacks and to perceive them negatively. A "retired" Klansmen remarked, "I became a racist because I grew up in the South, was taught to hate niggers, was taught that they were the enemy, and I was taught that they were trying to steal the white woman" (McConville, 1973:361).

Contrary to the claims of Klan historians and social scientists, the Klan is not a southern organization populated by "red-neck high school dropouts." The Klan is an American phenomenon and its membership rosters include a proportionate representation from every social class, region of residence, religious organization, and level of education. Klansmen are birthed, groomed, and tolerated within the bosom of American culture. As long as racism remains an important feature of the socialization process the Klan will continue to rise and mock Democracy. Social factors like wars, depressed economies, immigration patterns, and ideological shifts do not create the Klan, rather, they only add fertilizer to the racist seeds planted in the American socialization process.

REFERENCES

Anonymous
   1965   "The Various Shady Lives of the Ku Klux Klan." TIME
           MAGAZINE. 84 (April 9):24-5.

Anonymous
   1968   Klan handout announcing cross burnings and public demon-
           stration. Indianapolis, Indiana. 1 page.

Anonymous
   1967   "The Klan as Sympton." CHRISTIAN CENTURY. 84
           (November 22) 1484.

Anonymous
   1984   "A Death Sentence for a Klansman." NEWSWEEK. 103
           (February):30.

Blalock, Hubert M.
   1982   RACE AND ETHNIC RELATIONS. New Jersey: Prentice-
           Hall.

Chalmers, David M.
   1965   HOODED AMERICANISM: THE FIRST CENTURY OF
           THE KU KLUX KLAN. New York: Doubleday and Company.

Fuller, Irving Edgar
   1925   THE MAELSTROM: THE VISIBLE OF THE INVISIBLE
           EMPIRE. Denver, Colorado.

Gove, P.B. (editor)
   1966   WEBSTER'S THIRD NEW INTERNATIONAL DICTIONARY.
           Springfield, Mass.: G & C Merriam Company.

Halsey, Ashley
   1984   "It's time to go on the attack." CHICAGO TRIBUNE.
           September 12, Section 2, pp. 1-2.

Harmon, Rick
   1984   "Grand Jury to continue Klan probe." THE ALABAMA
           JOURNAL AND ADVERTISER. December 22, p. 2A.

Henslin, James M. and Donald W. Light
1983   SOCIAL PROBLEMS. New York: McGraw-Hill Book Company.

Howson, Embrey B.
1951   THE KU KLUX KLAN IN OHIO AFTER WORLD WAR I. Master's Thesis. Columbus, Ohio: The Ohio State University.

Jackson, Kenneth T.
1967   THE KU KLUX KLAN IN THE CITY 1915-1930. New York: Oxford University Press.

Johnsen, Julia E.
1923   KU KLUX KLAN. The Reference Shelf Series. New York: The H.W. Wilson Company.

Johnson, Willis
1968   They Said They Were Friends: 1871. In, CHRONICLES OF BLACK PROTEST. Edited by C. Eric Lincoln. New York: A Mentor Book.

Katz, William L.
1967   EYEWITNESS: THE NEGRO IN AMERICAN HISTORY. New York: Pitman Publishing Company.

Keerdoja, Eileen et al.,
1982   "The Klan's New Pitch to Youth." NEWSWEEK 99 (June 28): 12.

Kent, Frank R.
1923   "Ku Klux Klan In America." SPECTATOR. 130 (Feb.): 279-80.

King, Wayne
1980   "The Violent Rebirth of the Klan." NEW YORK TIMES MAGAZINE, December 7, pp. 37-40.

Kitano, Harry
1974   RACE RELATIONS. New Jersey: Prentice-Hall.

Lester, J.C. and D. L. Wilson
1905   KU KLUX KLAN: ITS ORIGIN, GROWTH AND DISBANDMENT. Introduction by Walter Fleming. New York: Neale.

Lincoln, C. Eric
1968   CHRONICLES OF BLACK PROTEST. New York: A Mentor Book.

Lipset, Seymour Martin
1965   "An Anatomy of the Klan." COMMENTARY. 40 (Oct.):74-82.

McConville, Edward
1973   "Portrait of a Klansman: The Prophetic Voice of C. P. Ellis." THE NATION. 217 (October 15):361-66.

Morganthau, Tom and Stryker McGuire
1980   "The Boy Scout Boot Camp". NEWSWEEK. 96 (December 15):32.

Myers, Gustavus
1943   HISTORY OF BIGOTRY. New York: Random House.

Parrillo, Vincent N.
1985   STRANGERS TO THESE SHORES. New York: John Wiley and Sons.

Patterson, Barbara
1963   "Defiance and Dynamite," NEW SOUTH. 18 (May):8-11.

Shepherd, William G.
1921   "A Nightgown Tyranny". LESLIE'S ILLUSTRATED WEEKLY. 133 (September 10):329-31.

Simmons, William Joseph
1926   AMERICA'S MENACE OR THE ENEMY WITHIN. Atlanta: Ku Klux Klan Press.

Simmons, William Joseph
1916   ABC OF THE KNIGHTS OF THE KU KLUX KLAN. Atlanta: Ku Klux Klan Press.

Stampp, Kenneth
1965   THE ERA OF RECONSTRUCTION: 1865-1877. New York: Vintage Books.

Taylor, Alva W.
1927   "What the Klan Did in Indiana." THE NEW REPUBLIC. LIII (November 16):330.

Upton, James N.
1983   "The Violence and Vitality of the Invisible Empire." Community Extension Center (Summer).

U.S. Senate, Committee on Privileges and Elections
1924   Senator from Texas: Hearings. 68th Congress, 1st and 2nd Sessions, p. 424.

Vander Zanden, James W.
1973   "The Klan Revival." In, SOCIAL MOVEMENTS: A reader
        and source book. Edited by Robert Evans. Chicago: Rand
        McNally College Publishing Company.

Williams, Dennis A.
1977   "The Great White Hope." NEWSWEEK. 90 (Nov. 14):45.

Williams Dennis A. and Bob Dunnavant
1980   "THE KKK Goes Military." NEWSWEEK. 96 (Oct.6):52.

CONTRIBUTORS

James F. Barnes is Chairperson, Department of Political Science, Ohio University, Athens, Ohio. From 1965 to 1967 he served as a political officer at the United States NATO delegation in Paris. He is co-author of THE WORLD OF POLITICS, and is currently writing a book on the African country of Gabon where he was a Fulbright Professor during the 1983-84 academic year.

Abraham L. Davis is a Professor, Department of Political Science, Morehouse College, Atlanta, Georgia. He is the author of THE U.S. SUPREME COURT AND THE USES OF SOCIAL SCIENCE DATA. He has been a visiting Professor and/or Lecturer at Colgate University, Syracuse University, Purdue University, and North Carolina A & T University.

Henry E. Hankerson is Chairperson, Department of Curriculum and Teaching, Howard University, Washington, D.C. He has to his credit over forty research and scholarly publications and teaching aids in refereed journals and books. He has recently completed a study tour of England (British Infant Schools).

Lorene Barnes Holmes is Chairperson, Division of Business Administration, Jarvis Christian College, Hawkins, Texas. The author of numerous scholarly articles and essays, her major publications include: "The Black Female Administrator in Higher Education -- Myth or Miracle?" JOURNAL OF THE SOCIETY FOR ETHNIC AND SPECIAL STUDIES, Volume 3 (January 1979); and, "Black Colleges -- Miracle Workers!" THE JOURNAL OF BLACK ACADEMIA, (November 1980).

Anne Squarrel Jenkins is an Associate Professor, Department of Social and Behavioral Sciences, Cheyney University, Chester, Pennsylvania. This young scholar has received many awards, including American Sociological Association Fellowship, National Science Foundation Teaching Fellowship, and Maryland Senatorial Scholarship.

217

Huey L. Perry is an Associate Professor, Department of Political Science, Southern University, Baton Rouge, Louisiana. His most recent honors include a Rockefeller Foundation Research Fellowship and a Southern Education Foundation Adjunct Fellowship. He is the author of DEMOCRACY AND PUBLIC POLICY: MINORITY INPUT INTO THE NATIONAL ENERGY POLICY OF THE CARTER ADMINISTRATION.

David Pilgrim is an Assistant Professor, Department of Sociology, Saint Mary's College, Notre Dame, Indiana. He is the author of HUMAN ODDITIES: AN EXPLORATORY STUDY; and, DECEPTION BY STRATAGEM: SEGREGATION IN PUBLIC HIGHER EDUCATION.

Wornie L. Reed is Chairperson, Department of Black Studies, University of Massachusetts at Boston, Massachusetts. He has published twenty-three articles and one book, BEING SICK INSIDE: THE HEALTH CONSEQUENCES OF IMPRISONMENT.

Isaac A. Robinson is a Professor, Department of Sociology, North Carolina Central University, Durham, North Carolina. He is the author of several computer simulations in sociology, and he has published papers on the recent immigration of Blacks into southern and border states.

Joseph W. Scott is a Professor, Department of Sociology, Notre Dame University, Notre Dame, Indiana. He is a past President of the North Central Sociological Association. He has published over twenty scholarly articles and one book, BLACK REVOLTS: RACIAL STRATIFICATION IN AMERICA.

Ronnie Stewart is an Assistant Professor, Department of Sociology, Alabama State University, Montgomery, Alabama. A seasoned researcher, he has been a consultant for research projects in Alabama and Ohio.

Almose A. Thompson, Jr. is a Professor, Department of Educational Administration, Tennessee State University, Nashville, Tennessee. He is the Founder of the Northwest Journal of African and Black American Studies. He has published numerous scholarly articles and essays.

Alton Thompson is an Assistant Professor, Department of Agricultural Economics and Rural Sociology, North Carolina A & T State University, Greensboro, North Carolina. He is the author of ten articles and one book, QUALITY OF LIFE AMONG RURAL RESIDENTS IN NORTH CAROLINA: COMMUNITY AND LIFE SATISFACTION.

Betty J. Traub is a Research Assistant, Department of Agricultural Economics and Rural Sociology, North Carolina A & T State University, Greensboro, North Carolina. Her research interests are rural poverty and the psychology of racism.

James N. Upton is Director, Black Studies Community Extension Center, The Ohio State University, Columbus, Ohio. He has published in the area of urban politics, educational policy, and citizen participation. He has recently received a grant from the Southern Education Foundation to study the factors that facilitate or hinder Afro-Americans access to graduate schools.

Randall P. White is the Program Associate, Center For Creative Leadership, Greensboro, North Carolina. He is currently responsible for research projects at several Fortune 100 corporations.

Carlene Young is Chairperson, Department of Afro-American Studies, San Jose State University, San Jose, California. She is a past President of the National Council for Black Studies. A licensed Clinical Psychologist, she is the author of BLACK EXPERIENCE: ANALYSIS AND SYNTHESIS.

QUOTIENT OF BLACK INFORMATION TEST

"...the Q.B.I. Test..."

developed by David Pilgrim

This test is designed to measure one's knowledge about black Americans and the black American experience. The test has several sections: **Vocabulary**, **History**, and **Current Status**. Each section has twenty-five closed-ended questions. Please select only one answer for each question.

Vocabulary

1. Day's work refers to work done by a
   a. maid
   b. school teacher
   c. prostitute
   d. actress
   e. preacher

2. A case quarter is
   a. a quarter
   b. a small gun
   c. an appearance in court
   d. a winning racehorse
   e. an intelligent person

3. A sedidy woman is believed to be
   a. violence-prone
   b. industrious
   c. noisy and loud
   d. pretentious
   e. very friendly

4. Where are people most likely to get happy?
   a. in a bar
   b. at a football game
   c. in a church
   d. at a high school graduation
   e. in a bank

5. Miss Anne refers to
   a. very old women
   b. white women
   c. single-parent mothers
   d. black women
   e. hard-working women

6. If a man is looking for a red-bone, for what is he looking?
   a. a large steak
   b. a light-skinned black woman
   c. a white woman
   d. an Indian woman

A

        e. an expensive cigar

7. Drylongso means
        a. hopeful
        b. forgetful
        c. holy
        d. stupid
        e. ordinary

8. Mojo refers to
        a. service stations
        b. magical charms
        c. hardwork
        d. Christian living
        e. athletic prowess

9. If I sport you, what am I doing for you?
        a. paying your way
        b. teaching you basketball techniques
        c. helping you with schoolwork
        d. comforting you
        e. introducing you to someone important

10. How much is a yard?
        a. $1,000
        b. half of what you need
        c. a week's salary
        d. a unit of 100
        e. nothing; less than nothing

11. In which situation do you hear "l'il help?"
        a. when a basketball rolls off the court
        b. when collecting financial donations
        c. when you have a flat tire
        d. when you need advice
        e. when you want to be sarcastic

12. A peck-a-wood is a
        a. woodpecker
        b. derogatory term for Southern whites
        c. derogatory term for upper-class blacks
        d. a Christmas tree
        e. a wooden house

13. To chill means to
        a. put on one's best clothing
        b. stand up for one's rights
        c. relax
        d. get angry
        e. forget something

14. A man who can really burn is an expert at
        a. fighting
        b. boxing

B

c. preaching
d. running
e. cooking

15. A woman who can really <u>blow</u> is an expert at
    a. arguing
    b. orating
    c. running
    d. fighting
    e. singing

16. If you call someone a <u>'bama</u> you are saying that they
    a. were reared in Alabama
    b. have a Southern accent
    c. are country hicks
    d. are very friendly
    e. are intelligent

17. A <u>brim</u> is a
    a. hat
    b. car
    c. coat
    d. belt
    e. necktie

18. <u>Illin'</u> refers to
    a. silliness
    b. illness
    c. relaxing
    d. parenting
    e. shoplifting

19. If you <u>shoot that rock</u>, what is the <u>rock</u>?
    a. a gun
    b. an animal
    c. a basketball
    d. your mouth
    e. an enemy

20. If you are <u>clean</u>, what are you?
    a. well-dressed
    b. very happy
    c. rich
    d. freshly-bathed
    e. egotistical

21. If someone has a little <u>juice</u>, what do they have?
    a. groceries
    b. a baby girl
    c. an aching muscle
    d. any small child
    e. money

C

22. If I <u>bust your heart</u>, what have I done to you?
    a. defeated you in a race
    b. disappointed you in some way
    c. failed to show up for a date
    d. played the <u>dozens</u>
    e. deceived you

23. Which one of the following people have <u>got off</u>?
    a. a student who earns a "C" on an examination
    b. a pianist who plays well during a recital
    c. a man who argued with his brother
    d. someone who enjoyed an excellent meal
    e. an entertainer who left a recital early

24. If I <u>call you out of your name</u>, I have _____ you.
    a. praised
    b. encouraged
    c. insulted
    d. fired
    e. ignored

25. If I <u>play you to the left</u>, what have I done to you?
    a. helped you study for an examination
    b. tried to convert you to liberal politics
    c. asked you for a date
    d. treated you poorly
    e. proposed marriage

History

1. The history of blacks in English America began with the landing of "twenty negars" in Jamestown, Virginia. In what year did they land?
    a. 1492
    b. 1526
    c. 1538
    d. 1619
    e. 1624

2. The first colony to give statutory recognition to slavery did so in 1641. Which colony set the precedent for statutory slavery?
    a. South Carolina
    b. Virginia
    c. Massachusetts
    d. North Carolina
    e. Georgia

3. The first colony to ban marriages between blacks and whites did so in 1664. Which colony set the precedent for anti-miscegenation legislation?
    a. Maryland
    b. Delaware

D

c. Pennsylvania
d. South Carolina
e. New Jersey

4. Who is generally regarded as the first martyr of the American
Revolution?
   a. James Derham
   b. Crispus Attucks
   c. David Walker
   d. Richard Allen
   e. Frederick Douglass

5. The first black newspaper was published in 1827. What was the
name of this newspaper?
   a. Baltimore Sun
   b. Chicago Defender
   c. North Star
   d. Atlanta Daily World
   e. Freedom's Journal

6. The first novel published by a black American was Clotel, in
1853. The writer of this novel was also the first black American
to publish a play, The Escape, in 1858. Who was this writer?
   a. Langston Hughes
   b. James Weldon Johnson
   c. Harriet Tubman
   d. Jean Toomer
   e. William Wells Brown

7. In 1857, the United States Supreme Court ruled that blacks
were not citizens. This ruling was in response to which case?
   a. Brown v. Board of Education
   b. Dred Scott v. Sanford
   c. Hawkins v.Board of Control
   d. McLauren v. Oklahoma
   e. Plessy v. Ferguson

8. In 1859, the last slave ship, The Clothilde, landed a shipment
of slaves in a southern city. In which city did this slave ship
land?
   a. New Orleans, Louisiana
   b. Pensacola, Florida
   c. Mobile, Alabama
   d. Gulfport, Mississippi
   e. Miami, Florida

9. In 1870, Joseph H. Rainey became the first black to be sworned
in as a congressman in the House of Representatives. Which state
did he represent?
   a. Alabama
   b. Michigan
   c. Ohio
   d. South Carolina
   e. Mississippi

E

10. Who am I? I was born the son of a slave owner and a slave.
In 1871, I was elected president pro tem of the Louisiana State
Senate and became Lieutenant Governor when the incumbent died.
The following year I became acting governor while Governor
Warmoth was tried for impeachment.
    a. P. B. S. Pinchback
    b. Frederick Douglass
    c. Booker Taliaferro Washington
    d. W. E. B. DuBois
    e. David Walker

11. In 1884, Isaac Murphy became a hero to thousands of black
Americans by winning a major sporting championship. What did he
win?
    a. the Kentucky Derby horse race
    b. the flyweight boxing championship of the world
    c. the 100 yard backstroke in Olympic swimming
    d. the 100 yard dash in the Olympics
    e. the middleweight fencing championship in the Olympics

12. Who delivered the "Atlanta Compromise" speech?
    a. W. E. B. DuBois
    b. Booker Taliaferro Washington
    c. Frederick Douglass
    d. David Walker
    e. Martin Luther King, Jr.

13. In 1905, a group of black intellectuals and civic leaders
formed the Niagara Movement to improve the status of blacks in
the United States. This organization was short-lived but it laid
the foundation for the birth of another organization in 1909.
Which national civil rights organization owed its existence to
the Niagara Movement?
    a. the National Urban League
    b. the Southern Christian Leadership Conference
    c. the National Association for the Advancement of Colored
       People
    d. the Congress of Racial Equality
    e. the National Negro Congress

14. In 1920, the first authentic blues record, <u>Crazy Blues</u>, was
made by a black singer. Who was this gifted artist?
    a. Paul Robeson
    b. Ella Fitzgerald
    c. Mamie Smith
    d. Faye Adams
    e. Nat King Cole

15. In 1931, nine black youths were wrongly arrested and charged
with the rapes of two white women.   Their case became an
international cause celebre and an indictment of the southern
racial caste system. By what name were the defendants known?
    a. The Chicago Eight

b. Roosevelt's Black Cabinet
c. Tippling Toms
d. Scottsboro Boys
e. Haynes' Bunch

16. In 1932, Howard University began publication of a major
academic journal. What was the name of the journal?
a. the _Journal of Black Studies_
b. _Phylon_
c. the _Journal of Negro History_
d. the _Journal of Ethnic Studies_
e. the _Journal of Negro Education_

17. Who am I? In 1904, I established the Daytona Normal and
Industrial Institute for Negro Girls. I helped President
Franklin D. Roosevelt organize the National Youth Administration
and was Director of the Division of Negro Affairs between 1936
and 1944?
a. Sojourner Truth
b. Harriet Tubman
c. Mary McLeod Bethune
d. Phillis Wheatley
e. Charlotte E. Ray

18. In 1936, a black American undermined the doctrine of white
supremacy by winning four Olympic gold medals. Who was this
athlete?
a. Ralph Metcalfe
b. Jesse Owens
c. Rafer Johnson
d. John Woodruff
e. Wilma Rudolph

19. In 1944, a social scientific study created a national stir by
concluding that whites were responsible for the United States'
racial problem. This study was published under what name?
a. _An American Dilemma_
b. _The Autobiography of Frederick Douglass_
c. _Up From Slavery_
d. _From Slavery to Freedom_
e. _Uncle Tom's Cabin_

20. In 1947, a 27-year-old black man founded a publication to
highlight the accomplishments of black Americans. What is the
name of this publication?
a. _Jet_
b. _Esquire_
c. _Essence_
d. _Ebony_
e. _Negro Digest_

21. In the case of _____ the Supreme Court ruled the state
must provide legal education for blacks "as soon as it provides
it for whites." Clue: 1948.

G

a. Sweatt v. Painter
b. Shelley v. Kraemer
c. Gray v. University of Tennessee
d. Sipuel v. Board of Regents
e. Davis v. Schnell

22. According to researchers at Tuskeegee Institute, what was the first year that no blacks were lynched in the United States?
    a. 1948
    b. 1950
    c. 1952
    d. 1954
    e. 1958

23. In 1955, a 14-year-old black youth was kidnapped and lynched for whistling at a white woman. The lynching spurred black protests across the nation. What was the name of the black youth?
    a. Rufus Clement
    b. Hulan Jack
    c. Charlie Parker
    d. B. O. Davis, Jr.
    e. Emmett Till

24. In what year was Martin Luther King, Jr. assassinated?
    a. 1964
    b. 1968
    c. 1970
    d. 1973
    e. 1975

25. Who wrote the book Black Power?
    a. Stokely Carmichael and Charles V. Hamilton
    b. H. Rap Brown and Huey Newton
    c. Martin Luther King, Jr.
    d. LeRoi Jones
    e. Claude Brown

Current Status

1. Blacks make up approximately what percentage of all Americans?
    a. 5
    b. 8
    c. 13
    d. 16
    e. 20

2. Which one of the following cities does not have a majority black population?
    a. Washington, D.C.
    b. Atlanta, Georgia
    c. New Orleans, Louisiana
    d. Detroit, Michigan

H

e. Gary, Indiana

3. In 1988 a black-owned company achieved more than $1 billion in annual sales. What is the name of the company?
   a. Johnson Publishing Company
   b. Motown Industries
   c. Soft Sheen Products
   d. Philadelphia Coca-Cola Bottling Company
   e. TLC Beatrice International Holdings

4. Black household income is about ___ percent of white household income?
   a. 40
   b. 50
   c. 60
   d. 70
   e. 80

5. Which organization publishes an annual report entitled, The State of Black America?
   a. the National Association for the Advancement of Colored People.
   b. the National Urban League
   c. the Congress of Racial Equality
   d. the Southern Christian Leadership Conference
   e. the Society for the Prevention of Negroes Getting Everything

6. Who is the Executive Director of the National Association for the Advancement of Colored People?
   a. Benjamin Hooks
   b. Jesse Jackson
   c. John E. Jacob
   d. Roy Innis
   e. Joseph Lowery

7. In 1988, who was the President of the National Council of Negro Women?
   a. Regina J. Frazier
   b. Janet J. Ballard
   c. Hortense G. Canady
   d. Dorothy I. Height
   e. Rejesta V. Perry

8. According to a 1988 research study conducted at the University of South Florida, _____ percent of single black women would remain single before marrying non-blacks.
   a. 5
   b. 26
   c. 45
   d. 56
   e. 67

9. Of the 12,480 doctorates awarded to American graduates of

1

science and engineering programs in 1987, about ____ percent were black.
  a. 2
  b. 5
  c. 8
  d. 10
  e. 13

10. According to a 1988 Media General/Associated Press survey, race relations have improved in the past twenty years. Of the whites surveyed, 67 percent said they had close friends who are black. What percentage of blacks said they had close friends who are white?
  a. 4
  b. 24
  c. 44
  d. 74
  e. 94

11. What percentage of the delegates to the 1988 Republican National Convention were black?
  a. less than 1
  b. 4
  c. 8
  d. 12
  e. almost 15

12. Which one of the following black celebrities does not have a white spouse?
  a. Whoopi Goldberg
  b. Richard Roundtree
  c. Hank Aaron
  d. Diana Ross
  e. Sidney Poitier

13. _____ is Kitty Dukakis' Chief of Staff -- the first black woman to hold that position in a national campaign.
  a. Marilyn Anderson
  b. Suzette Charles
  c. Tawny Grodin
  d. Lorraine Williams
  e. Barbara C. Harris

14. On September 24, 1988, members of the nation's largest Episcopal diocese elected a black woman as biship. Who is she?
  a. Marilyn Anderson
  b. Suzette Charles
  c. Tawny Grodin
  d. Lorraine Williams
  e. Barbara C. Harris

15. Who directed the movie School Daze?
  a. Spike Lee
  b. Robert Townsend

J

c. Richard Roundtree
d. Syndey Poitier
e. Ossie Davis

16. Of the people arrested for arson, what percentage are black?
    a. 5
    b. 15
    c. 25
    d. 35
    e. 45

17. The religious denomination with the most blacks is
    a. Lutherans
    b. Methodists
    c. Pentecostals
    d. Baptists
    e. Congregationalists

18. The majority (55.5%) of blacks live in which region of the United States?
    a. Northeast
    b. Midwest
    c. South
    d. West

19. In 1970, there were 48 black mayors in the United States. By 1987, the number had risen to _____.
    a. 96
    b. 178
    c. 303
    d. 501
    e. 978

20. In 1988, Londell Williams made national news by
    a. attempting to free Nelson Mandela
    b. shooting several KKK members
    c. breaking the world record in the 200 meters foot race
    d. disrupting a Ronald Reagan political rally
    e. plotting to assassinate Jesse Jackson

21. Who is Frederick K. Price?
    a. the mayor of Gary, Indiana
    b. a televangelist
    c. the first black astronaut
    d. the editor of the Cleveland Plain Dealer
    e. the oldest man in America

22. In which city do blacks enjoy their highest median standard of living?
    a. Richmond, Virginia
    b. New York, New York
    c. Green Bay, Wisconsin
    d. Chicago, Illinois
    e. Detroit, Michigan

K

23. Where is Morehouse College located?
    a. Cleveland, Ohio
    b. Birmingham, Alabama
    c. Detroit, Michigan
    d. Houston, Texas
    e. Atlanta, Georgia

24. Of the juveniles arrested for violating liquor laws, what percentage are black?
    a. 3
    b. 9
    c. 29
    d. 45
    e. 65

25. In 1987, what percentage of black families were headed by a single woman?
    a. 22
    b. 32
    c. 42
    d. 52
    e. 62

L

KEY

VOCABULARY		HISTORY		CURRENT STATUS	
1.	A	1.	D	1.	C
2.	A	2.	C	2.	C
3.	D	3.	A	3.	E
4.	C	4.	B	4.	C
5.	B	5.	E	5.	B
6.	B	6.	E	6.	A
7.	E	7.	B	7.	D
8.	B	8.	C	8.	E
9.	A	9.	D	9.	A
10.	D	10.	A	10.	E
11.	A	11.	A	11.	B
12.	B	12.	B	12.	C
13.	C	13.	C	13.	A
14.	E	14.	C	14.	E
15.	E	15.	D	15.	A
16.	C	16.	E	16.	B
17.	A	17.	C	17.	D
18.	A	18.	B	18.	C
19.	C	19.	A	19.	C
20.	A	20.	D	20.	E
21.	E	21.	D	21.	B
22.	A	22.	C	22.	A
23.	B	23.	E	23.	E
24.	C	24.	B	24.	A
25.	D	25.	A	25.	C

75 to 64 correct: Excellent.
63 to 53 correct: Good.
52 to 45 correct: Fair.
44 to 0 correct: Poor.

M